The WTO and global governance

The WTO and global governance: Future directions

Edited by Gary P. Sampson

**United Nations
University Press**

TOKYO · NEW YORK · PARIS

United Nations University Press
United Nations University, 53-70, Jingumae 5-chome,
Shibuya-ku, Tokyo 150-8925, Japan
Tel: +81-3-3499-2811   Fax: +81-3-3406-7345
E-mail: sales@hq.unu.edu   general enquiries: press@hq.unu.edu
http://www.unu.edu

United Nations University Office at the United Nations, New York
2 United Nations Plaza, Room DC2-2062, New York, NY 10017, USA
Tel: +1-212-963-6387   Fax: +1-212-371-9454
E-mail: unuona@ony.unu.edu

United Nations University Press is the publishing division of the United Nations University.

Cover design by Joyce C. Weston

Printed in Hong Kong

ISBN 978-92-808-1154-4

Library of Congress Cataloging-in-Publication Data

The WTO and global governance : future directions / edited by Gary P. Sampson.
    p.   cm.
  Includes bibliographical references and index.
  ISBN 978-9280811544 (pbk.)
  1. World Trade Organization. 2. Commercial treaties. 3. Foreign trade regulation. 4. International economic relations. 5. Globalization. I. Sampson, Gary P.
HF1385.W77874   2008
382'.92—dc22   2008035768

Contents

Contributors

Gary P. Sampson is presently the John Gough Professor of International Trade at Melbourne Business School, Melbourne University, and Professor of International Economic Governance at the Institute of Advanced Studies, United Nations University, Tokyo. He was appointed Director at the General Agreement of Tariffs and Trade in 1987 and then at the World Trade Organization in 1995 where he served as Director until 2003. From 1984 to 1986, he was Senior Fellow in Economic Policy at the Reserve Bank of Australia, and Professorial Fellow at the Centre of Policy Studies at Monash University. He teaches on a regular basis at the Melbourne Business School and London School of Economics and has written extensively in both the popular and academic press on matters relating to the international economy and economic governance. His most recent books are *The WTO and Sustainable Development* and *Developing Countries and the WTO: Policy Approaches* (co-edited with W. Bradnee Chambers).

Pascal Lamy has been Director-General of the World Trade Organization since September 2005. He began his career in the French civil service at the Inspection Générale des Finances and the Treasury. A former advisor to Finance Minster Jacques Delors, and subsequently to Prime Minister Pierre Mauroy, Mr. Lamy served the President of the European Commission (Jacques Delors) as Head of Cabinet from 1985 to 1994. Mr. Lamy is also known for having been a member of the team in charge of rescuing Credit Lyonnais. He later became CEO of the bank until its privatisation in 1999. From 1999 to 2004, he worked as Trade Commissioner at the European Commission led by Romano Prodi.

Sylvia Ostry is the Distinguished Research Fellow, Centre for International Studies, University of Toronto. She has a doctorate in economics from McGill University and Cambridge University. Dr. Ostry has held a number of positions in the Canadian federal government, among them, Chief Statistician, Deputy Minister of International Trade, Ambassador for Multilateral Trade Negotiations and the Prime Minister's Personal Representative for the Economic Summit. From 1979 to 1983, she was the head of the Economic and Statistics Department of the OECD in Paris. She has received 19 honorary degrees from universities around the world and, in 1987, received the Outstanding Achievement Award of the Government of Canada. In December 1990, she was made a Companion of the Order of Canada, the highest award in the Canadian national system of honours. In June 1991, she was admitted as a Fellow of the Royal Society of Canada.

Bert Koenders was appointed as the Netherlands Minister for Development Cooperation in February 2007. Between 1997 and 2007, Mr. Koenders was a Labour Party (PvdA) Member of Parliament. He held the role of spokesman for international and European affairs and was on the boards of several Parliamentary organisations. Prior to becoming a politician, Mr. Koenders worked as a consultant and as the European director of Parliamentarians for Global Action in New York. From 1993 to 1994, he was a European staff member and political advisor to the Special Representative of the Secretary-General of the UN working in Mozambique, South Africa and Mexico. He subsequently became principal administrator of policy planning for the Director-General of external relations, conflict prevention and European Union enlargement at the European Commission in Brussels.

Daniel C. Esty is the Hillhouse Professor of Environmental Law and Policy at Yale University with appointments in the Environment and Law Schools. He serves as Director of the Center for Business and the Environment at Yale and the Yale Center for Environmental Law and Policy. He has published books and articles on the environment, and is the co-author of a recent prize-winning book, *Green to Gold: How Smart Companies Use Environmental Strategy to Innovate, Create Value, and Build Competitive Advantage*. Prior to taking up his current position at Yale, Professor Esty was a Senior Fellow at the Institute for International Economics and served in a variety of senior positions on the US Environmental Protection Agency.

Juan Somavia, a Chilean national, has been Director-General of the International Labour Organization (ILO) since March 1999. From 1990 to 1999, he was the Chilean Permanent Representative to the UN, during which time he was actively engaged with civil society organizations. He proposed the 1995 World Summit for Social Development and chaired its Preparatory Committee. Mr. Somavia is the first representative of the southern hemisphere to head the ILO. Under his leadership, the Organization has established "Decent Work" as its primary goal. It is a restatement of the ILO's historic mission to promote social justice through the world of work. Mr. Somavia's multifaceted career has been driven by a strong concern for social justice, peace, human rights and democracy.

Louise Arbour has been the United Nations High Commissioner for Human Rights since 1 July 2004. Ms. Arbour began a distinguished academic career in 1970, culminating in the positions of Associate Professor and Associate Dean at the Osgoode Hall Law School of York University in Toronto, Canada, in 1987. In 1996, she became Chief Prosecutor for the International Criminal Tribunals for the former Yugoslavia and for Rwanda. In 1999, she took up an appointment to the Supreme Court of Canada. She has published extensively on criminal law and given innumerable addresses on both national and international criminal law.

Shervin Majlessi is a human rights officer at the Office of the United Nations High Commissioner for Human Rights (OHCHR), focusing on trade/globalization and good governance/corruption issues. Prior to joining OHCHR, he worked at the World Bank and as a deputy counsel for the Independent Inquiry Committee into the UN Oil-for-Food Programme. He has conducted research and studied towards a doctorate degree in international economic law at the University of Teheran, Centre for Studies and Research in International Law and International Relations of the Hague Academy of International Law, McGill University and Harvard Law School.

Celso Amorim is the Brazilian Minister of External Relations, a position he has held since 2003 and previously from 1993 to 1995. Mr. Amorim has been working in government roles since 1987. In 1999, Mr. Amorim was named as the permanent representative of Brazil to the United Nations (a position he had also held from 1995 to 1999) and the World Trade Organization. He remained in these roles for two years before moving to the United Kingdom to serve as Ambassador to Brazil. Mr. Amorim completed post-graduate education at the Diplomatic Academy of Vienna and London School of Economics. He has published several works in the fields of political theory, international relations, cultural policy, scientific and technological development.

Supachai Panitchpakdi began his four-year term as Secretary-General of UNCTAD in September 2005, after being appointed by the UN General Assembly. He previously served as Director-General of the World Trade Organization and as Thailand's Deputy Prime Minister and Minister of Commerce. As Deputy Prime Minister, he was in charge of the country's economic and trade policy-making, signing the Uruguay Round Agreement in 1994 and contributing to the formulation of regional agreements. Dr. Supachai received his Master's degree in Econometrics and Development Planning and his Ph.D. in Economic Planning and

Development from Erasmus University in Rotterdam.

Dani Rodrik is Rafiq Hariri Professor of International Political Economy and faculty chair of the MPA/ID program at Harvard University. He has published widely in the areas of economic development, international economics and political economy. His most recent book is *One Economics, Many Recipes: Globalization, Institutions, and Economic Growth* (forthcoming from the Princeton University Press). His current research focuses on designing growth strategies for developing economies. In 2007, he was awarded the inaugural Albert O. Hirschman Prize of the Social Sciences Research Council. He is also the recipient of an honorary doctorate from the University of Antwerp and of the Leontief Award for Advancing the Frontiers of Economic Thought. His work has been supported by research grants from the Carnegie Corporation, Ford Foundation and Rockefeller Foundation.

Patricia R. Francis joined the International Trade Centre as Executive Director in June 2006. The ITC – a development partner for small business export success in developing countries – is a joint agency of the United Nations and the World Trade Organization. Ms. Francis formerly held the position of President of Jamaica Trade and Invest, and was a member of Jamaica's Cabinet Committee for Development. During her tenure, Jamaica attracted more than US$5 billion in foreign direct investment. Ms. Francis has served as the President of the World Association of Investment Promotion Agencies, and chaired the Organisation for Economic Co-operation and Development's Caribbean Rim Investment Initiative, as well as the China-Caribbean Business Council. She has received awards from the Washington DC-based Caribbean-Central American Action Council and from the King of Spain for her business advocacy and leadership.

Ted Turner has received recognition for his entrepreneurial acumen, sharp business skills, leadership qualities and his unprecedented philanthropy. Mr. Turner is chairman of the Turner Foundation, Inc., which supports efforts for improving air and water quality, developing a sustainable energy future to protect our climate, safeguarding environmental health, maintaining wildlife habitat protection, and developing practices and policies to curb population growth rates; co-chairman of the Nuclear Threat Initiative, which works to close the growing and increasingly dangerous gap between the threat from nuclear, chemical and biological weapons; chairman of the United Nations Foundation, which promotes a more peaceful, prosperous and just world; and a partner in the Ted's Montana Grill restaurant chain. Mr. Turner is also chairman of Turner Enterprises, Inc., a private company, which manages his business interests, land holdings and investments.

Mitsuo Matsushita is a professor emeritus of Tokyo University, a Tokyo lawyer (Daiichi Tokyo Bengoshi Kai) and a counsel to Nagashima, Ohno & Tsunematsu, a leading international law firm in Tokyo. Having earned a Ph.D. and a D.Jur., Prof. Matsushita became internationally known as a Japanese expert in the fields of competition law and international economic law. Prof. Matsushita has held professorships at Sophia University, Tokyo University and Seikei University in Japan and worked as a visiting professor at universities around the world, including Harvard Law School and the College of Europe. He has published extensively in the fields of international trade and competition and investment law. From 1995 to 2000, Prof. Matsushita served as one of the founding members of the Appellate Body of the World Trade Organization. He has held numerous posts within the Japanese government and is currently a member of the Industrial Structure Council attached to the Ministry of Economy, Trade and Industry.

Foreword

The world trading system – based originally on the General Agreement on Tariffs and Trade and now the World Trade Organization – celebrated its sixtieth anniversary on 1 January 2008. During its lifetime, tariffs have fallen to just one-tenth of what they were, while the volume of world trade has grown twenty-seven-fold and at a rate three times faster than world output, bringing unprecedented prosperity for many. Greater independence of nations is the result, with the WTO at the centre stage of globalization.

In terms of what governments were looking for in post-war institutions, the GATT – and now the WTO – have been an outstanding success story and the envy of many other international organizations. Nevertheless, views on the virtues of the WTO differ greatly.

Its objectives are ambitious: to raise standards of living and ensure full employment with growth in real income and trade while providing for the optimal use of the world's resources. The means available to the WTO to achieve these goals are trade liberalization and the conduct of trade according to multilaterally agreed rules. With its far-reaching mandate, both the liberalization of trade and the rules that govern it have become inextricably linked with economic growth and stability, the environment and social conditions. The area of commerce subjected to liberalization commitments has greatly expanded, and WTO rules are not only more expansive but also reach more deeply into domestic regulatory structures.

One salient feature of these developments is that many issues not normally considered to be in the domain of traditional trade policy are now being dealt with by the WTO. The WTO is not only an agent of global-ization but also an agent of global governance. This has raised many questions relating to the dividing line between WTO rules, national sov-ereignty and other international obligations. In short, what is the role of the WTO in global governance?

With these issues in mind, I invited a number of prominent people – all influential in their respective areas of international affairs – to contribute their views on the proper role of the WTO in global governance. A wide variety of views emerged (see the precursor to the current volume, *The Role of the WTO in Global Governance*).[1]

One called on the trade community to accept the fact that social norms are inextricably linked with the international economic system and that they provide the common moral and legal underpinnings for the formula-tion of policies relating to development, to the environment and to social objectives. Integrating social norms into all aspects of economic policy-making – including trade policy – would ensure that markets are not only open and efficient but also fair and just.

For others, the multilateral trading system at the beginning of the twenty-first century is the most remarkable achievement in institutional-ized global economic cooperation yet witnessed. It does not intrude on national sovereignty as charged by some. On the contrary, it protects na-tional sovereignty by denying more powerful countries the potential to impose their preferred social and political norms unilaterally via trade sanctions. For example, by denying the right of countries to discriminate between products on the basis of how they were produced, WTO rules prevent powerful countries from riding roughshod over less powerful ones, thus freeing the space for national regulations and multilateral trea-ties to deal with environmental and social matters. Viewed through this prism, the concepts, principles and rules of the WTO should be consoli-dated through experience – neither shrunk nor further stretched in any direction.

Pascal Lamy remarks that, in both public and academic discourse, analysis of the WTO generally results in either extreme criticism or ex-cessive praise, with the result that discussions are dominated by two op-posite positions. On the one hand, some globalization critics assert that the WTO holds a hegemonic grip on global issues, while others denounce the WTO's isolation as an international rule-setter and compliance-enforcer. Proponents of a rule-based view of international relations, on the other hand, promote the WTO as a model for global governance.

Notwithstanding advances made at the meeting of ministers in Geneva in July 2008, the Doha Development Agenda is struggling to conclude. For some, like Ted Turner, failure is unacceptable. If the Doha Agenda fails, he says it would be the last effort of its kind – a result that is out of the question. According to Turner, if we quit on the Doha Round, we may not ever try anything like it again. This would mean no more global trade agreements and the role of the WTO in global affairs would change for ever, with the WTO no longer fulfilling its role in global governance by liberalizing trade and bringing common sense to the structure of world trade and production.

With these types of reaction in mind, it seemed timely to review not only the role of the WTO but also its possible future directions within global governance. There have, of course, been important contributions to this in the past six years, and, as Louise Arbour and Shervin Majlessi note, the link between trade, development and human rights has been treated extensively in academic circles and beyond since the publication of *The Role of the WTO in Global Governance*. They conclude, however, that among both the human rights community and the trade practitioners these linkages are still not immediately obvious.

One of the principal objectives of this volume is therefore to consider the role of the WTO in global governance six years on. Once again, prominent personalities offer their thoughts, particularly with respect to the non-traditional trade issues that have gravitated to the WTO and that overlap with the goals of their own international organizations. However, the objectives of this book are more ambitious, involving the identification of the future directions of the WTO in light of the many options that emerge from their contributions.

What emerges clearly in this respect is the need for effective coordination between international institutions in dealing with non-traditional trade concerns. This in itself is a challenging task. However, is this enough to ensure a proper role for the WTO in global governance? Should the WTO use its powerful dispute settlement system to enforce widely accepted standards relating to the environment, labour or human rights? Is the WTO effective in achieving its stated goals of supporting economic development by integrating developing countries more fully into the international trading system? Does it promote sustainable development as mandated? Should it change the way it functions in order to gain greater public support for its actions? These and many related questions are addressed in the following chapters. Based on 18 years experience, as Director of several divisions in both the GATT and the WTO, my own view is that the WTO should not be responsible for the non-traditional trade issues that have gravitated towards it. This brings inappropriate pressure on rules and procedures designed for trade purposes. While the obvious solution is to provide other international organisations dealing with the environment, labour standards and human rights the enforcement powers of the WTO, governments have not been prepared to do so. Like it or not, the WTO will continue to deal with non-traditional trade issues.

The critical question is: how to constructively contribute to international objectives relating to the environment, human rights and labour standards while continuing to function effectively as a world trade organisation?

Many suggestions as to "the way forward" emerge in the following chapters. My own short answer to the above question is that the WTO already has the institutional and legal flexibilities to accommodate both the non-trade issues now confronting it, and those that may come its way in the future. Changing its rules to make it an enforcement agency for human rights, labour standards or the environment is to give it an authority in global governance that it has neither the mandate nor expertise to deal with. The Introduction and Overview elaborates on why the WTO, conceived as a trade organisation, must remain as such.

*   *   *

A number of people have been most helpful in the preparation of this book. I would like to single out a few in particular. I appreciate very much the enthusiasm of Professor Hans van Ginkel, former Rector of the United Nations University (UNU), in originally supporting the idea of a second volume. Professor Zakri, Director of the Institute of Advanced Studies (IAS) at the UNU, provided both institutional support and encouragement, which were also very much appreciated. In terms of substance, I would like to thank my former colleagues at the World Trade Organization – in particular, Serafino Marchese and Jorge Vigano for their advice, insights and wisdom based on long experience in both the GATT and the WTO. Bradnee Chambers of UNU-IAS was most helpful in many areas, notably in matters relating to the United Nations Specialized Agencies and non-traditional trade concerns, such as the relationship between trade and the environment. Gregory Sampson of the International Trade Centre carried out useful research and comments on earlier drafts. Robert Davis, Managing Editor of the United Nations University Press, was particularly patient and helpful through the editing process, and Liz Paton, as usual, was responsible for a most professional editing job for UNU Press. Chris Flegg, a long standing colleague at Melbourne Business School, helped greatly with drafting suggestions for my overview chapter.

Note

1. Gary P. Sampson (ed.), *The Role of the WTO in Global Governance*, Tokyo: United Nations University Press, 2000.

Abbreviations

ACP	African, Caribbean and Pacific
ACTPN	US Advisory Committee for Trade Policy and Negotiations
ACWL	Advisory Centre on WTO Law
AD	anti-dumping
AfT	Aid for Trade
ASEAN	Association of Southeast Asian Nations
CAT	Convention Against Torture and Other Cruel Inhuman or Degrading Treatment or Punishment
CED	Convention for the Protection of All Persons from Enforced Disappearance
CEDAW	Convention on the Elimination of All Forms of Discrimination against Women
CESCR	Committee on Economic, Social and Cultural Rights
CG18	Consultative Group of 18
CITES	Convention on International Trade in Endangered Species of Wild Fauna and Flora
CPD	Convention on the Rights of Persons with Disabilities
CRC	Convention on the Rights of the Child
CRS	Creditor Reporting System (OECD database)
CTD	Committee on Trade and Development
CTE	Committee on Trade and Environment
DAC	Development Assistance Committee
DDA	Doha Development Agenda
DSB	Dispute Settlement Body
DSU	Dispute Settlement Understanding
DWCP	Decent Work Country Programme

EC	European Communities
EC	European Community
ECOSOC	United Nations Economic and Social Council
EPA	Economic Partnership Agreement
EU	European Union (for legal reasons referred to as the EC, or European Communities, within the WTO)
EU-LAC	European Union, Latin America and Caribbean
FAO	Food and Agriculture Organization
FDI	foreign direct investment
FOGS	Functioning of the GATT System
G2	United States and the European Union
G3	China, India and Brazil
G6	group formed to find negotiating compromises in the DDA (Australia, Brazil, the European Union, India, Japan and the United States)
G10	ten countries vulnerable to increased agricultural imports resulting from the DDA
G20	group of developing countries (in fact 23) with a focus on agriculture in the DDA (includes Brazil, China and India)
G33	group of developing countries that coordinate on trade and economic issues
G77	coalition of developing countries created to enhance their negotiating capacity in the United Nations
G90	alliance in the WTO including the poorest and smallest developing countries, includes LDC and ACP countries
G110	G20 and G90
GATS	General Agreement on Trade in Services
GATT	General Agreement on Tariffs and Trade
GDP	gross domestic product
GEO	Global Environmental Organization
GHG	greenhouse gas
GMO	genetically modified organisms
GSP	Generalized System of Preferences
GSTP	Global System of Trade Preferences among Developing Countries
ICCPR	International Covenant on Civil and Political Rights
ICERD	International Convention on the Elimination of All Forms of Racial Discrimination
ICESCR	International Covenant on Economic, Social and Cultural Rights
ICMW	International Convention on the Protection of the Rights of All Migrant Workers and Members of Their Families
ICT	information and communication technology
IF	Integrated Framework for Trade-Related Technical Assistance
IFFIm	International Finance Facility for Immunization
ILO	International Labour Organization
IMF	International Monetary Fund
IPC	Intellectual Property Rights Committee
IPR	Intellectual Property Rights
ISO	International Standard Organization

ITC	International Trade Centre
ITO	International Trade Organization
ITUC	International Trade Union Confederation
LDC	least developed countries
MDG	Millennium Development Goals
MEA	multilateral environmental agreement
MFN	most-favoured-nation
MNE	multinational enterprise
NAFTA	North American Free Trade Agreement
NAMA	non-agricultural market access
NEPAD	New Partnership for Africa's Development
NGO	non-governmental organization
NIC	newly industrialized country
NTB	non-tariff barrier
NTC	non-trade concern
OECD	Organisation for Economic Co-operation and Development
PPM	production and process methods
PRS	Poverty Reduction Strategies
PSIA	Poverty and Social Impact Assessment
QUAD	Canada, the European Communities, Japan and the United States
R&D	research and development
RTA	regional trade agreement
SCM	Subsidies and Countervailing Measures
SDT	special and differential treatment
SEZ	special economic zone
SME	small and medium-sized enterprise
SPS	Sanitary and Phytosanitary Measures
TACB	technical assistance and capacity-building
TBT	Technical Barriers to Trade
TCBDB	Trade Capacity Building Database
TVE	township-and-village enterprises
TPRM	Trade Policy Review Mechanism
TRIMS	Trade-Related Investment Measures
TRIPS	Trade-Related Aspects of Intellectual Property Rights
TRTA	trade-related technical assistance
TSI	trade support institution
UDHR	Universal Declaration of Human Rights
UNCTAD	United Nations Conference on Trade and Development
UNDP	United Nations Development Programme
UNEP	United Nations Environment Programme
UNITAID	United Nations International Drug Purchase Facility
VER	voluntary export restraint
WHO	World Health Organization
WIPO	World Intellectual Property Organization
WTO	World Trade Organization

Introduction and overview: Future directions

Gary P. Sampson

Introduction

The General Agreement on Tariffs and Trade (GATT) had far-reaching objectives: full employment, higher standards of living, growth of real income and expanded production and trade. With the World Trade Organization (WTO) came the added goal of the optimal use of the world's resources in accordance with sustainable development. Taken together, these objectives on the part of more than 150 governments have created for the WTO a vast area of diverse responsibilities.

It is therefore not surprising that WTO rules impact widely on national and international policies and that they extend to what many consider to be non-traditional areas of trade policy. Sometimes this has been by design – with the incorporation of trade in services and intellectual property rights into the WTO; or sometimes on a de facto basis through the dispute settlement process. There are many examples of its extended reach.

The Agreement on Trade-Related Aspects of Intellectual Property Rights (TRIPS) raises a number of ethical questions, such as the patenting of life forms, the rewarding of indigenous tribes for the exploitation of local genetic resources and the provision of essential medicines to impoverished people. Governments placed negotiations to reduce subsidies that deplete fish stocks on the Doha Development Agenda at the WTO Ministerial Conference in Doha in 2001, along with the negotiation of the relationship between the WTO and multilateral environmental

The WTO and global governance: Future directions, Sampson (ed),
United Nations University Press, 2008, ISBN 978-92-808-1154-4

agreements. The WTO dispute settlement mechanism has been confronted with topics far removed from traditional trade policy; disputes have raised questions about the role of science in the management of risk, regulations relating to public health, the conservation of endangered species and trade in genetically modified organisms.

As with other multilateral treaties, governments have voluntarily circumscribed their national sovereignty by accepting WTO rules. And for good reason: having undertaken a commitment to a degree of market openness, market access commitments would be undermined – as would the predictability and stability of the trading system – if governments were free to afford protection to domestic producers arbitrarily. The reality is that the degree of national sovereignty forgone in accepting WTO obligations is far in excess of that under GATT.

Not only is national sovereignty circumscribed under WTO rules, but governments have also undertaken complementary or overlapping commitments in other international agreements. Determining the borderline between WTO rules and national sovereignty, as well as commitments under other international treaties, is an important consideration in the context of global governance.

As Pascal Lamy notes, "governance" is not "government".[1] Governance is a decision-making process based on permanent negotiation, an exchange of agreements and the rule of law. It implies not the transfer of political sovereignty but, rather, the organizing of cooperation between existing entities on the basis of agreed and enforceable rules. According to Lamy, governance takes the form of institutions generating permanent dialogue and debate as a prelude to common actions; *governance* generates common rules, whereas *government* commands political will.

The objective of this overview is to identify future directions for the WTO in global governance. I first discuss why the importance of the WTO has increased greatly in recent years. The reasons are many and varied, with some more obvious than others. They extend, however, far beyond the increased importance of the value and volume of trade between nations. I then examine some "fundamentals" in terms of concepts, principles and rules that underpin the WTO. I believe it is necessary to review these if future directions are to be discussed. These fundamentals extend to economic, legal and institutional considerations, as well as WTO relationships with other organizations.

The chapter then draws on the contributions of the authors to address possible future directions for the WTO. Many clear-cut proposals emerge. However, owing to the complexity of a number of the issues identified, clear-cut solutions are not evident. I nevertheless believe that, by exploring this complexity and flagging alternative approaches, well-informed decisions will be taken in the future and important mistakes avoided.

The changing role of the WTO

There are many examples of the changing role of the WTO in international affairs. Some are more obvious than others.

One obvious change is the dramatic increase in both the value and the volume of world trade to which WTO rules apply: world trade has grown more rapidly than world production in almost every year since World War II. Countries trade a far greater share of their domestic production, and trade rules apply to more than a quarter of world production. The rules extend to textiles, clothing and agricultural trade – which were hitherto outside the reach of the WTO – as well as to the critical sectors of services and intellectual property rights, which have been added to the WTO agenda. Admission to the WTO, unlike the GATT, requires all members to sign on to all WTO agreements. The original 23 members of the GATT have grown to over 150 with the final membership likely to surpass 170. The levels of development, specific cultures, political systems and past colonial or other histories differ greatly across these countries, rendering consensus-based agreement in the WTO all the more difficult.

Even the larger value of trade understates the reach of WTO rules because the rules themselves have become more demanding. Domestic regulations relating to patents, financial services, subsidies and support measures for agriculture are among those now subject to WTO disciplines. They reach deep into the domestic regulatory structures of WTO member countries and raise key issues of public concern that far transcend those associated with conventional trade policy. The Agreement on Trade-Related Aspects of Intellectual Property Rights and the Agreement on Sanitary and Phytosanitary Measures (SPS) raise ethical questions about, respectively, the patenting of life forms and the role of precaution and public health; and the agricultural negotiations deal with the multi-functionality of agriculture.

The role of the WTO has also been expanded by continuing negotiations. Limitations on subsidies that deplete fish stocks and the relationship between the WTO rules and multilateral environmental agreements are part of the Doha Development Agenda.

The WTO profile has also changed because of the greatly strengthened dispute settlement mechanism. Unlike the GATT, the WTO dispute process moves forward automatically with panel and Appellate Body reports adopted unless there is a consensus against them. The rule of negative consensus, backed by a mechanism providing for compensation and sanctions in the case of non-compliance, has greatly increased public awareness of the WTO. Recent high-profile disputes have dealt with sensitive areas such as the role of science in risk management, the conservation of endangered species and restrictions on the cross-border movement of genetically modified organisms (GMOs).

According to Bert Koenders, major policy issues such as precaution, the environment, biodiversity, labour standards and climate change could drift towards the WTO not by design but by default and, in his view, the WTO dispute settlement system is not properly equipped to deal with the emerging controversies and trade tensions that they generate. The relative weakness of other multilateral institutions in enforcing their rules has unfortunately, he says, increased the demands on the WTO to deal with issues that were not previously within its mandate.

The capacity of the WTO dispute settlement mechanism to limit national sovereignty is unique among international organizations. As Pascal Lamy observes, globalization critics assert that the WTO acts as a hegemon with respect to international rule-making. Its dispute settlement mechanism makes it the only international organization with an effective judicial tool to ensure compliance with its rules. According to Lamy, trade agreements gain an institutional superiority in the array of international norms. As a result of this de facto norm primacy, commercial imperatives and economic values are, he says, believed to trump other international concerns, including environmental protection, human rights and health concerns.

Two-thirds of WTO members are now developing countries. Having undertaken new and demanding obligations, they rightfully look to future market access to support their export-led growth strategies. Their legitimate expectation is that the WTO will provide a forum in which their views can be effectively expressed and their concerns adequately dealt with. They also look not only for improved market access through the Doha Agenda but for acceptance of the legal flexibilities needed to implement their appropriate development strategies.

At the same time, others – in particular the least developed countries – feel they have not been integrated into the trading system at all, and look to new initiatives to respond to their special needs, some of which have surfaced for WTO attention. For example, the WTO has gained a high profile because of the injustices that face the impoverished cotton-exporting countries of Africa. The difficulties of gaining access to essential medicines for AIDS-stricken victims have heightened the involvement of the least developed countries, development organizations, other public interest groups, researchers and some governments.

A further important change is that developing countries have greatly increased their negotiating clout. In the past, the Group of 77 (G77) rallied around their common problem of poverty rather than around common or agreed policy approaches to meet their individual country requirements and priorities. Things have changed. As Sylvia Ostry notes, a "new geography" in the form of coalitions of southern countries became evident at the WTO ministerial meeting in Cancun. The G20 included the Big Three – Brazil, China and India – as well as a number of other developing countries. Despite repeated efforts to eliminate it, the G20 has persisted, and the other coalition that emerged in Cancun – the G90 of African and other poor countries – has also endured.

Sylvia Ostry also makes the point that the complexity of the WTO agreements requires knowledge, that knowledge enhances power, and that the WTO houses what she calls a *knowledge trap*. The strong are stronger in the WTO because of their store of knowledge, and the weak are weaker because of their poverty of knowledge. The weak lack autonomy in any system, but in the WTO complexity creates reinforced asymmetry and diminished autonomy. However, as Pascal Lamy notes, the technical assistance afforded by the WTO and other institutions has gone a long way to rectifying this shortcoming.

According to Louise Arbour and Shervin Majlessi, the Doha Agenda, with its new negotiating authority, has placed development issues and the interests of developing countries at the heart of the WTO's work. However, whatever the result of this round of trade negotiations, they say the WTO must keep its focus on development but with an approach that takes into account human rights considerations.

Sylvia Ostry does not attach much likelihood to a successful conclusion to the Doha Development Agenda. The Round, which was supposed to deal with development, in reality does not. What is absent is the need to confront the profound asymmetry in the system. For Ted Turner, failure is not an option. If the WTO gives up on global trade agreements, we can predict the outcome: the big countries will go off and do separate bilateral and regional deals with their favoured trading partners, raising the inevitable question of who will be left out. It will be the very people the WTO was created to include – the developing countries, which will have to bargain alone against the giants of international trade, leading us right back to where we are today: to a world where billions of people live in poverty.

Although the WTO has increased its importance on a number of fronts, has it also been diminished through the proliferation of preferential trade agreements? According to Dr Supachai, global economic governance and the role of the WTO are being tested by the profusion of regional trade agreements. Trade between partners to these agreements reached 50 per cent of total trade during 2007, and, given the growing number of agreements, their membership and trade coverage will have a significant impact on the international trading system. For Dr Supachai, an inward-looking approach by these agreements must be avoided; it hampers trade with third parties and undermines the multilateral trading system.

There is no doubt that the continuing growth of preferential arrangements has sparked a new interest in their motivation and effect. Do they extend WTO commitments, consolidate them or undermine them? Although in the most general terms the answer for many is not clear, Celso Amorim notes that bilateral agreements between some developed and developing countries present a serious threat to access to medicines. A cursory glance, according to Amorim, reveals provisions that attempt to bring patent protection beyond the standard set by TRIPS; they ensure extended protection to expired patents via the granting of exclusive rights over undisclosed test data. These provisions, he claims, make it harder for producers of generic versions of medicines to enter the market after patent expiry, and present a serious obstacle to better access to medicines. This is particularly the case for developing countries, since cheaper generic medicines are responsible for ensuring access to medicines at affordable prices.

In some instances, the role of the WTO has changed through events over which it has no control. One example is genetic engineering, which creates concerns for many because it permits genetic information to be transferred between organisms too distantly related for natural cross-breeding. At the centre of concern are WTO rules that could constrain the regulation of the cross-border movement of GMOs. It is hard to imagine that such issues were foreseen at the time of negotiation of the relevant WTO agreements. Another example is the proliferation of multilateral environmental agreements (MEAs), such as the Kyoto Protocol, with important potential trade implications that could not have been foreseen at the creation of the WTO.

The heightened interest in the WTO has also come against the backdrop of an incredible revolution in the speed with which information – true or false – can be communicated globally and in the cost of that communication. Sylvia Ostry remarks that we are undergoing a new technological revolution in information and communication technology, a revolution that is creating a global market for goods, services, capital and labour. The speed and breadth of change are unprecedented. This "Great Transformation" has an ongoing effect on government, individuals, corporations and values, and its role in penetrating public awareness is of profound and increasing importance.

Non-governmental organizations (NGOs) are now linked through broad networks and coalitions that render them more effective and more sophisticated than their earlier counterparts. The public image of the

WTO – as well as public interest in it – has been greatly influenced by the information conveyed through these electronic means. Although many of these groups are not against trade per se, others are intensely protection-ist, putting them on a collision course with supporters of an open and liberal trading system. The events in Seattle, Hong Kong and elsewhere – fuelled by coalitions of NGOs built on the World Wide Web – placed the WTO for the first time at the centre of a vital public policy discussion hitherto dominated by governmental representatives in closed meetings.

Finally, the profile of the WTO has been raised in very general terms because of the increasing awareness of the crucial role it plays in world affairs. For Pascal Lamy, there is a widening gap between global chal-lenges and the traditional ways of devising solutions, and no country, no matter how powerful, can successfully tackle these challenges on its own. Therefore, not only is multilateral cooperation a more peaceful means of solving conflicts; it will become the only effective means of achieving results in the face of global challenges. Developing an effective frame-work for global governance will become increasingly necessary as these new challenges arise. It is our generation's responsibility to deliver. Given the WTO's economic and political dimensions, it can be a funda-mental player in the building of a system of global governance. It can build bridges. Yet it will not and cannot be the only one to do so.

Future directions: Some fundamentals

In this section, I review some of the fundamental aspects of the world trading system that are important in charting its future directions. It does not intend to be comprehensive in terms of identifying all relevant considerations, but it does seek to illustrate the complexities involved in looking at possible future directions.

Economic fundamentals

The basic premise of well-functioning market-based economies is that prices register the relative scarcity of resources and consumer prefer-ences. One of the results of market-based prices is that they allocate re-sources efficiently. The welfare of society can be undermined, however, through trade restrictions and distortions that send misleading signals re-lating to the optimal use of resources. Trade liberalization therefore has the potential to improve resource allocation and to increase national in-come and welfare. In the case of the environment, for example, econom-ists argue that trade liberalization leads to more efficient resource use; a more efficient relative price structure (because the trade restrictions themselves are market distortions); more resources available for environmental management programmes (owing to a growth in real income); and an increase in the availability of environment-related goods and services (through market liberalization). Thus, the removal of trade barriers is itself a goal to be pursued, based on its potential for improving the environment.

However, trade liberalization is far from a panacea in terms of social (and economic) objectives. It ensures neither an equitable outcome nor the optimal use of resources from a social perspective. According to Dan Esty, trade policy – and particularly trade liberalization – inescapably affects the natural environment. In particular, freer trade promotes expanded economic activity, which often translates into industrialization, increased pollution and the consumption of natural resources. If environmental regulations are optimized and all externalities internalized, environmental harm need not accrue. But where regulation is inadequate and externalities are not fully internalized, overexploitation of open-access resources and inefficiently high levels of pollution are likely to result, a fact that trade experts and the WTO itself have come to acknowledge.

Non-discrimination

The principle of non-discrimination in the form of national and most-favoured-nation treatment dictates that WTO members cannot discriminate between imported products that are "like" nationally produced products or "like" those coming from other countries. It is one of the most important determinants of the role of the WTO in global governance. It limits governments' use of trade measures to restrict imported goods produced through child labour or those that have caused unacceptable damage to the environment. In all of this, the key concepts are non-discrimination and the "likeness" of products.

Products have generally been considered to be "like" based on their physical characteristics, end-use, consumers' preferences or tariff classification. In colloquial language, "like" means having the same physical characteristics or qualities, such as identical shape, size or colour. However, it may also mean "similar", raising many interpretive questions about the characteristics or qualities that are important in assessing the likeness of products and, therefore, the nature of imports that can be discriminated against. A diesel bus and an electric tram, for example, are alike in that they both provide transport for the public, but they may be very different when it comes to polluting the environment. Adding one gene to many thousands of others can turn a non-offensive food product into an allergy-causing nightmare. Further, the additional question arises of just whose perspective should be used to judge likeness: a slug and a snail are like products to a vegetable grower but not to a French gourmet.

From a governance perspective, the interpretation of "like products" is critical; it determines the legality of a national restriction on an imported good. Nevertheless, "likeness" has never been definitively established in GATT and WTO jurisprudence, and it is open to interpretation.

One manifestation of the importance of the interpretation of "likeness" is that a government may wish to differentiate between products according to the manner in which they were produced. Perhaps a production process was considered offensive by the importer because it emitted excessive greenhouse gases. Should imported eggs be banned if they were laid by hens kept in battery cages rather than by free-ranging hens? Are these eggs "like" the eggs of free range hens? And what of imported fur products, banned because wild animals are caught in steel-jawed leg traps? Or what of food products derived from GMOs? Are they "like" non-modified products, and can they be banned if they are physically indistinguishable from them? Are imported carpets made by children under the age of 12 like carpets knotted by adults? Should imported shrimp – physically the same as any other be banned if caught in a manner that inadvertently kills turtles?

Not surprisingly, "likeness" means different things to different organizations. Louise Arbour and Shervin Majlessi make the point that discrimination in the trade field is not the same as in other disciplines; the trade principle of non-discrimination is primarily directed towards reducing trade protectionism and improving international competitive conditions rather than achieving substantive equality. Accordingly, "national treatment" does not permit discrimination in favour of nationals even if the national provider of a "like" product is in a weaker position. For them, treating unequals as equals is problematic for the promotion and protection of human rights and could result in the institutionalization of discrimination against the poor and marginalized. For example, the non-discriminative application of trade rules that do not take into account the need to alleviate rural poverty can increase the vulnerability of small farmers and the rural poor. Arbour and Majlessi conclude that, as two sides of the same coin, non-discrimination and equality should provide the foundations for the free and equal enjoyment of human rights.

Thus, some human rights activists, environmentalists, animal welfare groups and others maintain that the WTO should change its interpretation of "likeness" and legitimize trade restrictions on the basis of how goods are produced. For them, some social, environmental and other injustices are so obvious that if the WTO prohibits trade restrictions it is acting irresponsibly from a governance perspective.

Ideally, determinations as to whether discrimination in trade is appropriate for social or environmental reasons should not be the task of the WTO. Rather, the task of establishing and enforcing internationally accepted standards should be handled through international agreements outside the WTO.

Dan Esty maintains that, for the WTO to continue to play a leading role in global governance, it must further refine its structure of rules and procedures so as to accommodate environmental values, and other concerns such as poverty alleviation, within the trading system. According to Esty, the long-term legitimacy and durability of the international trading system will be enhanced to the extent that international economic policy evolves in ways that intersect constructively with other policy-making realms, such as the emerging regime of global environmental governance. WTO decisions will not win the degree of popular acceptance that they must have to keep the trade system functioning smoothly unless the organization's decision-making processes are seen to be authoritative, effective and fair, both procedurally and substantively.

Standards

As barriers to trade are removed, the relative competitiveness of countries is increasingly influenced by different national standards. Dr Supachai notes that environmental, health and food safety requirements in particular have become more stringent and complex – a trend set to continue given concerns about food safety, energy efficiency and climate change. Many such requirements are now imposed by the private sector, coexisting and interacting with mandatory governmental requirements. Private standards, he says, are widely believed to be outside WTO disciplines and thus pose challenges in terms of justifiability, transparency, discrimination and equivalence.

Although standards can both facilitate trade and protect consumers, they can also be protectionist in intent and unnecessarily restrict trade. If all countries adopted the same standards, there would not be a problem in determining the intention behind them.

The reality is that international standards do not exist to meet the needs of all countries, and regulations that bear on the competitiveness of traded products differ across countries for very good reasons. Physical conditions differ, meaning varying absorptive capacities for air pollution, different effects from water run-off on levels of artesian water basins, and different impacts of timber-cutting on deforestation and desertification. A further complication is that, even if physical conditions are identical across countries and the risks are well known, societies may well wish to manage these risks differently. North American consumers, for example, may be less concerned about the consumption of food products derived from GMOs than are consumers in the European Union,[2] even with the same scientific information at hand.

The key WTO agreements dealing with standards are the Agreement on Technical Barriers to Trade (TBT) and the Agreement on Sanitary and Phytosanitary Measures (SPS). Neither agreement obliges countries to adopt minimum standards. They do, however, create rules that are to be respected to ensure that market access rights are not undermined through regulations that are disguised restrictions on trade. They also recognize that, for many reasons, common standards, far from being barriers to trade, work to promote trade.

From a trade policy perspective it is important that governments have the autonomy to adopt measures necessary to meet their national requirements. The question then arises of whether or not a liberal, global trading system can coexist with the very different trade and non-trade regulations that have been adopted by governments and that bear heavily on the competitiveness of products and services. As with the discussion above relating to discrimination, the WTO enters on the scene not to determine whether national policy choices are appropriate but to determine whether measures used to implement national policy goals are used for protectionist purposes. This, however, is not an easy task.

Trade and development

Many developing countries have reaped very considerable benefits from the market access openings provided by the WTO. They have adopted outward-oriented development strategies and legally binding WTO obligations to lock in domestic policy reforms. Their legitimate expectation is that the WTO will provide a forum where their views can be effectively expressed and their concerns adequately dealt with. However, many least developed countries feel they have not been integrated into the system at all. As Pascal Lamy notes, whereas some emerging economies in the developing world – most notably in Asia – are reaping the benefits of trade, the poorest countries of the world still have difficulties benefiting from global growth. In his view, integrating the group of least developed countries into the global market will be of utmost importance to meeting the challenge of poverty reduction.

Developing countries look to the WTO – and the Doha Agenda – to improve their access to markets. However, from a rules perspective, it is also crucial that the WTO legal framework provides them with the flexibility to implement their "appropriate" development strategy, and that, in turn, requires a decision on what an "appropriate" development strategy might be. Addressing this question raises critical governance issues.

GATT recognized the need for infant industry protection, flexibility in the use of balance of payments measures, non-reciprocity in trading tariff concessions and preferential market access for the manufactured exports of developing countries. These provisions were based on the premise that equal treatment of unequals is unfair. The "needs" of developing countries were dealt with by absolving them from a number of obligations undertaken by their developed counterparts. Just as poor people pay lower taxes, developing countries should pay less when they are poor and more as they develop. The legal flexibility created in GATT constituted the core of what came to be known as special and differential treatment, with its withdrawal described as graduation.

Today, there are 155 specific provisions in the WTO aimed at addressing the various concerns of developing countries. They come in many forms. Some are directed at increasing developing countries' trade opportunities whereas others are aimed at safeguarding their interests. Others provide for flexibility in the implementation of commitments, permit the use of otherwise WTO-unacceptable policy instruments or involve technical assistance. These provisions may be mandatory or non-mandatory. A large number are considered completely useless by developing countries or excessive by developed countries. However, the important question from a governance perspective is: do these provisions sit comfortably with what is perceived as an "appropriate" development strategy in the context of the WTO legal framework?

Although there is a growing acceptance of the link between trade liberalization and economic growth, there is also a clear recognition that open markets do not automatically guarantee success in trade-led economic growth. Factors such as the availability of human resources, investment, sound macroeconomic policy and low corruption are crucially important. Dealing with this reality sets the scene for today's debate.

Multilateral environmental agreements

There is no doubt in my mind that MEAs are the best way to tackle global and trans-boundary environmental problems. WTO members have made clear on numerous occasions that they do not look to the WTO to become a policy-making organization or standards enforcement agency for environmental matters. WTO rules permit governments to adopt whatever trade measures they wish to protect their domestic environments. For environmental problems beyond their borders, however, WTO members agree that regulations should be devised and enforced through international agreements and not unilateral coercion.

Since the WTO's establishment, one of the most actively discussed topics has been the possible conflict between trade-related measures in MEAs and WTO rules. Because the WTO and MEAs represent two different bodies of international law, it is important that the relationship between them is coherent and fully understood by all concerned. This is not the case at the moment. Given the importance of the global trade and environment regimes, any clash over their rules would have unfortunate ramifications for both regimes. Behind the question of which rules would trump the others lies another real governance issue.

Trade in services

The General Agreement on Trade in Services (GATS) extends trade rules into a huge and still rapidly growing area of international commerce. It holds the potential to greatly change the global patterns of investment, production and consumption in services such as telecommunications, transport (air, maritime and inland), finance (banking, insurance and securities trading), professional services, tourism, construction and engineering, and many others. These sectors include sub-sectors such as medical and hospital services and other areas of public health, and infrastructural services such as the supply of water, electricity and public utilities. I am not surprised that the GATS provokes a great deal of interest – and anxiety – among some governments and interest groups.

Much of this is related to the fact that "trade" has a very different meaning in terms of the GATS compared with other WTO agreements. For example, according to the GATS, trade in services may well take place through a foreign commercial presence of the service provider, without anything crossing borders. Specific commitments are undertaken in sub-sectors identified by governments, with limitations and conditions placed on their liberalization. There is no parallel in any other multilateral, plurilateral or bilateral agreement dealing with international commerce of any kind. Clearly, the division of responsibility between national authorities and negotiated international commitments in the WTO is crucial.

Overlapping responsibilities

In the absence of a world government, the responsibilities of international organizations are not clearly delineated. Nowhere is this more evident than in the pursuit of sustainable development, now a core objective of the WTO. As a result, there are overlapping objectives across a number of international agreements. Indeed, the Director-General of the WTO has noted: "Given the evolution of the rules-based trading system, as well as the growing attention paid to policies designed to achieve sustainable development, there has been an increasing overlap between what have now become 'trade' policies and policies relating to sustainable development." He continues that, in this respect, a crucial question that emerges is "whether a clearer mission for the WTO in support of sustainable development implies major institutional reforms".[3]

At the most general level, the objective of sustainable development stands on the pillars of economic development, environmental management and social responsibility. In Doha in 2001, trade ministers stated that the dual objectives of upholding and safeguarding an open and non-discriminatory multilateral trading system and acting for the protection of the environment and the promotion of sustainable development can – and must – be mutually supportive. Less than one year later, at the World Summit on Sustainable Development in Johannesburg, environment ministers called for urgent action to promote an open, equitable, rules-based, predictable and non-discriminatory multilateral trading system that benefits all countries in the pursuit of sustainable development. They also called for the successful completion of the work programme of the Doha Development Agenda. There is clearly common ground in terms of political objectives in the areas of both trade and sustainable development, and this is as it should be.

However, in the respective declarations, there are more than 20 overlapping areas of activity.[4] They include the need to remove trade distortions that damage the environment; to clarify and improve WTO disciplines on fisheries subsidies; to deal with global environmental problems through international consensus; to promote the mutual supportiveness of MEAs and WTO rules; to avoid arbitrary or unjustifiable trade measures that are disguised restrictions on international trade; to avoid trade measures that deal with concerns outside the jurisdiction of the importing country; to ensure that the TRIPS Agreement does not prevent WTO members from adopting measures to protect public health; to recognize the importance of core labour standards in the International Labour Organization (ILO); and many more.

In a speech to the United Nations Environment Programme (UNEP) Global Ministerial Environment Forum in 2007, Pascal Lamy remarked: "Sustainable development should be the cornerstone of our approach to globalization and to the global governance architecture that we create. If I have come to this forum, it is to deliver a message: **the WTO stands ready to do its part**."[5] The governance question that emerges here is: how to ensure coherent and mutually supportive approaches to the common objective of sustainable development.

Future directions

According to Pascal Lamy, the WTO is only part of a more global system in which several sets of rights and obligations exist, and there is a need to ensure coherence between international treaties while preserving the necessary policy space to favour non-WTO concerns. However, while ensuring that "policy space" is available for other international institutions, some questions emerge: to what extent is the "policy space" filled satisfactorily by other international agreements; do they have a compliance mechanism to enforce obligations effectively; and can the WTO make a more useful contribution to meeting the objectives of other institutions by changing its own behaviour? Lamy's view is that, although the WTO is powerful and sophisticated, it remains imperfect and its institutions contain shortcomings. I believe that addressing them will be critical if the role of the WTO in global governance is to be effective.

Strengthening UN agencies and coherence

It would seem logical that, if non-traditional trade issues come to the WTO, they should be transferred to United Nations specialized agencies that have the mandate and expertise to deal with them. Although this would seem a natural course of action, there are shortcomings in this approach. Pascal Lamy observes that the most evident failure of the general international legal system lies in its limited enforceability, and cites the former UN Secretary-General Kofi Annan's address to the 2004 General Assembly in which he states that, although an impressive body of international norms and laws exists, it is "riddled with gaps and weaknesses. Too often it is applied selectively and enforced arbitrarily. It lacks the teeth that turn a body of laws into an effective legal system."[6]

Pascal Lamy notes that WTO rules are better enforced, but its framework by no means resolves the problem associated with the lack of an international hierarchy of norms. Each international organization creates its own set of rules, according to its specialized mandate. Yet, once negotiated, no single body adjudicates conflicts between these agreements. The international principle of "good faith", which obliges governments not to agree to contradictory rules, is not enforced. His view is that the WTO's dispute settlement system does not provide the answer to this normative chaos in international law, for an adjudicator can only apply existing rules.

If the WTO is the body with the "teeth", perhaps a case can be made that the specialized agencies of the United Nations should be strengthened and given the same enforcement powers as the WTO. The WTO could then deal with a narrower agenda than it is now acquiring. However, the reality is that the political will is not there for governments to give the same enforcement powers to the UN specialized agencies as has been given to the WTO. If this political will is lacking, the implications may be an even wider gap to be filled by the WTO. What is needed in this case is a coherent approach to common objectives.

In terms of common objectives, Bert Koenders questions whether anyone could be against compliance with basic labour standards; the prevention of child labour; the promotion of sustainable development and the protection of biodiversity; and environment and animal welfare. To which Koenders replies no, but the question then arises of how to promote these objectives effectively, and whether the use of trade measures should be allowed. Here Koenders notes that most countries have undertaken commitments in these areas in other international agreements such as those of the ILO and the conventions on human rights, biodiversity and environmental issues. To the question of whether or not that makes a convincing case to allow unilateral trade measures to pursue these objectives via measures not explicitly authorized in these agreements, his answer is again no. I very much agree. The question then turns to how to promote these objectives effectively, and whether there are circumstances in which trade measures should be allowed.

In a similar vein, Louise Arbour and Shervin Majlessi say the WTO has already made a very important contribution to enhancing multilateralism and a rule-oriented international trading system. The challenge facing the international community is the development of a system of trade liberalization that benefits everyone, leaving no individual, group or state behind in the globalization. The WTO, through coordination with other global governance actors, clearly has a crucial role to play in the development of such a system.

According to Juan Somavia, over recent decades the policies promoting globalization have been extremely coherent but the outcomes have been far from fair. So the issue is not about coherence in itself, but about coherence around what objectives. Policy coherence is a means to a goal, but, according to Somavia, policies also need to make sense in their own right and to be able to achieve what they are meant to achieve. Both of these conditions then – policy coherence on shared goals and policies that make sense – bear on countries' prospects to realize the benefits of globalization.

Somavia also notes that trade policies and labour and social policies interact, and that greater policy coherence in the two domains can help to ensure that trade reforms have significantly positive effects on both growth and employment. He points out too that those trade policies have a significant impact on the level and structure of employment, wages and wage differentials, as well as on labour market institutions and policies. At the same time, labour and social policies influence the outcomes of trade policies in terms of the growth of output and employment and the distribution of income. For Somavia, there is a less clear understanding of how the interaction between trade and labour market policies can be designed in a more coherent manner to allow countries to reap the benefits of trade while simultaneously achieving good labour market outcomes.

Similarly, Louise Arbour and Shervin Majlessi note that, whereas the legal framework for the economic aspects of the liberalization of trade is provided by the multilateral trading system, the legal framework for addressing the social dimensions of trade liberalization is provided by human rights norms and practices. Meeting the challenges of globalization requires a governance structure that provides for coherent multilateral cooperation.

Cooperation and coherence can come in many forms. Celso Amorim points to the Declaration on TRIPS and Public Health as an example. In the United Nations, the Millennium Development Goals adopted in 2000 provide a substantial basis to support the claims of countries that have concerns about the effect that too-stringent patent protection might have on access to medicines. He notes that, in 2006, the UN General Assembly adopted a Political Declaration during the Follow-up meeting on the Declaration of Commitment on HIV/AIDS, which reaffirms the importance of the Doha Declaration on the TRIPS Agreement and Public Health.

Sylvia Ostry notes that one of the intents of the Uruguay Round was to improve cooperation and coordination among the main international economic institutions. Driven largely by the experience of the wide exchange misalignment of the 1980s and its impact on trade, the euphemism "international coherence" was devised. In this context, a Functioning of the GATT System (FOGS) Group was created, which produced a Ministerial Declaration on the Contribution of the WTO to Achieving Greater Coherence in Global Economic Policymaking.[7] Ministers recognized that "difficulties the origins of which lie outside the trade field cannot be redressed through measures taken in the trade field alone". They acknowledged that the "interlinkages between the different aspects of economic policy require that the international institutions with responsibilities in each of these areas follow consistent and mutually supportive policies". The Declaration went on to state that the "World Trade Organization should therefore pursue and develop cooperation with the international organizations". This served as the basis for the comprehensive and formal agreements between the WTO, the World Bank and the International Monetary Fund.

In Sylvia Ostry's view, little has emerged from the objective of greater coherence apart from rhetoric and agreements about who should attend what meetings and when. Bert Koenders says it is high time that WTO members agreed to properly define the relationship of the WTO with other relevant international bodies that use trade instruments to pursue their objectives. The principle, he says, should be to avoid conflict between different bodies of international law, especially where not all the parties are members of the WTO. In my view, the basic thrust of the Declaration on greater coherence in global economic policy-making would appear to be equally applicable to bringing greater coherence to global trade and non-trade-related policy-making.

Sylvia Ostry proposes a "policy forum", and recalls the Consultative Group of 18 (CG18), established in 1975 on a recommendation of the Committee of Twenty Finance Ministers, which came after the breakdown of the Bretton Woods system. The composition of the membership was based on a combination of economic weight, regional representation and regular rotation. The forum involved senior officials sent from capitals to participate. The CG18 was never officially terminated but meetings ceased at the end of the 1980s. In her view, establishing a WTO policy forum would be a great step forward.

My own view is that the minimum that is called for is an inventory of issues that require a coherent approach to be successfully dealt with. This should of course extend beyond the WTO and the Bretton Woods institutions, as required as a result of the Uruguay Round Declaration on coherence. Identifying the relevant issues would facilitate the task of determining the appropriate process for dealing with them within the WTO.

The importance of process

As non-trade concerns have gravitated to the WTO, they have been dealt with through different processes with differing outcomes, and much can be learned from past experience.

Bert Koenders asks if WTO rules need to be changed in order to accommodate non-trade concerns and argues that exploring courses of action other than rule change and looking for mechanisms already available in the WTO would make sense and be less contentious than changing rules. He has in mind options such as interpretations of the existing rules or Ministerial Decisions and Declarations. Pascal Lamy observes that, when faced with a political stimulus, the WTO manages to put forward legislative solutions throughout the chain of decision-making to respond and adapt to the new realities faced by WTO members. He cites considerable evidence of the evolving institutional nature of the WTO and concludes not only that the WTO can decide on rules by negotiation and adoption of international agreements but that there already exists a domain for WTO bodies to complement these traditional treaties through "secondary legislation".

In attempting to identify the "way forward" for the WTO, I think it is particularly useful to look at the manner in which a selection of non-traditional trade matters has been dealt with in the WTO:

- Some issues have been addressed in **committees** specially created to deal with the area of contention. Examples include trade and environment – dealt with in the Committee on Trade and Environment (CTE) – and trade and development – dealt with in the Committee on Trade and Development (CTD). As elsewhere in the WTO, these committees are open to all member governments.
- Some issues emerge from legal **agreements**. For example, the Technical Barriers to Trade (TBT) Agreement deals with eco-labelling and environmental standards; the protection of plant and human life and health is dealt with by the SPS Agreement; obligations relating to patents and regional appellations are found in the TRIPS Agreement; and the GATS provides for negotiated access to education and other public utility services.
- Other non-traditional trade concerns are dealt with through **formal negotiation**. The Doha Development Agenda envisages negotiations on fishing subsidies and fish stock depletion, the relationship between WTO rules and MEAs, and the liberalization of trade in environmental goods and services.
- There are **disputes** that directly touch on non-traditional trade concerns relating to – inter alia – endangered species, public health and genetically modified organisms.
- There are also WTO **decisions** such as the Singapore Ministerial Decision on labour standards and the Doha Ministerial Declaration on TRIPS and Public Health.

In reality, the WTO has had a rich experience in dealing with non-trade concerns. A closer look at some of them throws useful light on alternative ways forward. The list is long, and the examples I have drawn on are indicative only:

Trade and environment

In the early 1990s, concern about the possible clash of trade and environment policies figured prominently on the trade agenda. "Greening of the GATT" became the catch cry, launched by Dan Esty[8] and taken up by many environmentalists. Esty called for a Green Round of trade negotiations aimed at refining WTO rules and procedures so as to ensure that the international trading system would work to promote both open markets and environmental protection.

Dan Esty recalls that the original GATT agreement of 1946 did not mention the word environment and, for decades, trade policy-makers did not recognize the intersection between their policy domain and the environmental realm. After considerable public discussion and negotiation between governments, the CTE was created along with the WTO. Its mandate was to recommend modifications to WTO rules to accommodate environmental concerns. With its first major report in 1996, and much to the chagrin of environmentalists, no rule change was recommended.

In the past decade, however, the situation has changed and, for Esty, it is now clear that, for policy-makers, trade and environmental policies cannot be kept on separate tracks. Today, trade policy-makers at both the national and global levels understand that the trade–environment link is inescapable and must be managed systematically. Esty goes on to note that, in the intervening years since *Greening the GATT* was published, the debate has shifted from *whether* to integrate trade and environmental policy-making to *how* to do it; the focus on the trade–environment relationship is not really a choice, but rather a matter of descriptive reality for those engaged in managing international economic interdependence.

The interesting question is why there has been this change in sentiment in both the trade and environment community. Based on my own experience as Director of the WTO Trade and Environment Division, the principal reason is a far better understanding on the part of both trade officials and environmentalists of the nature and complexity of the issues. This can be attributed to an active debate at the academic level, as well as to the process that handled the issue in the WTO.

Since the creation of the WTO there has been a sharing of information through reports of CTE meetings and public information seminars, which have greatly enhanced the understanding of the link between trade and the environment. These symposiums have been attended by academics and by representatives of government ministries, NGOs, MEAs and UN specialized agencies. There have also been joint technical cooperation missions involving both WTO and UNEP staff that have enhanced an understanding of the issues.

Another reason for the turnaround in sentiment is that the secretariats of those MEAs with trade provisions have regularly addressed the CTE. The end result is that, although many MEAs provide for potentially nonconforming WTO trade measures, no trade dispute relating to legal inconsistencies between trade and environment treaties has ever come to the WTO: nor will it in the future, in my view.

Fishing subsidies

It is clear why the WTO finds itself centre stage in dealing with fishing subsidies. The WTO Subsidies Agreement is the only multilateral agreement that monitors subsidies and provides for countervailing measures. The WTO has among its objectives the optimal use of the world's resources, including fish stocks. Moreover, it has a powerful dispute settlement system to enforce any eventual disciplines on fisheries subsidies.

There has been transparent discussion of fishing subsidies in the WTO, primarily in the CTE. Summary records and background documents have been freely available, and interested parties have conveyed their concerns to negotiators through WTO seminars. Research and policy analysis on fisheries resources and management information have been provided by intergovernmental organizations such as the Food and Agriculture Organization, the United Nations Environment Programme, Asia-Pacific Economic Cooperation, and the Organisation for Economic Co-operation and Development.

Had the matter been dealt with as a WTO dispute, the views of countries – including those not directly involved in the dispute – would have been far from transparent. Through negotiations, in contrast, the positions of all WTO members are revealed. Public interest groups can direct their energies to convincing the appropriate governments of their cause rather than lambasting the WTO. With national positions on the table, it is clear where pressure needs to be applied by NGOs and others for movement to be made in the direction they wish to take. Further, and without question, irrespective of the decision by the panel and/or the Appellate Body, there would have been dissatisfaction on the part of some. The WTO (and in particular the dispute settlement system) rather than the governments involved in the negotiations would have been the object of attack.

Not surprisingly, the Appellate Body has consistently made the point that negotiated agreement, not WTO litigation, is the way to deal with disputes involving non-traditional trade matters. This is clearly the way forward not only for fishing subsidies but for other similar issues.

Declarations

Other non-traditional trade issues have been dealt with through Ministerial Declarations. One example is patent protection that restricts access to essential medicines. Flexibility provisions in the TRIPS Agreement do provide for the production of pharmaceutical products under specified conditions and without the authorization of the patent-holder. Nevertheless, a number of developing countries sought assurances that these provisions would be interpreted in a sufficiently flexible manner. Thus, a Ministerial Declaration was negotiated to deal with this concern.

According to Celso Amorim, the Declaration on TRIPS and Public Health, adopted at the Doha Ministerial Conference, recognizes that "the TRIPS Agreement does not and should not prevent members from taking measures to protect public health" and, in particular, that countries enjoy "the right to grant compulsory licenses and the freedom to determine the grounds upon which such licences are granted". Amorim asserts that the Doha Declaration goes beyond the mere reaffirmation of provisions inscribed in TRIPS. It acknowledges that health issues have a precedence vis-à-vis patents and that countries enjoy the policy space to adopt measures aimed at ensuring access to medicines. His view is that this had fundamental consequences for negotiations of the Development Round as a whole, and to date is one of the few results of the Round clearly recognizable as "development friendly".

The relationship between trade and labour standards provides a further example of the use of Ministerial Declarations. Although there has been considerable pressure for some years for the WTO to play a role in the enforcement of minimum labour standards, this is seen by governments to be the role of the ILO. With a view to clarifying matters, trade ministers affirmed at the 1996 Singapore Ministerial that the ILO was the competent body to set and enforce labour standards, whereas the role of the WTO was to promote economic growth and development through trade liberalization, with trade-induced growth seen as a contributor to the promotion of core labour standards. They correctly rejected the use of labour standards for protectionist purposes, and affirmed that the comparative advantage of low-wage developing countries must in no way be put into question.

There are many options for dealing with non-traditional trade matters in the WTO. In my view, past experience is important in this respect because it indicates that other options of a less confrontational and more transparent nature can be resorted to before calling for rule change or engaging in financially and politically costly disputes.

National responsibilities

There is no automatic process that accompanies trade liberalization to ensure a positive impact on social conditions, the environment or income distribution. The question then emerges of whose responsibility it is to deal with potential problems. The WTO view – and that of the GATT before it – has been that, when adverse production and consumption externalities are adequately integrated into decision-making processes, trade liberalization and the attainment of non-trade-specific objectives can be mutually supportive.[9] For trade-induced growth to be sustainable, appropriate domestic policies need to be in place. The predominant view of WTO members is that this is a national choice, with differences in domestic policies properly regarded as domestic choices reflecting domestic trade-offs. In my view, this approach must be preserved.

Thus, Juan Somavia notes that, if trade is being liberalized, then countries with well-designed social and labour market policies are better positioned to reap the benefits and cope with possible adverse effects. Louise Arbour and Shervin Majlessi point to a link between trade, development and human rights: trade can help guarantee the enjoyment of human rights by improving opportunities for economic growth, job creation and the diffusion of technology and capital, and can contribute to development and the eradication of poverty. Trade can, however, also threaten human rights in some situations. Their conclusion is that it is a national responsibility to promote and protect human rights when negotiating and implementing international rules on trade liberalization. In order to ensure the most appropriate human rights regulations, assessments of the impact of trade policies are fundamental. It is the role of national governments to study the impact of trade agreements and liberalization.

Dani Rodrik argues that, in terms of globalization more generally, a range of institutional complementary measures in both rich and poor countries is required in order to deliver its benefits in full and remain sustainable. In the advanced countries, the complementary measures relate in large part to improved social safety nets and enhanced adjustment assistance. In the developing countries, he continues, the requisite institutional reforms range all the way from anti-corruption to labour market and financial market reforms.

Rodrik argues that the greatest bang for the global reform buck lies in pushing for increased openness and market access, while ensuring that the adverse consequences of openness are taken care of; the challenge becomes not "how do we liberalize further" but "how do we create the *policy space* for nations to handle the problems that openness creates". His argument is that it is lack of policy space – and not lack of market access – that is the binding constraint on a prosperous global economy. There should be sufficient policy space to allow rich nations to address issues of social insurance and concerns about the labour, environmental and health consequences of trade; and to allow poor nations to position themselves better for globalization through economic restructuring and diversification.

Louise Arbour and Shervin Majlessi note that, in the trade policy community, trade expansion is often viewed as an end in itself and is used to measure the success of these policies; a view that in turn can be reflected in the methodologies, agenda and review mechanisms of the organization. They argue that, to ensure the sustainability of trade law and policy from a human rights and development perspective, WTO bodies and mechanisms – including the Trade Policy Review Mechanism and the Dispute Settlement System – should adopt a methodology and view that examines trade law and policy comprehensively, focusing not only on economic growth, markets or economic development but also on health systems, education, water supply, food security, labour, political processes and so on.

The bottom line is that the way forward, as Juan Somavia observes, is for each country to find its own way to best address the challenges posed by trade liberalization. For example, social dialogue between workers, employers and governments at the national level can be an effective way to find solutions that take the needs of each side into account. He also poses the question of whether traditional trade theory downplays some of the important implications of trade liberalization that can be observed in many countries: greater inequality that results from increased skill premiums and/or a shift from labour to capital incomes, and a loss of employment security in industrialized countries. If left unaddressed, both create opposition to globalization and can make it politically and socially unsustainable. Somavia argues moreover that labour and social policies are required in order to redistribute some of the gains derived from trade from winners to losers.

The role of discrimination

If the WTO were to legitimize trade discrimination without all WTO members agreeing to forgo their rights in this respect, it would profoundly change the nature of the WTO. However, it is precisely here that the greatest pressure is brought to bear on the WTO to create linkages with non-traditional trade areas. There are those who argue that there currently exists a strong multilateral rules-based trade regime, attained through the WTO, which is essential to developing a system of governance of global markets. It is reasoned that the trading system cannot act in isolation when there exists a wide variety of issues that rightfully belong on the trade agenda.

The thought of importing goods that have degraded the environment, accelerated the extinction of endangered species or been produced with child labour is clearly anathema to many. The question is not whether such matters should be dealt with at the international level; the controversy turns on whether the WTO is the appropriate body to deal with them.

As Bert Koenders points out, pleas can be heard to add policies in the country of origin as conditions for market access; conditions such as the local labour conditions or the implementation of national laws in line with international agreements in other areas. He cites as current examples the European Union's minimum sustainability criteria – currently in the making – for biofuels based on meeting minimum savings of greenhouse gas emissions over the whole lifecycle (compared with the fossil reference product) and the protection of bio-diversity. He also includes pleas for import prohibitions on products produced with the worst forms of child labour, or on agricultural products that fail domestic animal welfare standards in the European Union.

Similarly, as Louise Arbour and Shervin Majlessi note, the WTO mechanisms entrusted with the task of implementation and interpretation of the rules and settlement of disputes involving human rights considerations and obligations of states should ensure that these two processes – progressive realization of socio-economic rights and progressive trade liberalization – can be implemented simultaneously and coherently. This will require, according to Arbour and Majlessi, at a very minimum, that the states' international trade commitments not be interpreted in a manner that will undermine the fulfilment of their international human rights law obligations.

The way I see it is that if governments agree on when to discriminate in trade, then there is no problem: they agree that narcotics and stolen goods should be discriminated against. However, what weight should be assigned to other agreements if all WTO members are not parties? Or what if countries decide to act unilaterally in restricting trade, even if there is no multilateral agreement to do so?

For Bert Koenders, governments will always, for different reasons, search for linkages between issues and policies that may be unrelated to considerations of market access and competition. Although such linkages will undoubtedly complicate negotiations in the WTO, they could still deliver beneficial outcomes. From the perspective of global governance and enhancement of global welfare, he says such linkages should therefore not be rejected out of hand; cross-linkages between trade and climate change negotiations, for example, have become very topical and require urgent attention.

As Dan Esty points out, environmental programme and policy choices often affect trade, and in some cases become intertwined as a function of ecological realities. Furthermore, a number of environmental challenges are global in scope. Esty cites numerous examples that cannot be dealt with on a national basis, from the depleted fisheries in many of the world's oceans, to the need to protect the ozone layer, to the build-up of greenhouse gas emissions that may produce climate change. In such cases, says Esty, countries that seek to address worldwide problems unilaterally inevitably find that they cannot resolve the issue through their own efforts: international cooperation is essential. From the perspective of public goods economics, successful "collective action" requires mechanisms to promote collaboration and to discipline "free riders".

Indeed, a unique provision of the WTO is that the Dispute Settlement Understanding rules out all unilateral measures, with only the WTO able to decide whether a member's measures or actions are inconsistent with WTO rules. For Pascal Lamy, forcing powerful members to abide by dispute settlement rulings and generating a rules-based mechanism for dealing with disputes represent a major achievement of the WTO, placing it ahead of other organizations, where compliance is most often the result of diplomacy and the balance of powers.

WTO processes do in fact defer to other agreements (e.g. in the SPS Agreement) or take into account "soft law" or "best endeavour" commitments. The Appellate Body is a case in point. It determined that certain turtles should be considered an "exhaustible natural resource" because they were listed in Appendix 1 of the Convention on International Trade in Endangered Species of Wild Fauna and Flora (CITES). With respect to the Precautionary Principle, the Appellate Body noted that "it is unnecessary, and probably imprudent, for the Appellate Body in this appeal to take a position on this important, but abstract, question".[10] The Precautionary Principle had not yet "crystallized" to become a general principle of law.

The Appellate Body has taken the view that WTO provisions cannot be read in clinical isolation from public international law, and that the international rights and obligations of WTO members are to be taken into account when reading and interpreting their respective WTO obligations. This recognizes that the WTO is only part of a more global system that includes several sets of rights and obligations. No priority can be given to WTO norms over other international norms; there is a need to ensure global coherence in the interpretation and application of all values, rights and obligations. Lamy believes that, in leaving members with the necessary policy space to favour non-WTO concerns, the WTO also recognizes the specialization, expertise and importance of other international organizations.

The Appellate Body does indeed use discretion in its rulings and takes public opinion into account. In reality, WTO exceptions referring to non-trade concerns are to be interpreted according to the ordinary meaning of the non-trade policy invoked. In its interpretation of the important concept of "likeness", the Appellate Body says "likeness" evokes "the image of an accordion which stretches and squeezes in different places as different provisions of the WTO Agreement are applied. The width of the accordion ... must be determined by ... the context and the circumstances that prevail in any given case".[11] Similarly, in terms of sustainable development, the Appellate Body believes that in its rulings sustainable development "must add colour, texture and shading to our interpretation of the agreements annexed to the WTO Agreement".[12] The Appellate Body is responsible for "squeezing" the accordion and the "colouring in" exercise. Assigning an importance to "soft law" is a sensitive course of action because it necessarily interjects a subjective element into rulings. A judgement call is required.

So what is the way forward? Some wise advice is offered by the late Bob Hudec.[13] His view is that, in circumstances where discretion is required, most tribunals decide the case as best they can by making a "seat-of-the-pants judgment" about whether the defendant government is behaving correctly. Once the tribunal comes to a conclusion about who should win, it fashions an analysis – in terms of the criteria it has been asked to apply – that makes the case come out that way. So long as the tribunal gets it right most of the time – that is, decides its cases according to the larger community's perception of right and wrong behaviour – Hudec says the decisions tend to be accepted.

Viewed from this perspective, the eventual political acceptability of the WTO's policing function over domestic regulatory measures depends not on the persuasiveness of the legal standards being applied but on the ability of WTO tribunals to find the right answers; in other words, their ability to know when to prohibit regulatory measures viewed as illegitimate by the larger community, and when to let pass those measures that the community views as bona fide regulation. If the answers are largely right, according to Hudec, the "occasional absurdity" of the legal rationale will probably not matter.

In the final analysis, although many would like to see WTO rules changed to permit trade measures to be used to enforce preferred standards relating to production processes outside the importing country, I am quite convinced this would seriously undermine the credibility and usefulness of the WTO. If countries will not agree to forgo their rights not to be discriminated against and for the WTO be the adjudicator of whether discrimination is appropriate in the absence of agreement, the WTO would find itself at the top of a slippery slope dealing with social, environmental and other non-trade concerns.

MEAs and WTO rules

The potential problems surrounding the inconsistency of measures, trade agreements and MEAs fall into two groups.

The first covers trade-related measures taken by a party to an MEA against another party, where the measure is not specifically provided for in the MEA. The party taking the measure may justify it in terms of achieving the objectives of the MEA. Both parties could be members of the WTO, in which case the measure could then be challenged as being WTO inconsistent. Professor Matsushita provides the example of WTO members that are also parties to the Cartagena Protocol and find themselves faced with a serious conflict between the SPS Agreement and the

Protocol; the former requires a measure to prohibit GMO products based on scientific evidence, whereas the latter permits the application of the precautionary principle. In his view, although panels and the Appellate Body have no choice but to apply the SPS Agreement over the Cartagena Protocol, the eventual conflict should be resolved through negotiations as to the proper scopes of each agreement.

The second group of problems relates to WTO-inconsistent measures that are specifically provided for in an MEA, and taken by a party to the MEA against a non-party that is a WTO member. The WTO member may challenge the legitimacy of the measure in the WTO dispute settlement process. The defending government could seek an exception for the WTO-inconsistent measures and cite the existence of the MEA as a justification.

Matsushita remarks that the scope for exemptions from WTO obligations is not entirely clear, and it is left to panels and the Appellate Body to decide this relationship. The problem for the dispute settlement process is deciding on the importance to ascribe to the existence of the MEA. Ultimately, he says, this issue also needs to be addressed as a subject matter of future negotiations.

Professor Matsushita also predicts that tensions may arise between WTO agreements and MEAs – such as the Kyoto Protocol – even though WTO disciplines and the Kyoto Protocol may not themselves be in conflict. For example, to reduce carbon dioxide, a member of the WTO may introduce a measure to encourage electric cars by taxing cars that run on gasoline more heavily. If cars run on gasoline were then to be imported, this preferential tax could be challenged by other members as a violation of the national treatment principle if the cars are like products.

These potential problems are well known to governments. In such instances, the WTO finds itself in the role of an arbiter in environmental matters, something members have specifically stated that they wish to avoid. This concern finds its expression in the Doha Development Agenda, where governments are mandated to conduct negotiations in order to clarify the relationship between WTO rules and those found in MEAs. The way forward is to bring these negotiations to a successful conclusion.

The reality of the situation is that MEAs do – and should – have the power to invoke WTO-inconsistent measures to achieve their goals. Given the importance of the global trade and environment regimes, any clash over the application of rules agreed to among nations would have unfortunate ramifications for both regimes. To remove this possibility, and to avoid the WTO being the arbiter of environmental disputes, any WTO-inconsistent measures should be clearly spelled out and agreed to by the parties to a broad-based multilateral environmental agreement.

Disagreement about the legality of MEA measures in any MEA should then be dealt with by the compliance mechanism in the MEA itself, and should not be left to interpretation by a WTO dispute panel or Appellate Body report. This course of action requires effective MEAs, characterized by clearly specified trade measures that may be taken for environmental purposes, broad-based support in terms of country membership, and a robust dispute settlement system. My opinion is that effective MEAs are critical to avoid environmental disputes gravitating towards the WTO and inhibiting the smooth functioning of the WTO itself.[14]

Developing countries

In looking to future directions for the WTO, Dr Supachai observes a need for a fundamental reassessment and renewal of global governance and identifies a number of issues that are priorities for debate: what should be the objectives of governance, including what should be the optimal weighting and mix of values and objectives related to efficiency and market competition, on the one hand, and equity and development solidarity, on the other; what, and how far, to govern or leave to market outcomes; how best to achieve coherence in the governance of interrelated issues such as trade and finance, and across different levels of governance – national, bilateral, regional, plurilateral or multilateral – taking into account questions of sovereignty and interdependence; what types of governance norms, institutions and mechanisms to utilize, and how to design or reform these in a manner that enables all stakeholders, including weaker players, to have their interests or viewpoints taken into account.

The answer to many of these questions is heavily influenced by the development model adopted by the country in question. For some years, the "Washington Consensus" has been the mainstream prescription for economic development, with liberalization as the trade policy component. However, not all subscribe to the "Washington Consensus". In the view of Dani Rodrik, for example, successful developing countries are not those that have adhered to the Washington Consensus. According to Rodrik, even the simplest of policy recommendations – "liberalize your trade" – is contingent upon a large number of judgement calls about the economic and political context in which it is being implemented. He says the tendency in international trade negotiations has been to reduce the scope for government action with respect to industrial policies and productive restructuring. For these reasons, he concludes that maintaining the necessary policy space to pursue development strategies that reflect the human and institutional infrastructures in developing countries will be key to the success of any future trade round.

Dr Supachai notes the importance of developing countries' ability and scope to use national policies to pursue trade and development goals, something that was increasingly reduced as the WTO embraced and legislated deeper "behind the border" trade regulations. These rules and commitments, which in *legal* terms are equally binding for all countries, in *economic* terms might, according to Supachai, impose more binding constraints on developing than on developed countries. This is owing to differences in their respective structural features and levels of industrial development, which limit the possibility for developing countries to have recourse to certain development policies in areas such as subsidies, balance of payment measures, infant industry support, trade-related aspects of investment measures (TRIMS) and TRIPS. These rules, he concludes, make it more difficult for developing countries to create the competitive supply capacity needed to take advantage of improved export opportunities.

Although the debate on the virtues of the Washington Consensus will continue, what is increasingly apparent is that each country is unique. The simple reality is that the term "developing countries" masks very different country characteristics, to which the relevance of any development model is inextricably linked. They include natural resource endowments; cultural heritage; characteristics of leadership; and institutional and other arrangements. Successful reforms are those that package sound economic principles around local capabilities, constraints and opportunities. As these local circumstances vary, so do the reforms that work. An immediate implication is that growth strategies require considerable local knowledge.

Based on past experience, I am convinced that special treatment for developing countries should come in the form of special and *differentiated* treatment that depends on the country-specific circumstances. The challenge is to identify the legal flexibilities that are appropriate for individual country circumstances.

In this respect, Dr Supachai posits the view that "development" must be explicitly mainstreamed into the multilateral trading system of rights and obligations – including by way of reinvigorating and strengthening the concept of special and differential treatment. According to him, allowing developing countries – with a wide diversity of levels of development – effectively to manage their domestic economic policies in the light of national development and public policy objectives, within the multilateral framework of rights and obligations, would signify an adequate degree of policy flexibility for economic governance.

According to Patricia Francis, negotiations that improve access to potential markets do not automatically result in expanded trade. For Francis, trade can promote economic development only if we get the framework right, and the right framework is one that is broad enough to address legitimate concerns about globalization and to help developing countries build the skills they need to be competitive in world markets.

Francis goes on to emphasize the role of the private sector and says that accessing markets requires the skills of private enterprises to take advantage of the market opportunities. This calls for an ability to listen to business leaders, trade institutions and policy-makers and to design a range of innovative approaches that are targeted to the needs at hand.

Patricia Francis stresses the importance of the Aid for Trade initiative. The term "Aid for Trade" means different things to different people, as Francis rightly points out, and needs to be properly defined to facilitate the dialogue among so many players. For her, there are four broad areas that constitute Aid for Trade.

The first relates to policy, by which she means national, inter-country and global dimensions of policies needed to support trade development. Along with cross-border facilitation, global facilitation and rule-making, national strategies for trade – including export strategies – are required as part of national development plans. The second relates to physical infrastructures, which must be created and improved to support trade, including assistance to industrial facilities. Third, there must be compensation for tariff reduction, preference erosion, the cost of conforming to standards and the like. Finally, trade-related technical assistance is critical to help with supply-side constraints and to build the human and institutional capacity to trade effectively.

In my opinion, the importance of special and differential treatment within the WTO legal system lies in the fact that it is the mirror image of not only the physical, institutional and other characteristics of the country in question, but also the human and institutional infrastructure of the country itself. Developing countries require special and *differentiated* treatment that provides them with the necessary legal flexibility to pursue their appropriate development strategy, in line with their national human, physical and institutional characteristics.

Trade in services

The GATS is frequently criticized by special interest groups. One of the main reasons is the perception that countries – particularly developing countries – undertook more commitments in joining the GATS than is the case. The reality is that the GATS is very much a bottom-up agreement with only minimal obligations undertaken at the outset. Any additional commitments are undertaken according to national preferences and are inscribed in the national schedule. These are selective with respect to the sectors concerned and permit a wide range of limitations and restrictions to be placed on market openings.

The fact that commitments have been minimal is not surprising. Given the sensitive and strategic nature of many services regulations, governments took care in negotiating the GATS not to undertake general commitments that would restrict national policy objectives. The way forward is for negotiators to give substance to their commitment to liberalize trade in services progressively, to pay special attention to the needs of developing countries and to allay fears that the GATS is by its nature a particularly intrusive instrument.

Dispute settlement

It has been argued that the Appellate Body has extended its authority beyond what was granted to it. The Dispute Settlement Understanding (DSU) limited the jurisdiction of the Appellate Body to issues of law covered in panel reports and to legal interpretations developed by panels. It prohibited the Appellate Body from changing the rights and obligations provided for in WTO Agreements. A number of countries have argued – in a disapproving manner – that there has been an "evolutionary" interpretative approach adopted by the Appellate Body, which has given a new interpretation to certain DSU provisions and overstepped the bounds of its authority by undermining the balance of rights and obligations of members.

Professor Matsushita proposes a small group of experts on WTO law and economics to periodically review rulings of the Appellate Body. This group would be established within the WTO as a sort of advisory group, with no power to overturn the rulings of the Appellate Body. Its function would be limited: to review the decisions of the Appellate Body, assess them for jurisprudential and economic soundness, and publish its views. It would be composed of academics, lawyers, judges and economists of established renown and authority. Reviews of decisions of the Appellate Body made by this group should, in his view, be based on neutral, jurisprudential and economic theories and not on the political desirability of the rulings of the Appellate Body.

Matsushita also makes the useful point that the WTO dispute settlement procedure is premised on the assumption that all members are equal in their legal capacity to present their position in dispute settlement. In this regard, the WTO dispute settlement procedure is likened to the process in civil and commercial litigation in which parties are equal and it is their responsibility to adduce sufficient evidence and to present persuasive legal arguments. If a party is unsuccessful in producing good evidence and persuasive legal arguments, that party fails. The question, however, is whether WTO members are truly equal in their legal capacity in dispute settlements. In fact, there is a great deal of difference between developing country members and developed country members with respect to their legal capacity – despite the Advisory Centre on WTO Law established in 2001 – and this may hamper developing country members in effectively utilizing the WTO dispute settlement procedure.

Institutional considerations

It is often argued that participation in the WTO should be broadened to include non-state actors. In this respect, the WTO has no mandate from members to enlarge official membership beyond governmental representation. The organization thus faces the inherently difficult task of striking a subtle balance between preserving the inter-state nature of WTO talks while opening up to new actors. States promote their national interests whereas civil societies pursue issues-based objectives. I share the view of Pascal Lamy that because the WTO remains first and foremost a negotiating forum in which states express interests of the utmost importance to them, the admittance of civil society groups to negotiation bodies would be inappropriate.

Because the WTO is an intergovernmental organization, its members are presumed to be acting in the collective interests of their diverse constituents. Although governments liberalize trade and agree to rules to secure benefits for their economies as a whole, they are aware that some interest groups may be adversely affected in this process. The WTO is frequently the object of adverse public opinion.

One reason for the expression of adverse public sentiment has been a lack of understanding about what the WTO can and does do. The reasons for this are many, not the least being the non-transparent workings of the GATT, many of which were carried over to the WTO. Matters have, however, greatly improved in recent years. In addition, the Doha Declaration emphasizes that members will "continue to promote a better public understanding of the WTO and to communicate the benefits of a liberal, rules-based multilateral trading system", particularly "through the more effective dissemination of information and improved dialogue with the public". This is certainly one important "way forward".

Understanding of the WTO by public interest groups has increased greatly, and many are particularly well informed. One frequently heard complaint is that the WTO has extended its reach "too far".

Celso Amorim sums up the situation with respect to access to essential medicines. According to Amorim, the fact that the WTO was increasingly meddling in issues that transcended the sphere of trade, when millions of people were left unprotected in terms of their health necessities, gave rise to a significant change in the way world public opinion perceived the WTO in general, and the relation between intellectual property and health in particular. In his capacity as Ambassador in Geneva, Amorim witnessed how public opinion began to put trade issues in perspective, especially when it came to matters affecting access to medicines. This, he says, was due in part to the involvement of NGOs such as Oxfam and Médecins sans Frontières. To a certain extent, this change signalled that the prevailing view during the Uruguay Round – that trade liberalization would bring development – had shifted to one more prone to fulfil social concerns and development needs. Thus, in his view, the NGOs played a crucial role in this change.

But what does "too far" mean precisely? Does it relate to subject matter, the nature of the regulations the WTO enforces, its country membership, the non-trade issues that are gravitating towards it, or some other feature of its operations? In addition, "too far" in whose eyes? The 150-plus governments that have set its parameters or the public interest groups that find its role intrusive in national affairs? Or has its reach been extended not by design but unwillingly or unwittingly by governments themselves? For example, have major issues gravitated towards the WTO on a de facto basis, or have the implications of the agreements for which the WTO is now responsible turned out to be more far-reaching than originally foreseen?

In this context, sight is often lost of the fact that all WTO decisions are made on the basis of consensus, thereby taking in the views of all members. Agreements are negotiated by national officials, agreed to by trade ministers and signed off by domestic parliaments or some equivalent procedure before coming into force.

It is an unfortunate fact of life, however, that not every WTO member has the same power in the negotiating process. The more economically powerful countries are listened to more carefully. And, because agreement is by consensus frequently achieved by trade-offs, powerful countries have more bargaining chips and therefore greater leverage in reaching decisions by consensus. Nevertheless, smaller countries have an authority in the WTO through recourse to the dispute settlement process, the consensus rule and the new-found success in forming negotiating coalitions.

The question that arises for me is why sovereign states would spend years negotiating agreements that excessively undermine their sovereignty. If the answer is that nation-states unwittingly erred in joining or creating the WTO, then the option is there to leave. All that this requires is six months' notice; yet no country has ever expressed an interest in leaving either the GATT or the WTO. And if WTO agreements mean a loss of national sovereignty, why would 25 sovereign nations be so intent on acceding to the WTO and forgoing this sovereignty?

Policy conclusions: The way forward

A principal reason for the support for the WTO from both large and small governments is that they see adherence to multilateral rules – rather than political or commercial power – to be in their national interests. Rules bring predictability and stability to the world trading system and, although rule-governed trade may not guarantee peace, it does remove a potent cause of conflict, offering an alternative to reliance on unbridled force in the trading relations among states. Although sovereignty is forgone on becoming a member of the WTO – as with any significant international agreement – what is gained is the opportunity for participation in the global economy through cooperation.

The increasing role of the WTO in global governance comes from the confidence that governments have placed in it. This in turn is attributable to the certainty that comes from the legal enforcement of trade rules adopted on the basis of consensus, along with legally binding commitments to liberalise trade. Changing these rules to permit discrimination in trade to enforce labour, environment or human rights standards would further increase its role in global governance. To my mind, this is not at all desirable.

However, the WTO agenda has acquired many non-traditional trade issues, and more will come. This will further increase its governance role. In my view, the "way forward" rests on four pillars. All have been explored in detail in the foregoing paragraphs.

First, there must be a strong resistance on the part of governments to changing rules that would alter the role of the WTO as a trade organisation. In the case of challenges to rules, to the extent possible, this should be dealt with through negotiation and not litigation. Negotiations on fishing subsidies provide an example.

Second, the continued creative use of new and existing mechanisms to deal with non-trade issues is the pragmatic way forward. Discussions in specially created committees, Ministerial Declarations and many other avenues have so far been successfully used to deal with these complex issues. The Ministerial Declaration on TRIPs provides an example.

Third, there is a need for greater coherence across international organisations dealing with overlapping issues. The areas of overlap should be clearly identified, and a means to address them agreed on. This has certainly been the case in what was the very controversial area of trade and environment.

Finally, governments must maintain their right to implement domestic policies to meet national goals. However, policy measures should not be protectionist in intent, unnecessarily trade restrictive or be resorted to when a bilateral, regional or multilateral agreement is the proper way to go. The Shrimp-turtle dispute provides an example.

The WTO is far from perfect, and there are many proposals for change in the foregoing chapters. But at the most fundamental level, it must remain a **trade** organisation based on **non-discrimination** while retaining its **inter-governmental** character based on **consensus** decision making.

Notes

1. Unless specifically indicated otherwise, all references to authors relate to their chapters in this volume.
2. In formal terms, the European Union is referred to as European Communities within the context of the WTO. In the following chapters it is also referred to as the European Community.
3. See the "Foreword" by Pascal Lamy in Gary P. Sampson, *The WTO and Sustainable Development*, Tokyo: United Nations University Press, 2005, pp. vii and xi.
4. These can be found in Sampson, *The WTO and Sustainable Development*, pp. 38–51.
5. Pascal Lamy, address to the UNEP Global Ministerial Environment Forum, Nairobi, 5 February 2007, original emphasis; available at ⟨http://www.wto.org/english/news_e/sppl_e/sppl54_e.htm⟩ (accessed 10 June 2008).
6. Kofi Annan, "Address by Kofi Annan at the Opening of the General Debate of the Fifty-Ninth Session of the General Assembly", New York, 21 September 2004, at ⟨http://www.un.org/Pubs/chronicle/2004/issue3/0304p4.asp⟩ (accessed 10 June 2008).
7. See "Declaration on the Contribution of the World Trade Organization to Achieving Greater Coherence in Global Economic Policymaking", in WTO, *The Results of the Uruguay Round of Multilateral Trade Negotiations: The Legal Texts*, Geneva: WTO Secretariat, 1994, p. 386.
8. Daniel C. Esty, *Greening the GATT: Trade, Environment and the Future*, Washington, DC: Institute for International Economics, 1994.
9. Since the publication of a GATT Secretariat study requested for the proceedings of the United Nations Conference on Environment and Development in 1972.
10. WTO, *European Communities – Measures Concerning Meat and Meat Products* [EC Hormones], WT/DS26/AB/R, WT/DS48/AB/R, adopted 16 January 1998, para. 123.
11. WTO, *Japan – Alcoholic Beverages*, Appellate Body Report, WT/DS8,10,11/AB/R, adopted 1 November 1996, p. 114, fn 58.
12. *United States – Import Prohibition of Certain Shrimp and Shrimp Products* [Shrimp-Turtle], Panel Report, WT/DS58/R, circulated 15 May 1998, and Appellate Body Report, WT/DS58/AB/R, circulated 12 October 1998. Paras 152–154.
13. Robert E. Hudec, "GATT/WTO Constraints on National Regulation: Requiem for an 'Aim and Effects' Test", *International Lawyer*, Vol. 32, No. 3, 1998; reprinted in Robert E. Hudec, *Essays on the Nature of International Trade Law*, London: Cameron May, 1999, pp. 359–395.
14. For an elaboration of this approach, see Gary P. Sampson, "Effective Multilateral Environment Agreements and Why the WTO Needs Them", *The World Economy*, Vol. 24, No. 9, 2001, pp. 1097–1108.

Part I

The bigger picture

1

The WTO's contribution to global governance

Pascal Lamy

Introduction

The World Trade Organization (WTO) is only 13 years old, and is by far the youngest of the international economic organizations. Whereas its predecessor, the General Agreement on Tariffs and Trade (GATT), was the product of the post–World War II era, in many people's minds the WTO is synonymous with globalization in the twenty-first century. Looking back, it is fair to say that the 1999 WTO Seattle Ministerial Conference first launched this organization into world headlines. For better or worse, trade opening – which is the WTO's core business – now embodies the globalization process. As a result, opinions on the organization encompass the widest range of viewpoints on the issue of globalization. The Geneva-based institution is both hailed as a rudimentary form of globalization management and denigrated as responsible for the sins of globalization.

The challenges of globalization

With the acceleration of market integration and increased interdependence, the need to harness globalization has become a defining policy goal for decision-makers worldwide. Globalization in and of itself is not a new phenomenon. Yet its current speed and imbalances are generating anxieties across the globe.

The WTO and global governance: Future directions, Sampson (ed),
United Nations University Press, 2008, ISBN 978-92-808-1154-4

In the developed world, protectionist tendencies are making a come-back. The United States and the European Union, which had been advocates of trade liberalization, have to accommodate increasingly sceptical constituencies. The possibility that public opinion could drive governments towards a fortress Europe or an isolationist America can no longer be totally dismissed. Citizens are feeling politically dispossessed from basic democratic principles. The notion that each ballot grants a say in the direction of events no longer holds for all. As a result, although globalization has brought about the highest degree of prosperity worldwide, it has also generated mutations over which citizens desire control.

In the developing world, some emerging economies – most notably in Asia – are reaping the benefits of trade, but the world's poorest still have difficulties benefiting from global growth. Integrating the group of least developed countries into the global market will be of the utmost importance if we are to meet the challenge of poverty reduction. Aid alone is not the answer. This was recognized by world leaders when the latest round of WTO global trade talks was launched in 2001. Concluding the Doha Round will be key in defining whether the inequities that continue to characterize world trade are addressed. Making trade and globalization work, in particular for the world's poorest, is the challenge of our age.

Globalization creates new challenges, such as climate change or global terrorism. It also amplifies existing ones, among which are resource scarcity and migration flows. These share a common constraint: interdependence, which is the most important phenomenon by which globalization alters the foundations of international public policy. The current order is rooted in the Westphalian system, whereby the sovereign nation-state is bestowed with the power to take public action. Yet today this structure appears insufficient to respond to the global challenges. Globalization is both a reality and an ongoing process that cannot be met by nation-states alone. There is a widening gap between global challenges and traditional ways of devising solutions. No country, no matter how powerful, can successfully tackle these challenges on its own. Not only is multilateral cooperation a more peaceful means of solving conflicts; it will become the only effective means of achieving results in the face of global challenges. Developing an effective framework for global governance will become increasingly necessary as these new challenges arise. It is our generation's responsibility to deliver.

Global governance

Global governance is sometimes equated with the emergence of a world government. Yet the two notions have very different meanings. A world government would imply a transfer of decision-making prerogatives to a new political centre, endowed with international popular legitimacy. In its ideal form, this world political entity would emerge in place of current nation-states, by way of a transfer of sovereignty. From a liberal stand-point, it would take the form of a world democracy entrusted with all the powers inherent in government. Most notably, it would hold "the monopoly on the legitimate use of physical force".[1]

But "governance" is not "government". Governance is a decision-making process based on permanent negotiation, an exchange of agreements and the rule of law. It does not imply not the transfer of political sovereignty but organizes the cooperation of existing entities on the basis of agreed and enforceable rules. It takes the form of institutions generating permanent dialogue and debate as a prelude to common actions. In short, governance generates common rules, whereas government commands political will. In philosophical terms, global governance would be an heir to Kant's *cosmopolis*, whereas a world government would equate with a giant *Leviathan*.

The WTO in the debate on governance

Where does the WTO stand in this debate over global governance? How does the WTO fit into this archipelago of global governance?

In both public and academic discourse, analysis of the WTO generally results in either extreme criticism or excessive praise. Thus, two opposite approaches dominate discussions. On the one hand, globalization critics assert that the WTO holds a hegemonic grip on global issues. Others denounce the WTO's isolation as an international rule-setter and compliance-enforcer. In addition, proponents of a rule-based view of international relations promote the WTO as a model for global governance.

At one end of the political spectrum, globalization critics assert that the WTO acts as a hegemon with respect to international rule-making. The WTO's dispute settlement mechanism makes it the only international organization with an effective judicial tool to ensure compliance with its rules. Trade agreements thus gain an institutional superiority in the array of international norms. As a result of this de facto norm primacy, commercial imperatives and economic values are believed to trump other international concerns, including environmental protection, human rights or health concerns.

From this viewpoint, the WTO's alleged hegemony has resulted only in further advancing the interests of business, with no regard for other policy priorities. In the public health realm, the influence of multinational firms on negotiations has supposedly induced excessively stringent intellectual property rules that sacrifice the health of developing country populations. On the environment, advocacy groups allege that WTO rules favour resource-intensive production methods instead of promoting a growth model conducive to sustainable development. By supporting competition at the global level, trade rules reinforce the quest for the lowest possible production costs ("race to the bottom"), thereby further increasing the cost of environment-friendly strategies. On cultural issues, WTO rules would lead to increased uniformity by limiting the reach of cultural products unable to compete within the global entertainment industry.

Other critics, in contrast, point to the flaws associated with international rule coordination. Although WTO rules are better enforced, its framework by no means resolves the problem associated with the lack of an international hierarchy of norms. Each international organization creates its own set of rules, according to its specialized mandate. Yet no single body adjudicates conflicts between international agreements, once negotiated. The international principle of "good faith", which obliges governments not to agree to contradictory rules, is not in fact enforced. The WTO's dispute settlement system does not provide the answer to this normative chaos in international law, for an adjudicator can apply only existing rules. Labour norms that governments commit to at the International Labour Organization are nowhere to be found in WTO agreements. The Food and Agriculture Organization has a mandate to ensure the availability of food worldwide, but there is no mention of food security in the WTO's Agreement on Agriculture. The WTO Appellate Body's jurisprudence would consequently only highlight the incoherence of the current international framework of rule-making.

On the optimistic front, some liberals view the WTO as a model of global governance. The success of the dispute settlement system in delivering compliance is hailed as proof that international relations can indeed be rules based. Contrary to realist assumptions, there could be an alternative to anarchy as a foundation of international relations. The WTO's institutional architecture is an example of how such an order can be framed to achieve the pre-eminence of the rule of law in the inter-state sphere. The limited clout of major powers in the WTO – as compared with the United Nations Security Council – and the growing influence of developing countries – in comparison with the Bretton Woods institutions – prove that power can indeed be reined in. Having been effective in such a sensitive field as trade relations, it should serve as an example for other policy realms requiring multilateral cooperation. Alternatively, it could extend its scope to regulate a wider array of global public goods.

Although these positions may carry part of the truth, the reality is more nuanced. The WTO is neither a tool created to impose neo-liberalism on policy-makers worldwide, nor a ready-made model for global governance.

Governance within the WTO

In my view, the WTO is indeed quite powerful and sophisticated: its legislative basis is important and it has the institutional capacity to produce new rules, amendments and implementing instruments. Above all, it has an adjudicative body to enforce member compliance. Yet the WTO is not hegemonic and remains imperfect. Addressing its institutional shortcomings will be key if global governance is to become effective.

The WTO maintains a unique governance framework, which clearly distinguishes it from other international organizations. Its institutional architecture is more sophisticated as a result of building on the long tradition of rule-making in the field of international trade, and the creation of an enforcement mechanism that has proven effective and rests on an internal structure of governance that allows for a more equitable representation of members.

A long tradition of trade negotiation and legislation

As an heir to the GATT, the WTO inherited a long tradition of rule-making that had generated a complex set of agreements. The WTO treaty has some 500 pages of text and more than 2,000 pages of scheduled commitments. In addition, 50 years of GATT practice and decisions – what the WTO calls the "GATT acquis" – are included as part of the WTO treaty. However, in the WTO, trade rules are always being negotiated. In the jargon of the WTO, the ongoing trade talks under the Doha Development Agenda (DDA) are a "round" of negotiations in which previously agreed rules are updated and clarified. In these rounds, a wide range of issues is open to negotiation.

The Charter of the WTO is clear: the WTO provides a permanent forum for negotiations among its members concerning their multilateral trade relations. States need permanent forums for discussions and negotiations and, from that perspective, the institutional structure of the WTO is well developed. There are various levels and forms of decision-making that can be multi-stage and sequential. In all, the structure ensures that issues brought to the WTO cannot simply be swept aside.

An example of these legislative marathons is the series of phased decisions that enabled countries formally to amend the WTO Agreement on Trade-Related Aspects of Intellectual Property Rights (the TRIPS Agreement) in order to respond to the urgent needs of developing countries. The process began in Doha in November 2001, when ministers declared that it was important to implement and interpret the TRIPS Agreement, which had been negotiated 10 years previously, in a way that supported public health – by promoting both access to existing medicines and the creation of new medicines. Ministers also issued a separate

Declaration on TRIPS and Public Health, designed to respond to concerns about the possible implications of the TRIPS Agreement for access to medicines. That declaration left some unfinished business, and so the work continued. Indeed, in August 2003, the WTO General Council successfully adopted a Waiver to make it easier for poor countries lacking the capacity to manufacture medicines to obtain cheaper generic versions of patented medicines.[2] But the work was still not over – the waiver was temporary and needed to be transformed into a permanent amendment. Finally, in December 2005, WTO members in Geneva agreed on the wording that transformed the provisions of the waiver into a permanent amendment.[3] Once two-thirds of WTO members have ratified the change, this amendment will be formally incorporated into the TRIPS Agreement.

One conclusion can be drawn from this episode. When faced with a political stimulus, the WTO manages to put forward legislative solutions throughout the chain of decision-making to respond and adapt to the new realities faced by WTO members.

But there is more. One benchmark to assess the power and level of institutional sophistication of an international organization is the capacity of that organization to produce legislative material – to adopt norms that can affect members' behaviour and choices. Although it is true that the WTO Secretariat and the WTO bodies do not have any general power formally to adopt binding legislation, there are some cases where WTO bodies are able to adopt effective decisions that ensure pragmatic responses to specific needs. In this sense, these bodies produce forms of *droit dérivé*, or secondary treaty legislation. For example, the WTO treaty bestows upon the General Council the treaty power to adopt amendments, waivers, interpretations and accession protocols through decisions that do not necessarily require any additional ratification by members. These decisions constitute, in my view, a form of lawful exercise of secondary treaty legislation. Certain other WTO bodies also appear to have the treaty-bestowed authority to adopt certain decisions or to take certain actions that could have a direct bearing on members' WTO obligations.

Among the many examples, two are particularly relevant. For instance, the WTO Agreement on Sanitary and Phytosanitary Measures (the SPS Agreement) provides that the relevant Committee "shall carry out the functions necessary to implement the provisions of the agreement". On this basis, the SPS Committee adopted a decision that implements and complements the provisions of the Agreement. That decision provides that: "In the context of facilitating the implementation of Article 4 [of the SPS Agreement], the importing Member should explain the objective and rationale of the measure and identify clearly the risks that the relevant measure is intended to address. The importing Member should indicate the appropriate level of protection which its SPS measure is designed to achieve."[4] This decision has positively added to the WTO by effectively adopting more detailed and specific rules to implement broad treaty provisions.

Another example is the action by the Subsidies Committee to terminate environmental subsidies that could not be challenged in the WTO dispute settlement system. The Agreement on Subsidies and Countervailing Measures (SCM Agreement) provided that this Committee has the power to decide whether to continue such green subsidies. In December 1999, the Subsidies Committee implicitly decided not to extend such provisions beyond their expiry date of December 1999 by not making an agreement to that effect. This decision has had significant consequences by effectively terminating several Articles of the Subsidies Agreement. This is another legal action by a WTO body that can be viewed as a form of law-making.

There is also evidence of the evolving institutional nature of the WTO. Not only can the WTO decide on rules through the negotiation and adoption of international agreements, but there already exists a domain for WTO bodies to complement these traditional treaties with "secondary legislation".

The enforceability of WTO rules

Norms cannot, however, accomplish much on their own if they are left only to the good will of members. Enforcement mechanisms are vital if a rules-based system is to prove effective. The most evident failure of the general international legal system lies in its limited enforceability. In short, states agree to rules that they most often do not comply with. Then UN Secretary-General Kofi Annan underlined this shortcoming in his address to the 2004 General Assembly:

> At the international level, all States – strong and weak, big and small – need a framework of fair rules, which each can be confident that others will obey. Fortunately, such a framework exists. From trade to terrorism, from the law of the sea to weapons of mass destruction, States have created an impressive body of norms and laws. This is one of our Organization's proudest achievements. And yet this framework is riddled with gaps and weaknesses.
>
> Too often it is applied selectively and enforced arbitrarily. It lacks the teeth that turn a body of laws into an effective legal system.[5]

At the WTO, one of the enforcement mechanisms is concerned with the formal adjudication of disputes between members: the dispute settlement mechanism. The existence of a dispute settlement mechanism confers binding force on the WTO rules agreed to by members: non-observance of the rules may give rise to litigation and the litigants must accept the decision of the eminent persons appointed for that purpose. Otherwise, sanctions can be imposed, which is a considerable step to take. That change, which was instituted when the GATT became the WTO in 1995, has had the effect of raising the profile of the WTO, which is not without inconvenience.

The WTO's dispute settlement mechanism can be triggered easily and quickly, and panels and the Appellate Body will often be expected to make rapid rulings on any WTO-related grievance. Allegations that WTO trade is affected generally suffice to formally trigger the regular WTO dispute settlement process through a simple written request for consultations. Procedural steps take place automatically, within predetermined time-limits. When requested, a panel must be established, reports of the panel and Appellate Body must be adopted by the Dispute Settlement Body (which is composed of all WTO members) and retaliatory sanctions must also be authorized. After adjudication, the entire WTO membership maintains surveillance and monitors the implementation of the dispute conclusions by the losing country. Importantly, if implementation fails, the winning party is entitled to obtain permission to impose trade sanctions and even to retaliate.

Another unique provision of the WTO is that the Dispute Settlement Understanding (DSU) rules out all unilateral measures. Only the WTO can decide whether a member's measures or actions are inconsistent with WTO rules. The WTO embodies a rare achievement: it successfully regulates countermeasures by powerful states by subjecting their exercise to prior approval by the collective membership. This is perhaps the most interesting success. That it has happened in the regulation of trade relations only adds to the interest. Indeed, trade relations have a direct and immediate impact on the jobs of ordinary workers around the world. Although the regulation of trade relations carries welfare gains on aggregate, there are visible and concentrated pockets of national economies that, as a result of increased competition, suffer from lay-offs and restructuring. Trade policy is also subject to intense lobbying by interest groups (e.g. agriculture groups in the developed world, industry or service monopolies in developing countries), which imposes high political costs on governments that choose to stand up to vested interests. As a result, forcing powerful members to abide by Dispute Settlement Body decisions and generating a rules-based mechanism for dealing with disputes should be seen as a major achievement. On this issue, the WTO is ahead of other organizations, where compliance is most often the result of diplomacy and the balance of powers. In this light, the WTO stands out as an island of a Kantian rules-based international system in an otherwise Hobbesian world.

Given its record, it is fair to say the WTO's dispute settlement mechanism has provided its members with an effective legal system to enforce compliance with agreed trade rules.

Equal representation of individual members

The distribution of power between members within the WTO also amounts to a major step forward from other international economic institutions. It rests on the principle of the equal representation of individual members, regardless of size, power or contribution to the organization.

In the Bretton Woods institutions, for example, membership is represented by a board, with each member given voting rights proportional to its contribution to the institution's budget. As a result, rich industrial countries are given a *de jure* driving seat in these institutions. By contrast, the WTO Agreement stresses that all members have a right to representation in all of the WTO's governing bodies, ranging from the Ministerial Conference (which meets at least once every two years) to the General Council (the permanent decision-making body composed of permanent representatives accredited to the WTO), as well as all other councils and committees. All decisions are taken by consensus on the basis of a "one government, one vote" principle. Requiring consensus, however, does result in somewhat slower negotiations. Yet it appears to be a price worth paying, considering the objective of granting each member an equal say in the rules that govern international trade.

Equal membership has succeeded in empowering developing countries in the multilateral negotiation process. Major developing countries have become real drivers in the process, which now requires more than just an agreement between the European Union and the United States. In addition, developing countries have formed ad hoc issue-based negotiating groups to coordinate their positions and hence enhance their clout in the multilateral process. The G-20 and G-33 groups of developing countries on agriculture, the African Group, the group of least developed countries (LDCs) or the African, Caribbean and Pacific group of countries, among others, have become familiar names in Geneva. Their effectiveness in advancing their interests and taking advantage of equal representation should be stressed.

Furthermore, the WTO Secretariat has made every effort further to strengthen the negotiation potential of developing countries. The Secretariat's Technical Assistance programme is designed to equip developing country staff with expertise in negotiation.

Equal representation also corresponds to the core substantive principles that serve as the cornerstones of international trade law. It stands as the backbone of the non-discrimination principle and its manifestations in the form of the "most favoured nation" and "national treatment" clauses. It is also represented in the reciprocity principle, which lies at the heart of the multilateral negotiation process.

WTO institutional flexibilities to address the special needs of certain members

WTO rules further innovate in that they go beyond requiring strict conformity. For decades, multilateral trade agreements have striven to meet the benchmark for equity, recognizing the differences that exist between WTO members – rich or poor, large or small. In trade relations, less developed economies need flexibilities in order for trade and development to go hand in hand. WTO rules recognize that developing countries need more time to open markets and that depriving them of certain protective barriers would entail high social costs. This recognition has different legal manifestations.

Non-reciprocal mechanisms have long been included in trade agreements, embodied in the concept of "special and differential treatment". This recognition of developing country needs is by no means new, although it has expanded over time. It dates back to 1964 when GATT contracting parties added a fourth part to the GATT agreement, exclusively encompassing the issues related to "trade and development". In addition, Article XXXVI:8 of the GATT states that "developed contracting parties do not expect reciprocity for commitments made by them in trade negotiations to reduce or remove tariffs and other barriers to trade of less-developed countries". Also, the "Enabling Clause" authorizes the Generalized System of Preferences – through which developed countries may provide preferential market access to developing countries – as an exemption from the most favoured nation requirement. Taken together, this set of rules stands out as a means of ensuring that the integration of developing countries into the multilateral trading system does not carry excessive or undue costs. As a result, WTO membership provides a set of unique flexibilities in order for developing countries to take full advantage of increased trade flows. Far from being unfair or ideological in essence, WTO rules demonstrate pragmatic assessments of differences in development. In this respect, I would stress that they embody a unique determination to bind members to equitable rules, which are essential to level the playing field.

In addition to maintaining fair rules between members, the WTO has also proven flexible in opening up its institutional framework. In international law, only sovereign states can be equal. As a result, the membership of most international organizations is exclusively made up of states. Accordingly, the WTO is by law an inter-state institutional framework. Yet it has endeavoured to face up to realities in trade relations. It has opened itself up to new actors as they have emerged in the real world. In addition to states, WTO members can be "custom territories". This provision has enabled Chinese Taipei to join the WTO and Hong Kong to continue existing as a separate entity after it reintegrated with China in 1997. A separate path paved the way for fully fledged membership by the European Communities along with its individual members. The EC became a member *sui generis*. Beginning in the 1970s, it not only took part in all GATT meetings, but began to substitute itself for individual EC members. It became their sole representative in expressing and defending the common decisions taken under Article 133 of the Rome Treaty establishing the European Communities.

Some of the WTO's institutional features are unique. In matters of rule-making, power allocation or dispute settlement, the WTO provides potential guidelines for an effective framework for global governance. But the WTO's role should not be overstated. It remains a specialized organization focused on opening and regulating trade. The unique nature of its dispute settlement mechanism should not lead observers to over-stress its potential. Its competence lies in resolving trade disputes, not in imposing trade values over other policy objectives.

In comparison with other organizations, the WTO stands out as a sophisticated system. Contrary to what critics assert, the WTO does not consider itself to be more important than other international organizations and WTO norms do not necessarily supersede or trump other international norms. It faces the problem of coherence within its own jurisdiction. In fact, the WTO Appellate Body has endeavoured to reconcile value conflicts in accordance with principles of international law.

The recognition of important non-trade values within the WTO legal system

In international law, all norms are equal except (i) those included in the so-called "peremptory norms", or *jus cogens*, and (ii) those that would be in conflict with the UN Charter (Art. 103).[6] None of the work done in the WTO corresponds to either of those two exceptions; so, generally, it is fair to say that WTO norms are equal to other international norms. In fact, the GATT, and now the WTO, recognizes that trade is not the only policy that members can favour. The WTO contains various exception provisions referring to policy objectives other than trade, where policy matters are often under the responsibility of other international organizations.[7] The Appellate Body has managed to operationalize these exception provisions to provide members with policy space for non-WTO concerns.

A few examples help to shed light on how the system deals with non-trade concerns. First, WTO members are entitled to determine their own level of protection for the environment, health and morality if they wish, even if such national standards are higher than existing international standards.[8] Second, in the WTO, exceptions referring to such non-trade concerns are to be interpreted according to the ordinary meaning of the non-trade policy invoked. In this context, the Appellate Body has insisted that exceptions cannot be interpreted and applied so narrowly that they have no relevant or effective application. There must always be a balance between WTO market access obligations and the rights of governments to favour policies other than trade.[9]

Under the WTO rules, the Appellate Body has extended the availability of WTO exceptions that refer to non-WTO concerns through its development of a so-called "necessity test". When assessing whether a measure is "necessary" for the protection of health or some other non-trade concern, a new balancing test is to be used. Such an assessment will have to balance (i) the relative importance of the value at issue – greater importance will mean it is easier to justify a trade restriction as "necessary"; (ii) the contribution of the measure to the value; and (iii) the trade impact of the restriction.[10] Once a measure is considered to be "necessary", there is also an assessment of whether that measure is actually applied in a non-protectionist manner. Under this approach, members' restrictions that are based on important non-trade values and implemented in good faith will prevail over WTO market access obligations. That is why, in *US – Shrimp*, the United States was permitted to maintain its import restriction against shrimp from Asia, based on the environmental need to conserve and preserve turtles as natural resources.[11]

In several disputes involving the health of human beings and animals, the Appellate Body has repeated that members can set very high standards of health protection as long as they are consistent and coherent. Another example is the dispute between Canada and the European Communities over the importation of asbestos-related material. The European Communities' import restriction was upheld since it was based on authentic health risks and there were no alternative measures that could guarantee zero risk as sought by the European Communities regulation. Again, in the *US – Gambling* dispute, the Appellate Body confirmed that the United States can maintain the level of protection of "public morals" that it chooses, so long as the measure is not protectionist and is coherent (a requirement that the United States was found to violate).[12]

The Appellate Body went further when it decided that the provisions of the WTO cannot be read in "clinical isolation from public international law".[13] This recognized that the WTO is only part of a more global system that includes several sets of rights and obligations, emphasizing that no priority can be given to WTO norms over other international norms. By implication, the WTO is now obliged always to take into account other international rights and obligations of WTO members when reading and interpreting their respective WTO obligations. Hence, there is a need to ensure global coherence in the interpretation and application of all values, rights and obligations. Moreover, I believe that, in leaving members with the necessary policy space to favour non-WTO concerns, the WTO also recognizes the specialization, expertise and importance of other international organizations.

Improvements are required

Yet many shortcomings also exist. The WTO is far from having addressed the wide array of complex questions associated with global governance. It shares similar challenges with other international organizations. One of those challenges is the surveillance of member policies and actions. This is an essential part of the overarching objective of ensuring compliance with agreed rules. The WTO's binding dispute settlement system is one side of the token that has proved successful. But the transparency–surveillance–monitoring mechanisms have produced limited results and could benefit from improvements.

The WTO Agreement contains multiple notification and legislation review exercises to be conducted by the entire membership. An interesting feature of the WTO is the opportunity for cross-notification, whereby a member notifies the WTO of a measure not notified by its originating member. This process ensures further transparency by generating an obligation for the originating member to justify its position regarding such cross-notified measures. All notifications and cross-notifications are reviewed and commented on by members in relevant committees/councils. So far, however, these surveillance mechanisms have proved limited. Notifications of agriculture subsidies are lagging behind for key WTO members. On regional trade arrangements, the WTO surveillance mechanisms have exercised only limited control over whether any of them meet the conditions set forth in GATT Article XXIV. New mechanisms have been instituted to improve this situation.

The Trade Policy Review Mechanism (TPRM) is one of those new mechanisms. It is a peer review process that covers the full range of an individual member's trade policies and practices and their impact on the functioning of the multilateral trading system. The purpose is to enable a collective appreciation and evaluation of these policies and practices. The reviews are set against the background of each country's wider economic and developmental needs, policies and objectives, and of its external economic environment. Through greater transparency and understanding of trade policies, this review mechanism contributes to improved adherence by all members to rules, disciplines and commitments made under the WTO agreements.

In 2005, members expanded the reach of the WTO surveillance/monitoring mechanisms. At the Ministerial Conference in Hong Kong, it was agreed that at least 97 per cent of the rich countries' LDC imports would be duty free and quota free – that is, without any trade restrictions – with the aim of achieving full coverage at a later stage.[14] To monitor the situation, a new review process was set up. The Hong Kong decision provides that the Committee on Trade and Development shall annually review the steps taken to provide duty-free and quota-free market access to LDCs and report to the General Council for appropriate action. Members are now discussing where and how to implement this new review process. This is again a very innovative process that is evidence of the level of legal and institutional sophistication of the WTO, which may explain why states – weak and strong – make great use of this forum.

A recent decision has also been adopted to improve the transparency of regional trade agreements (RTAs) concluded by WTO members. The decision provides for early announcement of any RTA and notification to the WTO. Members will consider the notified RTA on the basis of a factual presentation by the WTO Secretariat.

Progress has undoubtedly been made. But further improvements will inevitably have to be made in order to meet the obligation of transparency, which stands out as a defining principle of the GATT.

Accountability and legitimacy as necessary elements of global governance

The final challenge for the WTO and global governance is that of accountability and legitimacy. News headlines are full of stories reporting massive demonstrations held against the backdrop of international economic gatherings. WTO Ministerials and annual meetings of the World Bank and the International Monetary Fund have become regular gathering spots for protesters. For all their internal differences and disagreements, critics converge in denouncing not only global capitalism but also the illegitimacy of international rule-makers.

Like any international organization, the WTO is faced with two distinct legitimacy issues. One is accountability to its members; that is, national governments. The other is its legitimacy vis-à-vis non-state actors. On the former, whereas many would argue that the WTO has problems of accountability, I tend to disagree. On the contrary, accountability towards members, including developing countries, is rather high.

New alliances between countries have emerged to engender more effective negotiations

The proposition that the WTO is a forum dominated by rich countries no longer holds true. The old club of the GATT has now given way to new groupings of states and coalitions: a new G-6 (Australia, Brazil, the European Union, India, Japan and the United States) has replaced the old QUAD (Canada, the European Communities, Japan and the United States). The proposals of the G-20 – an alliance of developing countries on agriculture – are now the benchmarks in many areas of the ongoing negotiations. There are also important new actors such as the G-33 group of developing countries and the African Group of nations. As mentioned before, the WTO Secretariat has acted to enhance the ability of developing countries to make better use of the opportunities associated with membership.

The WTO is efficient in fulfilling its role as a locus for discussion. It is important to recall that global governance requires that states increase their exchanges and negotiations. Since the WTO provides a permanent environment for such negotiations, it thus promotes the evolution of global governance opportunities.

Those who attack small-format meetings – for example, "green room" meetings – ignore the fact that, with around 150 members today, decisions to be taken by the entire WTO membership need first to be prepared in smaller formats, like committees in a parliament. In fact, diplomacy in general is also about informal discussions and bilateral encounters. This by no means takes away from the legitimacy of official negotiating bodies; it only helps to fuel the multilateral process when that stalls. Most importantly, the institutional framework ensures that all members agree. Consensus among all members for the adoption of decisions ensures legitimacy.

Representation of non-state actors within the WTO system

The situation is more problematic vis-à-vis non-state actors and world public opinion. Global governance legitimacy indeed faces inherent hurdles. It is quite distinct from the legitimacy bestowed upon national democratic governments. Because legitimacy depends on the closeness of the relationship between the individual and the decision-making process, the first challenge of global governance is distance. The other legitimacy challenge relates to the so-called democratic deficit and the accountability deficit, which arise when there are no means for individuals to challenge international decision-making. The specific challenge of legitimacy in global governance is therefore to manage the perception that decision-making at the international level is too distant, unaccountable and not directly challengeable. It is a daunting task. Even the most integrated inter-state organization, the European Union, has not succeeded in filling its legitimacy gap.

At the WTO there is no mandate from members to enlarge official membership beyond governmental representation. The organization faces the inherently difficult task of striking a subtle balance between preserving the inter-state nature of WTO talks while opening up to new actors. States promote their national interests whereas civil society pursues issues-based objectives. Because the WTO remains first and foremost a negotiating forum in which states express interests of the utmost importance to them, the admittance of civil society groups to negotiation bodies would be inappropriate. By the same token, these groups – whether business, non-governmental organizations (NGOs), national parliaments or labour organizations – have no formal role in the dispute settlement process.

Efforts within the current system have nonetheless been made. An annual Public Forum, open to all, is held in Geneva for both states and non-state actors. Regular WTO briefings are held for NGOs and parliamentarians. NGOs also have the opportunity to influence the dispute settlement process through the submission of *amicus curiae* briefs, a procedure developed following the *US – Shrimp* case.[15] Most importantly, NGOs' involvement in the WTO has been formalized. Article V:2 of the Agreement Establishing the WTO states that "the General Council may make appropriate arrangements for consultation and cooperation with non-governmental organizations concerned with matters related to those of the WTO". Although no detailed arrangement has been signed to date, the General Council has adopted guidelines defining the nature and extent of the relationship between the WTO Secretariat and NGOs.[16] They provide a legal basis and political stimulus for greater transparency towards these organizations. Since I took over as WTO Director-General, I have regularly addressed, consulted and discussed with NGO representatives, national parliaments, and labour and business organizations, because I believe dialogue is key to a better mutual understanding. As a result, the WTO has taken steps towards promoting a progressive shift from an international society to an international community.

The WTO is neither a hegemonic monster, acting like a Trojan horse for the primacy of trade over policy choices, nor a perfect model that has solved all issues relating to the regulation of globalization. In fact, its scope of action is quite limited. It is a specialized international organization committed to opening and regulating trade on the basis of multilaterally agreed rules. Trade is only one aspect of globalization, albeit an important one. Many impending global challenges go beyond commercial flows.

The WTO as a laboratory for global governance

Yet, within its limited sphere of competence, the WTO has gone a long way in introducing institutional innovations that have proved effective. In comparison with other international organizations, it is ahead of those in the wider UN system. It has turned out to be a laboratory for global governance.

Far from being a perfect model, the WTO is a laboratory for harnessing globalization and contributing to the construction of a system of global governance. It is a place where evolving global governance can find some roots in ensuring legitimate decision-making. In addition, it is an institution that can evolve to provide for the increasing participation of non-traditional international and domestic actors. It is a forum where values can be discussed, which is crucial as trade restrictions become more and more values based. Given its economic and political dimensions, the WTO could be a fundamental player in the building of a system of global governance. It can build bridges, yet it will not and cannot be the only player to do so.

In the end, the key lesson to be drawn from the WTO's limited existence is that a rules-based international system is viable. Contrary to realist assumptions, the world does not have to remain anarchic even when important interests are in play. In fact, the more interdependence becomes the norm, the more a rules-based multilateral order will be in the interest of states. For the time being, however, the decision remains in the hands of sovereign states. Global governance will be for states to build, for we still live in a Westphalian order.

Notes

1. Max Weber, "Politics as a Vocation", translated and edited in H. H. Gerth and C. Wright Mills, *From Max Weber: Essays in Sociology*, New York: Oxford University Press, 1946.
2. WTO General Council, Decision of 30 August 2003, *Implementation of Paragraph 6 of the Doha Declaration on the TRIPS Agreement and Public Health*, WT/L/540 and Corr.1, 1 September 2003, at ⟨http://www.wto.org/english/tratop_e/trips_e/implem_para6_e.htm⟩ (accessed 7 January 2008).
3. WTO General Council, Decision of 6 December 2005, *Amendment of the TRIPS Agreement*, WT/L/641, 8 December 2005, at ⟨http://www.wto.org/english/tratop_e/trips_e/wtl641_e.htm⟩ (accessed 7 January 2008).

4. Committee on Sanitary and Phytosanitary Measures, "Decision on the Implementation of Article 4 of the Agreement on the Application of Sanitary and Phytosanitary Measures", G/SPS/19, adopted 24 October 2001.

5. Kofi Annan, "Address by Kofi Annan at the Opening of the General Debate of the Fifty-Ninth Session of the General Assembly", New York, 21 September 2004, at ⟨http://www.un.org/Pubs/chronicle/2004/issue3/0304p4.asp⟩ (accessed 7 January 2008).

6. Report of the Study Group of the International Law Commission, "Fragmentation of International Law: Difficulties Arising from the Diversification and Expansion of International Law", UN Doc. A/CN.4/L.682, 13 April 2006, section E.

7. See, e.g., Article XX of the General Agreement on Tariffs and Trade, 1994.

8. WTO Appellate Body Report, *United States – Measures Affecting the Cross-Border Supply of Gambling and Betting Services* [*US – Gambling*], WT/DS285/AB/R, 7 April 2005, para. 308; Appellate Body Report, *Australia – Measures Affecting Importation of Salmon*, WT/DS18/AB/R, adopted 6 November 1998, DSR 1998:VIII, 3327, para. 199; Appellate Body Report, *European Communities – Measures Affecting Asbestos and Asbestos-Containing Products*, WT/DS135/AB/R, adopted 5 April 2001, DSR 2001:VII, 3243, para. 168.

9. Appellate Body Report, *United States – Standards for Reformulated and Conventional Gasoline*, [*US – Gasoline*], WT/DS2/AB/R, adopted 20 May 1996, DSR 1996:I, 3, p. 22; Appellate Body Report, *United States – Import Prohibition of Certain Shrimp and Shrimp Products*, [*US – Shrimp*], WT/DS58/AB/R, adopted 6 November 1998, DSR 1998:VII, 2755, para. 156.

10. Appellate Body Report, *Korea – Measures Affecting Imports of Fresh, Chilled and Frozen Beef*, WT/DS161/AB/R, WT/DS169/AB/R, adopted 10 January 2001, DSR 2001:I, 5, paras 161–164.

11. Appellate Body Report, *US – Shrimp*; Appellate Body Report, *United States – Import Prohibition of Certain Shrimp and Shrimp Products – Recourse to Article 21.5 of the DSU by Malaysia*, WT/DS58/AB/RW, adopted 21 November 2001, DSR 2001:XIII, 6481.

12. Appellate Body Report, *US – Gambling*; Appellate Body Report, *United States – Measures Affecting the Cross-Border Supply of Gambling and Betting Services – Recourse to Article 21.5 of the DSU by Antigua and Barbuda*, WT/DS285/RW, adopted 22 May 2007.

13. Appellate Body Report, *US – Gasoline*, p. 17.

14. Sixth WTO Ministerial Conference, *Ministerial Declaration*, adopted 18 December 2005, WT/MIN(05)/DEC, 22 December 2005, at ⟨http://www.wto.org/English/thewto_e/minist_e/min05_e/final_text_e.htm⟩ (accessed 7 January 2008).

15. Appellate Body Report, *US – Shrimp*, paras 101, 104, 107–110.

16. WTO General Council, Decision adopted on 18 July 1996, "Guidelines for Arrangements on Relations with Non-Governmental Organizations", WT/L/162, 23 July 1996, at ⟨http://www.wto.org/english/forums_e/ngo_e/guide_e.htm⟩ (accessed 7 January 2008).

2

The WTO, global governance and policy options

Sylvia Ostry

In the postwar golden decades of the 1950s and 1960s, trade issues hardly made headlines. The General Agreement on Tariffs and Trade (GATT) was described even by policy wonks as "a better soporific than hot milk" and known as "the General Agreement to Talk and Talk". By the end of the 1990s the World Trade Organization, the institution created by the Uruguay Round negotiations, had become a magnet for dissent. Not only was the street theatre of the Seattle Ministerial Meeting in 1999 big news on television but the debacle emerging as the meeting collapsed fed newspapers around the world.[1]

Perhaps most important is that we are undergoing a new technological revolution in information and communication technology (ICT). This revolution is creating a global market for goods, services, capital and labour. The speed and breadth of change are unprecedented. It is, indeed, a new Great Transformation. In terms of the trading field, we are most concerned with economic globalization – the deepening integration among countries through trade, financial flows, investment, and so on. But we must also be aware of the ongoing effect of the Great Transformation on government, individuals, corporations and values. The role of ICT in penetrating public awareness is of profound and increasing importance. We will be looking at this in more detail, but let us start with the new multilateral trading system housed in the World Trade Organization (WTO). It is best to begin with a brief account of the radical system change resulting from the Uruguay Round and then to examine some of the main issues affecting the role of the WTO and some reform proposals.[2]

The WTO and global governance: Future directions, Sampson (ed),
United Nations University Press, 2008, ISBN 978-92-808-1154-4

The Uruguay Round legacy

The Uruguay Round was the eighth negotiation held in the context of the GATT, which came into force on 1 January 1948 as part of the post-war international economic architecture. The primary mission of the GATT was to reduce or eliminate the border barriers that had been erected in the 1930s and had contributed to the Great Depression and its disastrous consequences. The GATT worked very well through the concept of reciprocity (denounced as mercantilist by trade purists) and because of rules and other arrangements to buffer or interface between the *international* objective of sustained liberalization and the objectives of *domestic* policy stability. This effective paradigm, termed "embedded liberalism,"[3] was also aided by the virtual exclusion of agriculture (by an American waiver and the near-sacrosanct European Common Agricultural Policy) and by the Cold War. From the 1960s, the rounds were essentially managed by the European Community and the United States, with a little help from some of their industrialized-country friends. The developing countries were largely ignored as players (although this began to change in the 1970s, largely as a consequence of the OPEC oil shock).

The Uruguay Round was a watershed in the evolution of the system. Agriculture was at the centre of the negotiation as US exports to the European Community diminished and the European Community's heavily subsidized exports flourished and even penetrated the US market. A US call for negotiations started in 1981 but was stalled by the endless foot-dragging by the European Community, aided by a small group of developing countries led by Brazil and India, and strongly opposed to the so-called "new issues" of services, intellectual property and investment demanded by the Americans. The Round was finally launched in September 1986, at Punta del Este, Uruguay. It concluded in December 1994, four years beyond the target date agreed at the launch.

So the negotiations were almost as tortuous as the launch. The Grand Bargain, as I have termed it,[4] was completely different from old-time GATT reciprocity. It was essentially an implicit deal: the opening of markets in the countries of the Organisation for Economic Co-operation and Development (OECD) to agriculture and labour-intensive manufactured goods, especially textiles and clothing, in exchange for the inclusion in the trading system of services, intellectual property and (albeit to a lesser extent than originally demanded) investment; as well as – a virtually last-minute piece of the deal – the creation of a new institution, the WTO, with the strongest dispute settlement mechanism in the history of international law and virtually no executive or legislative authority.

The Grand Bargain tuned out to be a Bum Deal. There was far less opening in agriculture than expected and the reduction of restrictions on textiles and clothing was back-loaded and more than offset by the impact of China. The South side of the deal would require a major institutional upgrading and change in the infrastructure of most Southern countries. Such changes take time and cost money. The new issues involved not border barriers but domestic regulatory and legal systems. The barriers to access for service providers stemmed from laws, administrative action or regulations. The intellectual property inclusion covered comprehensive standards for domestic laws and detailed provisions for enforcing corporate property rights. Social regulation covering product standards and health and safety involves sophisticated administrative procedures law as well as highly trained scientific human resources. Implementation thus involves considerable investment and uncertain medium-term results. In effect, the trading system was transformed from the negative regulation of the GATT – what governments must not do – into positive regulation – what governments must do. Most importantly, there was no reciprocity in the new issues. It was all one way – from poor to rich.

It is important to note that the inclusion of the new issues in the Uruguay Round was a US initiative and this policy agenda was largely driven by US multinational enterprises (MNEs). These corporations made it clear to their government that without a fundamental rebalancing of the GATT they would not continue to support a multilateral policy but would prefer a bilateral or regional track. But they didn't just talk the talk, they also walked the walk, organizing business coalitions in support of services and intellectual property in Europe and Japan as well as in some smaller OECD countries. The activism paid off and it is fair to say that American MNEs played a key – perhaps even *the* key – role in establishing the new global trading system. This merits a brief digression.

In the United States, the private sector advisory process established in the 1970s for the Tokyo Round of Multilateral Trade Negotiations was designed to cope with or broker interest group pressures acting on Congress. But in the Uruguay Round its impact spread well beyond its original objective. The US service sectors were world leaders and the same was true in investment and technology. American MNEs controlled 40 per cent of the world's stock of foreign investment at the outset of the 1980s and the US technology balance of payments was well over US$6 billion when every other OECD country was in deficit. This was high-stakes poker and the MNEs launched the game. The US Advisory Committee for Trade Policy and Negotiations (ACTPN), in cooperation with other US business groups, undertook the task of convincing European and Japanese corporations to lobby for the new issues. In the services sector, US activism extended well beyond the two trading powers. Nine country service coalitions were organized and met regularly with the GATT secretariat. In the case of intellectual property, the US group, called the Intellectual Property Rights Committee (IPC), worked through the Union of Industries of the European Community and the Keidanren in Japan. At first the Japanese were reluctant to join the IPC. They feared that intellectual property was too new a subject to become part of the GATT, and they felt initially that intellectual property was, in any case, ill suited to the Uruguay Round of trade discussions. But the IPC persuaded their counterparts to table, in Geneva in 1988, a detailed trilateral proposal for an intellectual property agreement drafted by US legal experts. This bore a remarkable resemblance to what came out of the Uruguay Round. The strategic skills of the American MNEs were aided by the role of the US government. A multi-track policy including the North American Free Trade Agreement helped by locking in high standards and undermining Latin American cohesion in opposition to the Agreement on Trade-Related Aspects of Intellectual Property (TRIPS). Even more effective was the use of unilateralism in the form of a new Special 301 of the 1988 Trade and Competitiveness Act targeted at developing countries with "inadequate" intellectual property standards and enforcement procedures. In the case of Brazil, the 301 worked and so India was left isolated.

Because of some clever legalistic juggling by the United States and the European Community in the end game, the Uruguay Round consisted of a "single undertaking". There were no "escape hatches" for the Southern countries: it was a take it or leave it deal. So they took it but, it is safe to say, without a full comprehension of the profoundly transformative nature of the new system, to say nothing about the Bum Deal. As one of the Southern participants was reported to have said, "TRIPS was part of a package in which we got agriculture".[5]

There were significant unintended consequences of the Uruguay Round. The rise in profile of the MNEs owing to their crucial role in securing inclusion of the "new issues" helped catalyse the activist non-governmental organizations (NGOs) and launch the anti-corporate globalization movement (of which more below). But equally important and not unrelated, the Round left a serious North–South divide in the WTO. Although the South is hardly homogeneous, there is a broad consensus that the outcome was seriously unbalanced. A key feature of this aspect of the Uruguay Round's systemic transformation is *asymmetry*.

Asymmetry

The member countries of the WTO vary widely in power and always will. Power is linked to autonomy, which is understood to combine the availability of choice with the capacity to act. The power of the United States was unique in the post-war years when the GATT was created, so the autonomy of the other members of the "club" that managed the system was, for the most part, deferential to the hegemon and all went well. But the WTO houses a very different system, which can be described in many different ways but the word "complexity" is quite appropriate. The need for knowledge – advanced and sophisticated – is essential. Complexity requires knowledge and knowledge enhances power. The strong are stronger in the WTO because of their store of knowledge and the weak are weaker because of their poverty of knowledge. The weak lack autonomy in any system but in the WTO system complexity creates reinforced asymmetry and diminished autonomy. The WTO houses a *knowledge trap*.

A number of case studies by the World Bank demonstrate both the capacity deficit in poor countries and the heavy costs of implementation.[6] There was very little participation by the African countries in the Uruguay Round because of both the lack of secretariat staff in their Geneva delegations and the lack of coordination and expertise at home. The situation in Geneva has not improved very much, as Table 2.1 demonstrates. It has been estimated that the WTO councils, committees, working parties, etc. involve over 2,800 meetings per year – which it is impossible for the poorer countries to attend. One WTO official said: "we set up a Subcommittee with a Chair and a Secretary who turned up for the first meeting on trade needs of LDCs [least developed countries]. No LDCs came. No developed countries came. No one came. Not one country showed up".[7] Worse, the WTO delegates often have to cover the United Nations in Geneva as well as the WTO. There is still serious weakness in *domestic* coordination mechanisms among a number of ministries and this institutional deficiency is not confined to the poorest countries but affects many developing and transition economies. Finally, there is little if any coordination between Geneva and the home country. A former delegate noted: "During the entire duration of the Uruguay Round our Geneva-based WTO team received *two* instructions from our capital".[8] The lack of resources and capabilities in poor countries virtually eliminates policy choice and participation.

Because the poorest countries are primarily dependent on agriculture, and often on only a few commodities, the disappointing results of the Uruguay Round in agriculture have ensured that agriculture remains at the centre of the Doha agenda. But what is equally important and far less studied is the impact of the Agreement on Sanitary and Phytosanitary Measures (SPS). Case studies from the World Bank provide incredible examples of the imposition of new standards for alleged (minor) health reasons that cut African exports of nuts and grains by 60 per cent.[9] The poor countries play no role in the setting of international standards such

Table 2.1 African countries with permanent missions at the United Nations Office in Geneva as of April 2005

Country	No. of WTO Geneva-based delegates	No. of WTO delegates *not* in UN Directory	Remarks
Nigeria	7	7	
Congo, Democratic Republic	4	2	
South Africa	9	0	
Tanzania	9	0	
Kenya	4	0	
Uganda	4	0	
Ghana	3	0	
Mozambique	2	0	
Cameroon	7	1	
Cote d'Ivoire	5	0	
Madagascar	3	0	
Angola	4	0	
Burkina Faso	4	0	
Zimbabwe	8	0	
Malawi	0		
Mali	3	0	
Niger	0		
Senegal	5	0	
Zambia	8	0	
Chad	4	unknown	No UN delegation list found
Guinea	3	0	
Rwanda	2	0	
Benin	8	0	
Burundi	2	0	
Sierra Leone	0		
Togo	0		
Central African Republic	0		
Congo	4	0	
Lesotho	4	1	
Mauritania	3	0	
Namibia	1	0	
Botswana	8	0	
Djibouti	1	unknown	No UN delegation list found
Gabon	5	0	
Gambia	0		
Guinea-Bissau	0		
Swaziland	0		
Mauritius	7	0	

Sources: WTO Directory (*circa* May 2005) and "Missions Permanentes auprès des Nations Unies à Genève", No. 96, United Nations, Geneva, April 2005.

as the Codex Alimentarius because they lack both the monetary and the human resources to participate. So standards developed by a limited number of countries can get the status of international standards.

The situation is likely to worsen as developed countries increase regulation for high-valued-added products and as large multinational buyers increasingly dominate the retail market. These large retailers will likely determine standards and the small and medium enterprises in poor countries, lacking information about export markets, are unable to compete. The gap between domestic and international regulation is widening. The need to reform agriculture by moving up the value-added scale would require major changes in institutional infrastructure. The cost would be high and the poor countries do not have the resources. Similar problems exist in the Technical Barriers to Trade Agreement (TBT) covering trade in goods. Although both the TBT and the SPS were supposed to provide technical assistance, this has been inadequate and, in any case, significant infrastructure investment is required. Once again, however, some case studies demonstrate that, where investment in technology and institutional-building have been undertaken, successful export-driven growth is feasible.[10]

These are but a few examples of how the complexity of the global trading system requires more than "trade policy" to integrate the poor countries. Although the Uruguay Round agreements included some recognition of the need for technical assistance and the Doha Agenda is littered with references to technical assistance and capacity-building, it has been repeatedly emphasized that the true jewel in the crown was the creation of the WTO and the Dispute Settlement Understanding. For the first time in international law a truly effective institutional constraint on the powerful has been achieved. So is the increased legalization a welcome offset to asymmetry? Not exactly – as this brief review shows.

As Professor J. H. H. Weiler terms it, the WTO involves "the juridification of the process, including not only the rule of law but the rule of lawyers".[11] And since it is said that, whereas the United States has only 4 per cent of the world's population, it has 50 per cent of the world's lawyers, the legal culture of the WTO is, by and large, American. Be that as it may, the main focus of concern in the context of asymmetry is whether the paradigm shift of juridification benefits the poorest countries. Data on the number of legal experts in LDCs' Geneva missions or in their domestic ministries are not available, but one can safely assume the numbers are very small or even non-existent. And, as may be seen from Table 2.2, none of the poor African countries participates either as complainant or as respondent in WTO dispute settlement cases. This is asymmetry writ large. But further analysis as to the reasons for this opt-out is worthy of a brief review.

Table 2.2 Participation in WTO dispute settlement cases, 1995–2005

Complainant	No. of appearances	Respondent	No. of appearances
United States	79	United States	89
EC	69	EC	55
Canada	26	Argentina	17
Brazil	21	India	17
India	16	Japan	14
Mexico	15	Korea	13
Korea	12	Canada	12
Thailand	11	Mexico	12
Japan	11	Brazil	12
Chile	10	Chile	10
Argentina	9	Australia	9
Australia	7	Turkey	7
Honduras	6	Egypt	4
New Zealand	6	Peru	4
Guatemala	5	Philippines	4
Hungary	5	Ecuador	3
Philippines	4	Belgium	3
Switzerland	4	Ireland	3
Colombia	4	Belgium	3
Poland	3	Venezuela	2
Indonesia	3	South Africa	2
Costa Rica	3	Romania	2
Pakistan	3	Pakistan	2
Turkey	2	Slovak Republic	2
Ecuador	2	Dominican Republic	2
Peru	2	France	2
Pakistan	2	Czech Republic	2
Norway	2	Trinidad and Tobago	2
China	1	Nicaragua	2
Chinese Taipei	2	Malaysia	1
Antigua and Barbuda	1	Croatia	1
Bangladesh	1	Slovakia	1
Nicaragua	1	Uruguay	1
		Greece	1
Czech Republic	1	Netherlands	1
Sri Lanka	1	Panama	1
Hong Kong	1	Thailand	1
Uruguay	1	China	1
Venezuela	1	Sweden	1
Singapore	1	Denmark	1
		UK	1
		Portugal	1
		Poland	1

Source: WTO Dispute Settlement, "Chronological List of Disputes Cases", May 2005; see ⟨http://www.wto.org/english/tratop_e/dispu_e/dispu_status_e.htm⟩ (accessed 24 January 2008).

There have been a number of studies on dispute settlement and the poorest countries in the WTO, many sponsored by the World Bank. Although much more remains to be done, the research clearly documents the absence of African countries in this essential "crown jewel" of the trading system. What accounts for the mystery of the "missing cases"?

One reason is clear and very simple – lack of money. The absence of government legal services either at home or in Geneva would require the hiring of private lawyers, which is far too expensive. A conservative estimate of attorney fees in trade litigation runs from around US$90,000 to US$250,000, depending on the complexity of the case, plus another US$100,000–200,000 for data collection, economic analysis, travel, administrative assistance, and so on.[12] An Advisory Centre on WTO Law (ACWL) was established in December 1999 and entered into force in July 2001 to provide some legal assistance for poor countries. It requires a membership fee based on per capita income and share of world trade. It is funded mainly by European governments plus Canada. The United States refused to join or provide funding. Although the ACWL is certainly a welcome initiative, it will require further funding and coordination with both enterprises and governments in developing countries as well as capabilities in economic research.[13] The role of sophisticated econometric research and economic evidence in WTO dispute settlement is another example of the reinforcement of power by complexity in the mechanism designed to constrain power. And it does not end there. For example, a prominent Washington-based law firm states on its website that its specialty involves advising "numerous governments and companies in over 175 WTO disputes on intellectual property, government procurement, subsidy, trade, remedy, environment, taxation, telecommunication, and investment matters". The WTO's dispute settlement mechanism is thus great for business because it is the supreme court of international tribunals.[14]

But the cost side of the cost/benefit model for dispute participation often includes more than money or legal service subsidies. Political costs – threats by richer countries to reduce development aid or to remove trade preferences – may also be very powerful deterrents to initiating a WTO dispute or rejecting a threat of retaliation. An example of political deterrence is provided by a former US trade official, who argued in an African capital that "the U.S. might withdraw food aid were the country's Geneva representatives to press a WTO complaint".[15]

Finally, the concept of asymmetry is treated here in terms of the poorest countries, but, as noted earlier, it is also a facet of the new issues. In the case of services, the emerging economies – especially India – are moving ahead. But no liberalization under the General Agreement on Trade in Services (GATS) has occurred since 1997. No reciprocity?

How about technical training (as suggested by the secretary-general of the WTO) to help correct some asymmetry in the WTO?

Even though these are just a few examples, the structure of the WTO is inherently asymmetric. Nothing much changed after Uruguay. The next step was Doha.

After Uruguay: Doha

After the Uruguay Round, there was a virtual consensus that there had been serious imbalance in the outcome and this view was clearly seen in Seattle. This was the first attempt to launch what some have called a "Millennium Round". It ended with a walkout by a coalition of virtually all the developing countries from Latin America, Asia and Africa. There were many reasons for this, not least the US President's inclusion of labour standards to be enforced by trade sanctions. Whatever the complex developments in Seattle, with all the street theatre and the "teamster turtles" and what many NGOs called "The Big Bang" of a new movement, the North–South aspect cannot be ignored. The round was finally launched in Doha, Qatar, in November 2001. It is more than symbolic that the outcome of the Doha Ministerial was termed a "Development Agenda".

Although it is true that the Doha Declaration was a masterpiece of creative ambiguity, the major objective of the meeting was to avoid a repeat of the Seattle debacle. Thus the great success of Doha was that it did not fail, and this involved convincing many developing countries, especially the poorest in Africa, that trade was good for development. Delegations from both the United States and the European Union visited Africa to woo ministers, and the Declaration repeatedly referred to technical assistance and capacity-building, now called (only half in jest) "the new conditionality". Pushed by a successful NGO campaign on AIDS in Africa, the Americans were sort of willing to antagonize "big Pharma". The Europeans were most skilful in securing a waiver for their preferential arrangement with the African, Caribbean and Pacific states by wily deal-making with the Latin American banana exporters. So Doha was unique in its focus on the South and on development.

Originally, the Round was planned to finish in January 2005 but it has been moving in fits and starts – suspended, started, suspended again. What is clear at this point is that the Doha Round's outcome is very uncertain, even if there is fast-track renewal in an election year. I will use my favourite definition of Heisenberg, "We can know where we are but not where we're going, or we can know where we're going but not where we are". I think Doha is Heisenberg squared.

It seems that the European Union was much more interested than the United States in a Round. Possibly because of considerable domestic problems in the expanded Union and the endless problems with agriculture, the Europeans would have liked to have added the so-called Singapore Issues – investment, competition policy, transparency in government procurement and trade facilitation – to the Round. All except facilitation were dropped at the mid-term Ministerial Meeting at Cancun, Mexico, in 2003. The European Union also wanted to include trade and the environment. These issues might have been able to detract from some of the problems of agriculture. In fact, however, there was very little interest from business, either in Europe or in the United States, in a WTO Round.[16]

The Round was supposed to have been dealing with development issues. In fact, what the Round came down to was a concern with agriculture and with non-agricultural manufactured products. And there seems to be very little cohesion or coherence on either of these issues. Both the Americans and the Europeans are willing to undertake some reform of their domestic subsidies and the Europeans are willing to do something on their export subsidies, but they do not seem to be able to reach agreement with the developing countries. Moreover, there are quite significant differences among the developing countries on agriculture. What is even more interesting at this point is the lack of coherence concerning non-agricultural products. The OECD countries have made quite substantial demands on the emerging market countries for market access. One gets the impression that, in order to get any support for this Round from the business community, there must be some market opening. The emerging market countries seem unwilling to budge, which again seems curious but one of the rumours going around is that they are very worried about opening their markets because of China; true or not, they seem not to be willing to move on this very important issue. The lack of interest by the business community is quite widespread, except in the developing countries, where more business seems involved than in the past. However, looking at the data on trade and investment, which have been very good, one wonders whether business is saying, "Who needs the WTO and who needs rounds? I mean, we can either engage in our own arbitrage, or we have lots of bilaterals and regionals. Why would we have to worry about something like a WTO round?" That, of course, raises the question about the relevance of multilateralism in today's world. Furthermore, one wonders why the complex modalities chosen for tariffs in the Doha Round, which are almost incomprehensible except to the experts, are part of the endless ongoing conversations. Surely, a much more straightforward and simple approach would be slightly easier to deal with.

Be that as it may, I think the Doha Round, whatever happens, is unlikely to be a success. It was supposed to deal with development and it really does not. It does not confront the profound asymmetry in the system. Although there is a North–South gap, there are enormous differences among the developing countries and there does not seem to be any view of the purpose and future of the multilateral system.[17]

WTO: Whither or whether

Whither?

As has been noted, the Doha mid-term Ministerial Meeting was held at Cancun in September 2003. It ended with an impasse among the developed and developing countries over agenda items. But there also appeared to be an axial shift in the political economy of the policy game.

At Cancun a "new geography" became evident in coalitions of Southern countries. The G20 included Brazil, China and India, as well as a number of other developing countries. Despite repeated efforts to eliminate it, the G20 has persisted. The other coalition at Cancun – the G90 of African and other poor countries – has also endured but its role in the trade games is not clear, although the G20 and G90 were introduced as the G110 in Hong Kong! There are also a large number of coalitions (Gs) on different subjects. But the "new geography" and the rise of China and India have generated no new or coherent strategy.

One real danger of the new geography is that it could transform trade into a zero sum game. By blocking consensus, the G2 (the United States and the European Union) and the G3 (China, India and Brazil) can both exert power, but for what purpose? The G20 includes countries with considerable soft infrastructure, and the proliferation of NGOs is able to provide knowledge and policy analysis. One way of using the time available from the "pause" in the Doha Round would be to begin to confront asymmetry.

One of the aims of the Uruguay Round was to improve cooperation and coordination among the main international economic institutions. Driven largely by the experience of the wide exchange misalignment of the 1980s and its impact on trade, the euphemism "international coherence" was devised. But little emerged from the objective apart from worthy rhetoric and some subsequent agreements about who should attend what meetings and when.[18]

In 1997, however, a specific project was launched to coordinate trade and poverty reduction in the least developed countries. It was termed the Integrated Framework for Trade-Related Technical Assistance (IF) and involved the WTO, the World Bank, the International Monetary Fund (IMF), the United Nations Conference on Trade and Development, the United Nations Development Programme and the International Trade Centre, as well as a number of bilateral donors. Although there are still difficulties with the programme, this is one way to start.[19] This is new territory and policy innovation involves learning by doing, doing well and, often, doing not very well. Case studies are data and the task of absorbing and contextualizing will not yield to a minimalist mathematical model.

The promotion of international coherence by a specific project for Africa that involves the WTO, the World Bank and the New Partnership for Africa's Development (NEPAD) with the objective of integrating trade and development fits well into a "redefined" concept of technical assistance and capacity-building (especially since the precise meaning of both or either is rather fuzzy and flexible). Country "ownership" would be paramount. Such a project would require funding both for the WTO secretariat and for the physical and intellectual infrastructure of the countries. And some of the problems – governance, for example – may prove insurmountable. But, whatever the outcome of the Doha Agenda, it would be feasible and desirable to launch a genuine (not rhetorical) project to reduce poverty and stimulate development.

Indeed, in November 2007 the WTO hosted a Global Aid for Trade (AfT) Review in Geneva, where Director-General Pascal Lamy stressed that, at the Hong Kong Ministerial Conference in December 2005, the WTO mandate was to include help to build trade capacity for developing countries. The global review was more a reporting mechanism with no specifics on mechanisms. So existing mechanisms such as the IF should be used. And the concept of AfT in the WTO is highly significant. Supply-side capacity and trade-related infrastructure could change market access to market entry.[20]

Finally, there has been growing interest in the media on the issue of the appalling state of many African countries. We should not rely too much on celebrity diplomacy (in 1973 Robert McNamara, head of the World Bank, vowed to eliminate poverty in the world by 2000), but it is not to be ignored. A recent book, the *Bottom Billion*, by Paul Collier (2007) has received a great deal of attention. It is especially useful in exposing the formidable complexity of development in these countries. So getting AfT in the WTO is one small step on a long road. And there are other reform actions that should also be considered.[21]

Not to overuse the word, it is important to recognize that the *construct* of the WTO is asymmetrical: it is juridified, but without real executive or legislative power, and it has a very small secretariat and a very limited budget (one-third of that of a number of NGOs). These structural deficiencies greatly exacerbate the rich–poor asymmetries and knowledge trap. Not only do the OECD countries have a wide array of research resources, they also have their own well-endowed think-tank, the OECD. The substantive scope of the OECD is very broad and its secretariat is part of a government network with access to "soft" power – "the power of information, socialization, persuasion and discussion".[22] So the OECD is very effective in securing adherence to rules, fostering changes in rules and achieving agreement on policies.[23]

There is no policy forum in the WTO. There had been one – the Consultative Group of 18 (CG18), established in 1975 as a recommendation of the Committee of Twenty Finance Ministers after the breakdown of the Bretton Woods system. The composition of the membership was based on a combination of economic weight, regional representation and regular rotation. The forum involved senior officials from capitals. The CG18 was never officially terminated but meetings ceased at the end of the 1980s.

Establishing a WTO policy forum would be a great step forward. But it would be unlikely to function effectively without an increase in the WTO's research capability. Analytical papers on key issues are needed to launch serious discussions in Geneva and to improve the diffusion of knowledge in national capitals. The basic issues of trade and development need country-specific case studies. There is no agreed model – indeed there is growing dissent. A top priority for the forum should be to undertake a thorough analysis of the unsolved issue of special and differential treatment. Another priority is the environment. The WTO research secretariat would form part of a research or knowledge network linked to other institutions, including, of course, the World Bank as well as academics, NGOs and business and labour organizations.

The Report by the WTO's Consultative Board (2004) recommended there be more political involvement of ministers and senior policymakers from capitals in WTO activities and put forward a number of suggestions, among which is the establishment of a senior-level "consultative body" – CG18 redux. Obviously there will be opposition from some countries to these proposals. But the dissenters should be encouraged to consider the alternative – an ongoing erosion and decline of the multilateral rules-based system.

Finally, the membership of the policy forum will be the most contentious aspect of the proposal. This, of course, is the same issue as the conflict between "legitimacy" and "efficiency" in the negotiating modalities – the "Green Room" syndrome. Although in theory the consensus principle that governs the WTO should require that all 150 plus members (soon to be up to 170) be present in every negotiating group, paralysis by consensus is guaranteed. But the reality of the GATT/WTO decision-making rules has been aptly described as "organized hypocrisy in the procedural context",[24] with the Big Two – the United States and the European Union – running the shop. Green Rooms are essential whether "informal" or "formal". The organized hypocrisy worked in the past because of the transatlantic alliances. But what happens with the ongoing shift in the balance of power, the new geography? China's concept of organized hypocrisy and administrative process could be quite different!

There is one more reform that could enhance the legitimacy of the WTO. It concerns the critique by the NGOs of the lack of *transparency*. In WTO-ese, there are two kinds of transparency: internal and external. On the internal front, the main and increasingly contentious issue involves negotiating arrangements for Ministerial Meetings that involve the exclusion of many member countries (the Green Room). However, the NGOs have been most active with respect to *external transparency*, having three main requests: more access to WTO documents; more participation in WTO activities such as committee and ministerial meetings; the right to observer status and to present *amicus curiae* briefs before dispute panels and the Appellate Body.

The WTO has made considerable progress in providing information speedily and effectively on its website and through informal briefings. It has allowed NGO representatives to attend parts of Ministerial Meetings, has sponsored public symposia on trade and environment issues and, in the case of the Committee on Trade and Environment, has engaged civil society in discussions. But all these incremental developments have been opposed by many developing countries. The de-restriction of documents took four years of gridlocked negotiations and the policy passed only with continuing restrictions. Far more contentious has been the request to open up dispute settlements to *amicus* briefs. However, a dispute panel recently decided to allow closed-circuit television cameras into the courtroom. This was agreed by the three parties – Europe, the United States and Canada – as an experiment, perhaps in the hope of establishing a precedent.

Although there have been a number of proposals for WTO reform in the years since Seattle, the issue of transparency and participation at the national level has been raised only by a coalition of NGOs once, just before Doha, in October 2001. There was no response; a similar silence greeted a US proposal after Seattle. Yet a review of recent developments in other international institutions such as the OECD, the World Bank and the United Nations Economic Commission for Europe stressed the importance of engaging citizens in policy-making or what is often termed encouraging "ownership" of policy.[25] Further, a report of the Panel of Eminent Persons on United Nations Civil Society Relations[26] underlines the need to "emphasize and highlight the country level". Indeed, an entire school of international law based on "inter-actional theory" points out that "law is persuasive when it is perceived as legitimate by most actors and legitimacy rests on inclusive processes [that] reinforce the commitments of participants in the system".[27] In a Report to the Trilateral Commission, *The "Democracy Deficit" in the Global Economy: Enhancing the Legitimacy and Accountability of Global Institutions*, one of the authors, Joseph Nye Jr, suggested it might be a good idea to start at the national level.[28] The interlinking of national and global is an ongoing process and policy spillover is hardly surprising, although it has not yet reached the WTO. So maybe a small push could help. There is a mechanism in the WTO that lends itself to an avenue for external transparency. This is the Trade Policy Review Mechanism (TPRM).[29]

One of the original negotiating groups in the Uruguay Round was the Functioning of the GATT System (FOGS). It was designed to enhance the effectiveness of the domestic policy-making process through informed public understanding, i.e. *transparency*.

The TPRM is voluntary and flexible in subject matter and clearly em-braces the policy-making process; it thus seems the logical venue for launching this project – on a *voluntary* basis and as a *pilot to be assessed after an agreed period*. The WTO secretariat is already seriously overbur-dened, so it might be necessary for the volunteers to put up some funding in advance. But these costs should clearly come under the arrangements agreed at Doha on capacity-building. Enhancing capacity to improve and sustain a more transparent trade policy process sounds like a good invest-ment. The TPRM Reports could be published and a feedback mechanism would begin to operate. Transparency at the domestic level would create pressure for more information from Geneva. And information about one country could encourage stakeholders (especially NGOs) to pressure their governments to participate.

Moreover, by sharing information on national processes, stakeholders in many countries without adequate technical or financial resources – such as small and medium enterprises – could gain useful information on market opportunities. The policy process should be evolutionary, reflect-ing systemic changes and changes in the policy environment. And, of course, although benefits will accrue from a more participatory process there are also costs. There are costs for governments in terms of time, expertise and financial resources and there are significant differences in resources among stakeholders. This is another facet of asymmetry that is ignored and aid might be required.

A number of other ideas are being explored – parliaments, human rights, WTO "democracy", and so on. But it is time to reach a conclusion with just one more suggestion.

Whether

The suggestions for reforms during the "pause" are based on the assumption that negotiations will be relaunched when the new administration takes charge in the United States at the end of 2008 or start of 2009. But some countries or global elites (business, NGOs and others) are either indifferent or hostile to the WTO – or even to the multilateral rules-based system. The demonstrations at meetings still go on (but more anti-war than anti-WTO or anti-IMF), but no clear substantive message has emerged.

Who would lead a new multilateral negotiation? The new US government? The European Union? The new Gs? The business lobby? The NGOs? Where could we find the ideas for a new global system? Embedded liberalism is dead. The Washington consensus is dead. Shock therapy is dying. Utopianism is alive and well – but not much good for worn-out multilateralism. Global civil society has been called acephalous, i.e. headless. This sounds appropriate for more than civil society.

What is missing is leadership. The Italian philosopher Gramsci defined leadership as pessimism of the intellect and optimism of the will. So how about one more proposal – courtesy of Gramsci.

The power of middle powers

When the Bretton Woods system broke down in the 1970s, the response came from two middle powers, France and Germany. President Valéry Giscard d'Estaing and Chancellor Helmut Schmidt established the economic summit, the first important post-war institution since Bretton Woods.

The effort to launch the Uruguay Round proved very difficult because of opposition from the European Community over agriculture and from a group of developing countries over the "new issues". Once again, the middle powers came to the rescue. This story is worth telling here.

Despite endless infighting, a date was finally set for a Ministerial Meeting in Punta del Este, Uruguay, for September 1986. It was intended to launch a new Round – or so at least some hoped. During the summer several groups were formed to plan for Punta. The largest comprised the United States, the European Community and Japan (called the "Big Three"), most industrial countries and a number of moderate developing countries. They worked to prepare the Ministerial Declaration. This provoked the group of developing countries called the "G10 hardliners", led by Brazil and India, to prepare their own ministerial draft declaration. It looked like a rehearsal for a showdown. But the coalition of industrialized and developing countries – *without the Big Three* – won the contest for Punta. The Ministerial Declaration was prepared by the de la Paix group, named after the hotel where it met in Geneva.[30]

It is very important to understand that the de la Paix group had only one objective – to launch a multilateral round of negotiations. Unlike other coalitions – then and now – it was not activist on substantial issues. Many in the group understood that in the 1980s multilateralism was at stake and they rose to meet the challenge. It was the middle powers that prevented a terrible failure at Punta. Can there be a replay? Not without some change.

One big difference between the 1980s and today, of course, is the North–South divide. The role of Brazil and India was very important at Punta (and had a significant effect on the content and process of the Round) but there was no G110 (just the G10!). However, many members of the WTO recognize that multilateralism is at stake. And we are facing a world of unprecedented threats and challenges; for all our intellect, there is a lot of pessimism. Let us mobilize the optimism of our will.

What about putting together a coalition of middle powers to launch an analysis and discussion of trade and development without delay? It could (one hopes) meet at the WTO. The coalition could be serviced by the WTO secretariat. Funding could (one hopes) be secured from foundations or philanthropic individuals. The research and discussion should all be available on the Internet and briefings for the "Great Powers" should be arranged. Business groups, farm federations, NGOs and academics should be invited so that a knowledge network can be established. A representative from the coalition of least developed countries should receive financing to attend.

A very difficult problem is how to form the coalition. It should be voluntary so that there is no linkage with WTO rules or negotiations. And countries should be free to drop out and suggest a replacement. Indeed, since the coalition must be a reasonable size (not more than 30), a rotation might be a good idea. The simplest way to handle this would be for the Director-General to convene a meeting of the General Council and appoint an ambassador for multilateralism to head the procedure for selection. Geography is crucial, of course, but the issue of how to deal with the big, emerging markets (who is a middle power today?) will not be easy. Nonetheless, when there is a political will there is a policy way.

The really big change?

The key agenda item for these discussions should be trade and development. Whatever the argument that the WTO is "not a development agency", the cat is out of the bag and cannot be put back. This will be complex and contentious and it is very broad and far-ranging, including agriculture as central to many countries.

The agenda list could go on and on. But that would not be very helpful because the objective of this policy discussion would be to consider how to launch negotiations to create a more balanced WTO, involving development, in a changing global society. It is not utopian – just optimistic.

Notes

1. Richard Blackhurst, "Reforming WTO Decision Making: Lessons from Singapore and Seattle", in Klaus Günter Deutsch and Bernhard Speyer (eds), *The World Trade Organization: Millennium Round*, New York: Routledge, 2001, pp. 295–299.
2. See Jean-Marc Coicaud and Veijo Heiskanen (eds), *The Legitimacy of International Organizations*, Tokyo: United Nations University Press, 2001; Paul Collier, *The Bottom Billion – Why the Poorest Countries Are Failing and What Can Be Done about It*, Oxford: Oxford University Press 2007; Brendan McGivern, "Decision Making in the Global Market – Consumers International", Briefing Paper on the World Trade Organization, Consumer International, Brussels, 27 July 2004; Amrita Narlikar, "Fairness in International Trade Negotiations: Developing Countries in the GATT and WTO", Centre of International Studies, Cambridge University, mimeo, August 2006; Ernst-Ulrich Petersmann (ed.), *Preparing for the Doha Development Round: Challenges to the Legitimacy and Efficiency of the World Trading System: Conference Report*, Florence: Robert Schuman Centre for Advanced Studies, European University Institute, 2003; Roger B. Porter, Pierre Sauvé, Arvind Subramanian and Americo Beviglia Zampetti (eds), *Efficiency, Equity and Legitimacy: The Multilateral Trading System at the Millennium*, Washington, DC: Brookings Institution Press, 2001; Debra P. Steger, "The Culture of the WTO: Why It Needs to Change", *Journal of International Economic Law*, Vol. 10, No. 3, 2007, pp. 483–496; Ngaire Woods, "Global Governance in International Organizations", *Global Governance Builder*, Vol. 5, No. 1, 1999.
3. John Gerard Ruggie, "International Regimes, Transactions, and Change: Embedded Liberalism in the Postwar Economic Order", *International Organization*, Vol. 36, No. 2, 1982, pp. 379–415.
4. Sylvia Ostry, "The Uruguay Round North-South Grand Bargain: Implications for Future Negotiations", in Daniel M. Kennedy and James D. Southwick (eds), *The Political Economy of International Trade Law, Essays in Honor of Robert E. Hudec*, Cambridge: Cambridge University Press, 2002.
5. Peter Drahos and John Braithwaite, *Who Owns the Knowledge Economy? Political Organising behind TRIPS*, Dorset: The Corner House, 2004.
6. See J. Michael Finger and Philip Schuler, "Implementation of Uruguay Round Commitments: The Development Challenge", *The World Economy*, Vol. 23, 2000, pp. 511–525; Bernard Hoekman, *Economic Development and the World Trade Organization after Doha*, Policy Research Working Paper 2851, Geneva: World Bank, Development Research Group, Trade, June 2002.
7. Drahos and Braithwaite, *Who Owns the Knowledge Economy?*.
8. Gregory Shaffer, "The Challenges of WTO Law: Strategies for Developing Country Adaptation", *World Trade Review*, Vol. 5, No. 2, 2006: pp. 177–198.

9. See United Nations Millennium Project, *Investing in Development: A Practical Plan to Achieve the Millennium Development Goals*, New York: United Nations, 2005; South Centre, "WTO Sanitary and Phytosanitary Agreement: Issues for Developing Countries," *Trade-Related Agenda Development and Equity Working Paper*, Geneva, July 1999.

10. See United Nations Millennium Project, *Investing in Development: A Practical Plan to Achieve the Millennium Development Goals*, New York: United Nations, 2005, Chapter 10; Kym Anderson, Will Martin and Dominique van der Mensbrugghe, "Would Multilateral Trade Reform Benefit Sub-Saharan Africans?", World Bank Policy Research Paper 3616, Washington, DC, June 2005.

11. J. H. H. Weiler, "The Rule of Lawyers and the Ethos of Diplomatic Reflections on WTO Dispute Settlement", in Porter et al. (eds), *Efficiency, Equity, Legitimacy*.

12. Chad P. Bown and Bernard M. Hoekman, "WTO Dispute Settlement and Missing Developing Country Cases: Engaging the Private Sector", University of Wisconsin, May 2005.

13. Shaffer, "The Challenges of WTO Law".

14. Bown and Hoekman, "WTO Dispute Settlement and Missing Developing Country Cases".

15. Shaffer, "The Challenges of WTO Law", p. 193.

16. See Simon J. Evenett, "Reciprocity and the Doha Round Impasse: Lessons for the Near Term and After", Centre for Economic Policy Research Policy Insight, 11 September 2007; Gilbert R. Winham, "The Doha Round and Its Impact on the WTO", in Donna Lee and Rorden Wilkinson (eds), *The WTO after Hong Kong: Progress in, and Prospects for, the Doha Development Agenda*, London: Routledge, 2007, pp. 229–247.

17. P. Kleen, "The Uruguay Round and the Doha Round – So Alike and Yet So Different", Jan Tumlir Policy Essays No. 1, Brussels: European Centre for International Political Economy (2008, forthcoming).

18. See Sylvia Ostry, "Coherence in Global Policy-Making: Is This Possible?", Asia and the Future of the World Economic System, London: Chatham House, March 1999; available at ⟨http://www.utoronto.ca/cis/ostry⟩ (accessed 25 January 2008); Sylvia Ostry, "Institutional Design for Better Governance", in Porter et al. (eds), *Efficiency, Equity, Legitimacy*, pp. 374–375.

19. Manmohan Agarwal and Jozefina Cutura, *Integrated Framework for Trade-Related Technical Assistance, Case Study*, Washington, DC: World Bank Operations Evaluation Department, 2004.

20. BRIDGES, *Weekly Trade News Digest*, 28 November 2007, pp. 8–10.

21. See Collier, *The Bottom Billion*; Michael A. Clemens, "Smart Samaritans", *Foreign Affairs*, Vol. 86, No. 5, 2007, pp. 132–140; Niall Ferguson, "The Least Among Us", *New York Times Book Review*, 1 July 2007.

22. Anne-Marie Slaughter, *A New World Order*, Princeton, NJ: Princeton University Press, 2004.

23. Ibid.

24. Richard H. Steinberg, "In the Shadow of Law or Power? Consensus-Based Bargaining and Outcomes in the GATT/WTO", *International Organizations*, Vol. 56, No. 2, 2002, p. 342.

25. Sylvia Ostry, "External Transparency in Trade Policy", Occasional Paper 68, Group of Thirty, Washington, DC, 2004.

26. United Nations, *Report of the Panel of Eminent Persons on United Nations-Civil Society Relations*, UN General Assembly, Fifty-eighth session, 11 June 2005, New York: United Nations.

THE WTO, GLOBAL GOVERNANCE AND POLICY OPTIONS 77

27. Jutta Brunnée and Stephen J. Toope, "International Law and Constructivism: Elements of an Interactional Theory of International Law", *Columbia Journal of Transnational Law*, 2000–2001, p. 39.
28. Joseph S. Nye, Jr. and others, *"The Democracy Deficit" in the Global Economy: Enhancing the Legitimacy and Accountability of Global Institutions, A Report to the Trilateral Commission*, Taskforce Report No. 57, Washington, DC: Brookings Institution Press, 2003.
29. Ostry, "External Transparency in Trade Policy".
30. I served as a member of this group and it was agreed that the Big Three should be kept informed.

3

Enhancing the role of the WTO in global governance

Bert Koenders

Introduction: Setting the scene

At the start of 2008 it is still unclear whether the Doha Round in the World Trade Organization (WTO) can be concluded successfully by the end of the year or whether it will wither away owing to a lack of political courage to bridge relatively small differences on reciprocal market openings and the reduction of trade-distorting subsidies and to face down special interests. Yet it is easy to share Martin Wolf's observation that the "multilateral trading system at the beginning of the twenty-first century is the most remarkable achievement in institutionalized global economic cooperation that there has ever been".[1] As the multilateral trading system celebrates its sixtieth birthday in 2008, the contribution of the WTO to an emerging global governance system cannot be underestimated.

So there is something important at stake in the Doha Round. Looking at governance issues allows me to take some distance from the immediate Doha Round travails, though they are never very far away. The most relevant policy questions from a global governance perspective that I will address are:

- How to preserve the strengths of the multilateral rules-based trading system in global governance?
- How to allow the multilateral trading system to respond better to the new challenges and pressures being put?

In answering these questions I focus on two important challenges for the WTO:

The WTO and global governance: Future directions, Sampson (ed),
United Nations University Press, 2008, ISBN 978-92-808-1154-4

- How to better integrate developing countries and development into the multilateral trading system in a manner that is both effective and fair? Developing countries have legitimate expectations that the WTO should take their concerns into account and strike a balance between rights and obligations that ensures that trade contributes to their growth and development.
- How to improve the responsiveness of the WTO to new challenges, in particular sustainable development concerns? What should or could be the role and limitations of trade and for the WTO when governments pursue other legitimate policy objectives through internal measures that are intimately related to "behind-the-border" issues.

Functions of the WTO

The WTO is the embodiment of the multilateral trading system. It performs various functions that range from negotiation, monitoring, dispute settlement to cooperation with other (international) players.[2] Like all international organizations, its (historical) record is not perfect and deserves some justified criticism. The WTO is sometimes criticized for being undemocratic, non-accountable, non-transparent and overreaching its mandate.

Looking at the governance aspects of legitimacy and accountability of the WTO and how it builds consensus, important challenges remain to making global trade work optimally for development and poverty reduction. In the past, the right balance has not been always struck in individual trade agreements, mostly because of the dominance of developed countries in the rule-making process and sometimes because of the reticence of developing countries to engage fully in the negotiations. Developing countries feel that some substantive WTO rules have perpetuated the bias against their interests, such as in the rules for agricultural subsidies and the 10-year phase-out of quantitative restrictions for textiles and clothing (a forced 40-year derogation from the general prohibition of quantitative restrictions). Some commentators perceive the overall outcome of the Uruguay Round as unbalanced.[3]

But times are changing, albeit slowly and not without a fight. Pascal Lamy mentions in his foreword to the *World Trade Report 2007*: "much can be improved and much remains to be done".[4] I agree wholeheartedly with that statement. It is not guaranteed that the Doha Development Round will satisfactorily implement its promised development dimension. Yet governments of both small and large countries continue to support the WTO and its effective binding dispute settlement system. The principal reason is that they perceive adhering to multilateral rules and multilateral negotiations to be in their national interest rather than relying on the exercise of political or economic power or being the object of it.

Dealing with heterogeneity of interests and complexity in negotiations

In an uncertain and changing world, multilateral rules and a viable and credible international institution bring much-needed stability and predictability to world trade, globalization and the economic policies based thereon. After 60 years of negotiating reciprocal market opening and crafting trade rules, trade agreements are still incomplete contracts. They remain work in progress, as is worldwide trade liberalization for that matter. The heterogeneity of the interests at stake in the WTO, with a diverse membership of more than 150, is huge. The complexity of WTO negotiations is increasing ever more, even if certain hard-core issues such as market access, agriculture, regionalism and development reoccur regularly on the agenda. Some of them seem to form familiar obstacles to concluding the round, yet again. Neither heterogeneity nor complexity is insurmountable and both can be overcome if the right political will and flexibility are mobilized and a common vision developed.

I do not see bilateral and regional negotiations, though proliferating, offering a real alternative for effective multilateral trade cooperation. The poorer countries, which are likely to be excluded from such preferential trading arrangements, are exactly those that need the support of a robust multilateral trading system to help them integrate into the global economy. Development-friendly Economic Partnership Agreements (EPAs) between the European Union and the African, Caribbean and Pacific (ACP) countries, for example, could be supportive in this regard if they strengthen regional integration between developing countries, which is yet to be achieved. Moreover, most of the benefits of regulatory cooperation and the dismantling of the toughest distortions can be realized only in a WTO that offers developing countries a better arena for negotiations anyway. It is likely that most bilateral/regional negotiations will founder or leave untouched the same big controversies (e.g. agriculture, trade contingency rules and subsidies) that have caused the current impasse in the Doha Round.

Negotiating trade rules is rightly regarded as the most important function of the WTO. The *World Trade Report 2007* makes four key points about multilateral trade negotiations.[5] First, it may be difficult to strike a balance that offers something of equal worth to all parties, at least initially. Secondly, after the deal has been struck, parties have to deal with uncertainty arising from unforeseen circumstances, new complexity or unwillingness to stick with the original contract. Underlying national interests may also change over time. Thirdly, successful cooperation requires broad negotiating agendas that reflect the heterogeneity of interests and the different priorities of parties. So there has to be something of interest to everybody for negotiations and rounds to be worthwhile and to work. Fourthly and above all, successful international cooperation is an iterative process. Reaching a satisfactory compromise with more than 150 parties takes time and effort, especially when the decision-making is based on consensus, for which I see no real alternative in the WTO. If the process does not fully include all parties in a transparent manner and if the rules do not show sufficient flexibility to take account of different capacities to adjust, negotiations are bound to fail. This may ultimately jeopardize the correct implementation of the current contract and undermine the institution.

Governance of the WTO

In the WTO, process and decision-making procedures have always been important elements of governance and often difficult to separate from the substance of the negotiations. The institutional design of the organization and the modalities of the negotiations have played a significant role in determining the outcomes. The legitimacy of the multilateral trading system depends both on internal legitimacy (full participation of all members) and on external transparency (engagement of civil society in the member states). Indeed, if the rules are to legally bind all parties in a single undertaking, without the possibility of opting out of individual agreements, full participation and transparency become essential to enhance the sense of ownership of the substantive outcomes.

Relevant institutional questions in this regard are: Who defines the agenda? Who sets the priorities? Who participates in the negotiations? How transparent and inclusive are the negotiations? What is the proper trade-off between efficiency and inclusiveness (the presence of representatives of all members and interests) in the different phases of the negotiating process? How can mutual trust be enhanced through better procedures and working methods? Who monitors and evaluates the decisions and outcomes? How can the possibilities of democratic accountability in the WTO be expanded?[6]

An effective voice for developing countries in the WTO

Not all problems related to inclusiveness and internal transparency have yet been solved by the WTO. In negotiations among more than 150 parties it is of course inevitable that a balance must be struck between inclusiveness and efficiency if there are to be text-based results at the end of the day. In practice, the WTO has adopted new working modalities since the Seattle debacle that increasingly succeed in doing a better job on these scores. Even so, many developing countries still have only limited technical and human resources to participate meaningfully in the many and often parallel negotiating circuits. Empowering these countries to have an effective voice in the work of the organization remains part and parcel of governance. Increasingly, coalitions and intermediary support organizations are being used as methods to manage the complexity of the negotiations and to aggregate interests. Developing countries are successfully forming issue-based platforms as a form of joint representation to enhance their negotiating capacity.[7] Improving the negotiating and lobby capacity of such coalitions is a priority. Given the time and effort that is required to develop and coordinate well-defined positions, negotiations procedures in the WTO should accommodate the handicaps of such groups. Not everyone is blessed with the sophisticated coordination machinery of the European Union. An attempt to introduce formal country groupings, like the constituency structure of the Bretton Woods institutions, however, seems not to be the right answer in the WTO. It could easily reduce the flexibility and responsiveness to changing interests and circumstances that variable coalitions currently provide.

Learning, deliberation and surveillance

Adequate trade capacity to maximize the potential from WTO membership is needed not only in negotiations but also in the phase of implementation and monitoring of agreements, the enforcement of rights through dispute settlement and the exploration of new issues. As Robert Wolfe notes,[8] negotiating is first a process of learning about an issue and this requires participation. Learning to understand new issues properly – as, for example, in the case of trade-related intellectual property rights or investment – takes time and capacity. This is irrespective of the political desirability (or otherwise) of negotiating an issue. Allowing adequate time for learning is therefore an essential part of an effective governance process, like transparency and public deliberation. Deliberation in turn helps in learning and understanding the interests that affect the outcome of subsequent negotiations.

Effective global (trade) governance must facilitate not only bargaining over known interests but also learning about new issues and interests through arguing and deliberation before negotiations commence. Clearly this implies more than having a few informed delegates in Geneva and officials in capital. In order to enhance the legitimacy of the multilateral trading system, public deliberation will also require much stronger engagement with civil society and parliamentarians, in Geneva but primarily at home in the WTO member countries. This will contribute to more effective national trade policy processes that go beyond the trade ministry.[9] Some observers are concerned that asymmetries in access to information, research and analysis might actually be widening, not only between developed and developing countries but also between small and large delegations.[10] This gap could further marginalize smaller developing countries in the process of multilateral rule-making if not dealt with properly (see also the section on trade-related technical assistance and capacity-building commencing on page 96).

Constructive engagement of other policy communities

In view of growing apprehensions about the impacts of globalization, deliberation has to go beyond trade policy as purely an economic policy. This does not necessarily always need to be dealt with by (instant) rule change. Pascal Lamy rightly suggests that more thought should be given to enhancing the monitoring and surveillance functions of the WTO, without WTO members being engaged in negotiations or dispute settlement.[11] A larger part of those functions could be devoted to encouraging constructive discussion of and engagement in common interests and exploring the mutual supportiveness of various governmental policies. Between negotiations and dispute settlement he rightly sees a "missing middle" where governments should be fostering dialogue between various policy communities at home and internationally. This is partly related to the discussion about deepening and broadening the future agenda of the WTO, which should not be solely about negotiating new rules. New challenges related to other legitimate policy objectives such as health, environment and climate change are thrown up and require the constructive engagement of trade policy-makers and the WTO.

   The role and profile of WTO have become more important than those of the General Agreement on Tariffs and Trade (GATT) because of the greater weight of trade rules in national policies and global governance. Primary reasons are the broader coverage of the WTO's rules and their extension to behind-the-border issues and measures, as in the case of agriculture, services and intellectual property, and their coerciveness because of the effective dispute settlement system of the WTO. Some worry that the WTO has extended its reach too far and that its grip has become too deep. In their view, the WTO has become too intrusive and has (had) a chilling effect on the development of national policies and international regimes in other areas. At the same time, trade rules do not formally take precedence over other bodies of international law, such as international law on health, the environment and human rights. WTO agreements do take account of other legitimate policy objectives of governments, though the degree may be a matter for genuine debate. WTO litigation has also demonstrated the ability and sensitivity in maintaining a careful balance between trade and non-trade concerns (NTCs). Where the balance lies is probably in the eye of the beholder. According to some major developing countries, the Appellate Body has shown itself an activist judge by creating rather than interpreting WTO law in some rulings.[12]

The discussion about the relation between trade and NTCs, however, does not end there. Some major policy divergences on issues such as precaution, the environment, biodiversity, labour standards and climate change could drift towards the WTO, not by design but by default. The WTO and its dispute settlement system are not necessarily the most properly equipped to deal with the emerging controversies and trade tensions that they may generate. The relative weakness of other multilateral institutions in enforcing their rules has unfortunately increased the demands on the WTO to deal with issues that were not heretofore within its mandate, according to Peter Sutherland.[13] Seen from a perspective of global governance, this cannot be the correct response in dealing with these legitimate policy concerns. All policy communities within nation-states share a mutuality of interests, i.e. prospering, stable and rule-based societies. These policy-makers and regulators also form part of the same governments of sovereign nation-states. Even so, the WTO and its members may need to become more engaged and accommodating towards NTCs, though this does not necessarily have to lead (directly) to rule changes (see also below).

The WTO's place within global governance: The coherence mandate

The WTO is a part of a broader system of evolving global governance that is still far from complete or perfect. Policies in the (ever-broadening) arena of trade increasingly affect or intersect with other areas of policy-making. This can be in areas such as international finance, debt, exchange rates, security, human rights, environment or labour rights. The early recognition of substantive linkages between policies at the international level and of the need for their mutual supportiveness raised the desire to create cooperative arrangements between international institutions. The Punta del Este Declaration that launched the Uruguay Round in 1986 already called for action, at both international and national level.[14] Developing countries, however, feared a form of "ganging-up" by cross-conditionality of policy requirements of various international organizations or having their market access to developed countries dependent on meeting what they regard as extraneous conditions to trade. At the time, these countries insisted on better policy coordination at national level being a precondition for effective international coordination.

In the area of global *economic* policy-making, the linkages between trade, investment, finance, debt and exchange rates are quite obvious to most people. Here countries are also bound by a wider set of international obligations and rights. Flowing from its founding Agreement and the coherence mandate of the Uruguay Round,[15] the WTO has negotiated formal cooperation agreements with the Bretton Woods institutions – the International Monetary Fund (IMF) and the World Bank. The WTO, however, differs considerably from these institutions when it comes to internal governance issues, such as accountability to its members and the setting of priorities, mandate and objectives. Whereas the centrepiece of the IMF and the World Bank are the Secretariats, in the member-driven WTO it is the legal agreements that bind the members. The WTO Secretariat services the negotiations but proposals come from members only. I share Pascal Lamy's assessment that the WTO seems to have managed to adjust better to geopolitical changes in terms of enhancing accountability and the voice of developing countries in its decision-making procedures than the IMF and the World Bank have done so far.[16] Having consensus as the method for decision-making and accepting negotiating proposals from developing country coalitions such as the G-20 as the backbone of the new agriculture agreement in the making are clear illustrations of this. Inter-agency cooperation can improve the coordination of trade, debt and financial policies only at international level so far. It cannot correct policy incoherencies at country level.

The cooperation between the WTO and the IMF/World Bank is only one aspect of the wider network of improving international cooperation aimed at enhanced global welfare. This also incorporates humanitarian, environmental, labour and, increasingly, security issues. In this regard, the WTO maintains extensive relations with several other international organizations, such as the United Nations, the United Nations Conference on Trade and Development (UNCTAD), the United Nations Environment Programme (UNEP), the Food and Agriculture Organization (FAO), the International Labour Organization (ILO) and other international standard-setting organizations. This wider network can assist in achieving the Millennium Development Goals and encourage sustainable development and global governance when the work of these organizations is linked to trade and trade-related policies. Here we enter some uncharted waters as cooperation is still primarily between secretariats. Specialized international agencies derive their (limited) mandates from nation-states and their instructions from the competent departments in capitals. How can these international organizations be expected to show perfect cooperation at policy level if this does not happen in capitals between the relevant departments and policy communities? Hence coherence should indeed start at home in the nation-states through better coordination and preferably a "whole-of-government" approach to global governance. Most countries still grapple with this challenge of acting coherently, but progress on this front is the only way forward to get better global governance. WTO members will also have to consider seriously how to give coherence a better institutional place within the WTO system and, it is to be hoped, abstain from the usual defensive reflexes. Currently, the coherence mandate is the topic of the occasional debate in the General Council only when reports about cooperation between the secretariats of international organizations are being discussed.[17]

Integrating developing countries in world trade and the WTO

In my view the greatest challenge from a global governance perspective is how to ensure a better and more equitable integration of developing countries in global trade and the WTO. This should be done in a manner that contributes to their growth, sustainable development and poverty reduction. Developing countries now make up more than two-thirds of the WTO membership and they come in many sorts, with very different interests and capacities. As we know from experience, trade and trade openness can play a positive role in economic development. They allow countries and people to exploit their productive potential, promote economic growth, curtail arbitrary policy interventions and protect against economic shocks.

But trade liberalization does not automatically lead to poverty reduction or to a more equitable income distribution. Globalization and most trade reforms create winners and losers and may even exacerbate poverty in the short run. Trade reforms cannot work as isolated measures. The appropriate policy responses are to design tailored special and differential treatment, phase and sequence liberalization properly, put institutional domestic institutions in place in parallel, employ newly gained resources to alleviate hardships and (re)activate the losers in society. In short, the response should be to facilitate adjustment rather than abandon the reform process altogether.[18] As Minister for Development Cooperation of The Netherlands, I am particularly interested in how to deal with the impact of trade liberalization on development and poverty reduction and the potential role of multilateral rules to strengthen good (economic) governance and lock in positive domestic reform. I am also interested in exploring what we actually mean when we say that we want to strengthen the development dimensions in the Doha Development Round and rebalance the rules in favour of developing countries or enhance their policy space.

In responding to these questions, we should first take a look at the policy prescriptions and experience of dealing with the trade interests and concerns of developing countries over the past 60 years. Have they resulted in a better integration of developing countries in the multilateral trading system? Where do we stand now in pursuing the goal of more favourable treatment for developing countries? What is the appropriate way forward in the design of the trade rules and the building of trade capacity by developing countries themselves, international organizations and donors? Gary Sampson adds some fundamental questions:[19] What are appropriate development strategies for developing countries and what role should trade and trade openness play in them? And, subsequently, what are the right legal flexibilities and constraints and the kind of support that the WTO system should deliver to them?

Treatment of developing countries in the GATT

Most trade and development provisions foreseen in 1947 in the stillborn International Trade Organization (ITO) – when only a few developing countries were present at the table – did not become part of the GATT that emerged from the ratification failure of the ITO charter. The GATT started out with a vision of one global system of trade rules for everyone, with the developing countries present as full players. This vision changed dramatically during the decolonization era as a growing number of developing countries became independent and GATT-contracting parties in their own right. Most of them were reliant on the export of primary commodities that faced continuously deteriorating terms of trade. This trend and the creation of UNCTAD in 1963 strengthened the calls for industrialization policies based on import substitution and a focus on domestic and regional markets among developing countries. In the GATT, developing countries limited themselves largely to obtaining exceptions from the general rules to accommodate their special circumstances and economic policies and extracting non-reciprocal and preferential market access concessions from developed countries.

Legal flexibility in the GATT was created through an approach that became known as special and differential treatment (SDT) since equal treatment of unequals was regarded as unfair. Rules changes were secured for developing countries in the form of legal provisions for various purposes: infant industry protection, flexible use of trade measures for balance of payments reasons, non-reciprocity of tariff concessions by developing countries (through inclusion in the GATT of part IV on trade and development) and preferential market access arrangements, such as the Generalized System of Preferences (GSP) deviating from most-favoured nation (MFN) status in tariff reductions (codified in the Enabling Clause).[20]

For developing countries there was of course a flipside to being scarcely bound by the GATT rules in practice and their disengagement

from MFN-based tariff negotiations. The consequence was that the negotiating agendas and the reciprocal exchange of tariff concessions in
GATT rounds were set and dominated by developed countries and their
mutual trade interests. The effect of that unevenness in obligations, irrespective of its laudable objective, was considerably less progress in reducing tariffs on labour-intensive manufactures and agricultural products in
which developing countries have a comparative advantage and major export interests. Even now, after eight negotiating rounds, there is still
significant unfinished business in dismantling tariff protection in the
countries of the Organisation for Economic Co-operation and Development (OECD). This has serious repercussions for poorer developing
countries' efforts to achieve export-led growth.[21] Products such as textiles and clothing, leather and leather products, fish and fish products
and (processed) food still face huge and peak tariffs higher than for any
other product category. Treatment is often also characterized by tariff es-
calation (the more processed, the higher the tariff) in developed countries, making it more difficult for developing countries to add value
locally to commodities. This picture is also true – though to a lesser
degree – for the major developing countries, notably China, India, Brazil
and South Africa. These countries have become important export outlets
for other developing countries.

Another proof of the thesis that there are no free lunches was that developed countries forced protectionist exceptions to the GATT rules for
themselves. Most notable were the quantitative restrictions and the right
to provide export subsidies for agricultural products and the managed
trade in textiles and clothing in the form of the Multi fibre Agreements.
As for using economic development or the (political) sensitivity of certain industries as a reason for trade-distorting policies, developing countries were simply following in the footsteps of their colonial masters,
according to Robert Hudec.[22] This phenomenon of having a flipside to
less engagement in trade negotiations still continues in a sense, as least
developed countries (LDCs) and agricultural negotiators of the G-20 experience on a daily basis in the Doha Round.

Developing countries before and during the Uruguay Round

The 1980s showed a clear break with the treatment and the disengagement of developing countries in multilateral trade negotiations. In the
first half of the 1990s, negotiations in the GATT Uruguay Round culminated in a significant widening of their trade obligations. The single undertaking required all WTO members to accept all agreements ensuing
from this round. This included disciplines in the trade rules area evolving
from earlier Tokyo Round codes on subsidies, anti-dumping and tech-

nical regulations whose membership was previously limited to developed countries, significant tariff commitments and new obligations in the (until then) uncovered areas of services and the protection of intellectual property rights.

In order to enhance developing countries' participation in trade and ease the adjustment process and the implementation of new obligations, the following special and differential treatment (SDT) means were available: (i) exhortatory provisions aimed at increasing the trade opportunities of developing countries; (ii) best endeavour provisions under which WTO members should safeguard the interests of developing countries, for example by taking their special circumstances into account when designing and implementing technical regulations; (iii) legal flexibility in commitments, action and use of certain policy instruments, for example more lenient requirements to invoke certain rights in the area of export subsidies and contingency measures; (iv) transitional periods, for example to implement resource-intensive obligations as in the Agreements on Subsidies, Customs Valuation, Trade-Related Investment Measures and Trade-Related Aspects of Intellectual Property Rights (TRIPS), and extra time to phase in non-reciprocal tariff reductions; (v) best endeavour provisions and promises by developed countries to provide technical assistance; (vi) provisions related to preferential treatment of LDCs.[23]

The *World Trade Report 2007* mentions several factors to explain the change in attitude of major developing countries towards increased participation in trade negotiations since the 1980s and their willingness to adopt more obligations in the Uruguay Round.[24] The report also assesses the track record of the most prominent SDT rights in the areas of infant industry protection, export promotion, preferential market access and (temporary) exemptions from the rules to take account of adjustment difficulties or special circumstances. The two areas of infant industry protection and preferential market access and non-reciprocity continue to form the core of SDT demands by most developing countries. The thinking about the third area – how to take account of adjustment difficulties and special circumstances – has evolved over time, as has development policy in general.

Import substitution and export promotion

First, there was the recognition in the 1980s of both the failure of most import substitution policies and the spectacular export successes of East Asian countries in international markets. In many developing countries pursuing import substitution and infant industry protection policies, substantial distortions had been introduced in their economy. These distortions penalized the agriculture sector where the majority of the poor still reside and discouraged exports, and were often exacerbated by overvalued currencies. Widespread rent-seeking by special interest groups, corruption and long-term inefficiencies were often by-products of selective government intervention at the level of individual industries. Unbound tariffs or high tariff ceilings already provided considerable legal room for manoeuvre to increase applied tariffs in practice. Where further legal flexibility was needed, it was found by resorting to the easy-to-use balance of payments exemptions rather than the more cumbersome and costly route of infant industry protection of GATT Article XVIII.

On export promotion policies, the evidence of selective government intervention is less clear-cut according to the WTO Secretariat. Some developing countries such as Korea, countries of the Association of Southeast Asian Nations (ASEAN) and Mauritius were very successful in their export strategies. Encouraged by this success, other developing countries requested special rights to subsidize exports and the export promotion of manufactures to cover their trade policies in export-processing zones. However, many countries – in Latin America and Africa – failed in diversifying from traditional commodity exports, and often at huge cost. Sound macroeconomic policies and huge investments in education to create skilled labour forces were major explanatory factors for success in East Asia, in addition to market protection in the early phases. Notwithstanding certain sector-specific interventions, export-orientation policies in successful newly industrialized countries (NICs) such as Korea were generally characterized by the offer of uniform export incentives, which were enhanced by relatively stable exchange rates. The success of these export policies was also crucially dependent on access to developed countries' markets, at first through the preferential access of GSP programmes.

The international policy debate seems to have been almost resolved now. On the one hand, the simplistic "Washington Consensus" recommendation of pursuing outward-oriented development through trade liberalization with minimal government intervention has been shown not to work. On the other hand, the limited success in practice of active industrial policies owing to constraints on the budget, information, administrative capacity and political economy has been acknowledged, as well as the importance of functioning markets and institutions.[25] As for the legal treatment, Sampson notes that GATT failed to design the legal flexibility needed to accommodate the right economic policies for developing countries.[26] He concludes that the legal flexibility offered was counterproductive and legitimized the wrong policies.

Preferential market access

From the 1960s, preferential market access arrangements were boosted as a tool to improve exports from developing countries and the industrial development based thereon. In the 1980s, however, developed countries began to make the eligibility conditions of their GSP schemes stricter and to remove more advanced countries from preferential treatment. The contribution of preferences to export growth and the diversification of the exports of beneficiaries also show a mixed picture. Relatively small preferential margins, the exclusion of "sensitive" products and restrictive eligibility conditions – notably in the preferential rules of origin – limited utilization in practice and reduced the development impact. By introducing long-term inefficiencies in the allocation of productive resources, these preferences have also affected the way in which beneficiaries needed to restructure their economies in accordance with their comparative advantage. Overall, these schemes seem to have generated economic rents for special interest groups rather than fostered broad-based industrial and agriculture development.[27]

Several successful exporters realized that they could be better off by pursuing their offensive interests in multilateral negotiations. Partly because of the threat of unilateral (contingency) measures against their exports by major developed countries, they became demandeurs of stricter multilateral trade rules and further MFN-based trade liberalization. This concerned especially the heavily distorted markets for agriculture and textiles. Many developing countries were undertaking "autonomous" trade liberalization efforts, often in the context of structural adjustment programmes of the IMF and World Bank.

In parallel, the benign neglect of developing countries in GATT – whereby developing countries were accorded more lenient treatment in the rules and free-riding in market access negotiations was accepted – changed. In 1979, the Enabling Clause had already implicitly introduced the notion of the phasing-out of legal flexibility as the level of development of developing countries increased. Whereas this phasing-out initially implied less favourable tariff treatment in the markets of developed countries as developing countries develop, the phrase "increasing participation in world trade" acquired a new political meaning. It also started to mean a phasing-in of more obligations on more advanced developing countries and compliance with the general rules of the game in a multilateral trading system based on a balance of rights and obligations.

In the GATT Uruguay Round, developing countries increasingly faced difficulties in defining unified negotiating positions because of diversified economic interests across products, markets and trade disciplines. The Uruguay Round became a turning point in the traditional developing country solidarity in GATT. Nor did greater use of trade-defensive measures in South–South trade help to maintain their mutual solidarity. This trend for developing countries to pursue their individual trade interests is expected to continue in the future as many issue- and interest-based coalitions have now emerged. It may be seen as a healthy development.

The limited value of preferences will of course further erode as MFN liberalization of tariffs leaves less room to offer preferences. In the current Doha Round, the beneficiaries of these preferences are pitted against excluded developing countries that seek MFN liberalization in developed country markets. Unfortunately, this offers some political cover to developed countries to question the need for ambitious tariff reductions, particularly in agriculture. Except for ensuring duty-free quotas for the LDCs as part of the "single undertaking", I am doubtful about trade solutions to deal with preference erosion if that would imply less MFN liberalization. Somewhat longer periods to implement agreed tariff reductions may be needed for some products. In view of the relatively limited problem in terms of the number of countries and products affected, financial solutions by preference-giving countries to assist affected beneficiary countries to adjust seem to be the best way forward.

The approach of developing countries after 1995 and in the Doha Round

The Uruguay Round richly sprinkled some 155 SDT provisions over the many agreements. This was the result of negotiating efforts by developing countries, the willingness of developed countries to make "easy" concessions and the changing nature and the wider coverage of the WTO. This high number illustrates a form of inflation in WTO negotiations. Though some SDT provisions are mandatory, the majority remain "best efforts" or exhortatory in nature. Few of the mandatory provisions would be legally enforceable in dispute settlement. It is no surprise that most SDT provisions have had limited operational significance. The lack of success in the past did not end the calls for more favourable treatment of developing countries after the WTO came into existence and after the Doha Round started at the end of 2001.

Many developing countries faced considerable difficulties in implementing the resource-intensive obligations in new areas such as Technical Barriers to Trade (TBT), Sanitary and Phytosanitary (SPS) measures and TRIPS. This stretched beyond limited financial and administrative resources and many governments did not consider the required changes to be their highest development priorities. Developing countries also considered that the cost of compliance with the WTO went much further than just administrative and institutional costs. For example, the TRIPS Agreement has been estimated to have resulted in considerable net financial flows from developing countries to developed countries owing to higher royalty payments for licensing and higher-priced "IPR-related" goods such as medicines.[28] In addition, the negative effects of TRIPS on access to affordable medicines for life-threatening diseases in developing countries came to light. Developing countries took the view that developed countries were not fully meeting their commitments in the areas of technical assistance and were dragging their feet in the promised market openings, for example by back-loading liberalization obligations in textiles and clothing. So the actual implementation of the WTO agreements had not provided developing countries with the "promised" results, funding and improved market access, while unforeseen problems and high compliance costs had surfaced. In their view it demonstrated the unbalanced character of the overall Uruguay Round deal and they called for a reopening.

In the second half of the 1990s this concern first led to the implementation debate in the WTO. Developing countries called for more SDT provisions in the existing agreements to take better account of their special needs and capacity constraints. Having already paid for the Uruguay Round deal in full in the form of, amongst others, agreements such as TRIPS, they argued that correcting unforeseen problems in implementing the agreements should not be paid for twice by new concessions on their part. These problems needed to be fixed first before any negotiations about the agenda of a new WTO round could start. In the run-up to the Ministerial Conference in Seattle in 1999, developing countries tabled a large number of proposals that were intended to fix the implementation problems. Most proposals requested additional transition periods and a permanent loosening of substantive obligations, often on the basis of self-determination by developing countries.

This triggered fierce resistance from developed countries, which regarded the Uruguay agreements as a done deal. They could be reopened only as part of a new round and paid for by concessions in other areas. This also launched a fundamental debate about the need for the graduation of advanced developing countries from SDT provisions and for defining criteria to determine eligibility for additional flexibilities. Developed countries insisted that, if SDT rights were to remain available to *all* developing countries (irrespective of development level) on the basis of self-selection, there would have to be strict limitations on the exemptions from the uniform multilateral rules. Sampson poses the following relevant operational questions in this regard for allowing such legal flexibility: Which obligations should qualify for SDT? What type of flexibility should be provided? Which countries are eligible on the basis of what criteria? And who decides (self-determination or a multilateral procedure) and for how long should the SDT treatment last?[29]

A procedural compromise to defuse the stand-off on the implementation issue was found by making all SDT provisions part of the Doha Round negotiations after all. The Doha Ministerial Declaration on implementation-related issues and concerns instructed the negotiators to review all SDT provisions "with a view to strengthening them and making them more precise, effective and operational".[30] After Doha, the debate focused on exploring: (i) how to make developed countries' best endeavour commitments on providing technical assistance and taking account of developing countries' concerns mandatory; (ii) the need for so called "policy space" in developing countries to protect import-competing industries and to be able to subsidize export industries. The first approach did not get very far because developed countries did not envisage themselves making binding financial commitments on technical assistance in the WTO or not applying urgent technical regulations to developing country exporters. The second approach is still in play in the Doha Round.

In the Doha Round, one expression of the second approach became the offer of a "round for free" to the LDCs as a group. These countries – too small to matter in world trade – would get complete flexibility for their own policies and would not be expected to make market access concessions themselves. The second predictable expression of this approach in the SDT debate was to focus on the procedural proposals of the list of demands and to concede rather meaningless "rights" that cannot be enforced in dispute settlement. After the failure of the Cancun Ministerial Conference in 2003, an implicit trade-off or stand-off seems to have materialized. Developed countries have accepted taking three (investment, competition and transparency in government procurement) of the four Singapore issues off the table, and developing countries do not seem to be pushing the bulk of their implementation proposals very hard any more (the process had become unmanageable anyway).

A more promising approach: From special and differential treatment to special and differentiated treatment

Most of the above-mentioned questions posed by Sampson on how to make SDT more meaningful for development have not yet been adequately addressed in the negotiations. What remains outstanding is to get a satisfactory answer to the political question – as Sampson puts it – of whether the ability to accept more WTO obligations comes only as the result of economic development or whether accepting WTO obligations is seen as helpful to promote development. My answer is that functioning markets and institutions matter and well-designed WTO rules that take account of the circumstances in individual countries can promote development and strengthen both the enabling environment for the business sector and the hand of reforming governments against special and vested interests.

To move the SDT debate along, developing countries could abandon their sometimes defensive insistence to be treated as one group in these negotiations. Developing countries should recognize that they are not all equal, nor do they have the same needs and abilities. I acknowledge that it is difficult to abstract from the political economy and the negotiating positions of WTO members in the search for more consistent and development-oriented solutions, especially if major developed WTO members have sought in the past and still seek exemptions from uniform rules or tailor them to accommodate their own political sensitivities.[31]

Going for an alternative two-speed or variable geometry system with different rules applying to (poor) developing countries – in the form of either sectoral deals or plurilateral deals with stricter rules for clubs of limited membership – may seem appealing at first sight. There is, however, a clear risk of excluding poor countries completely from the negotiations of normative rules for the globalized economy that may be impossible to adapt later. From the perspective of inclusive global governance, I would not regard such a development as helpful or desirable.

As Robert Wolfe states, if the WTO is a central component of global governance, then its normative framework should apply to all members.[32] All members should be full participants in the negotiations on the evolution of the system and take ownership of the resulting rules. Where the problems lie in developing the regulatory negotiating agenda in the WTO and determining its depth and breadth, one answer is to build appropriate regulatory capacity in capitals in developing countries and to encourage their regulators to go to Geneva to learn and advance their interests. If this requires more time before negotiations can commence, this should be given rather than advance the WTO in the direction of a two-speed system.

As far as the future of the SDT debate is concerned, a *differentiated* treatment in certain rules that depends on the circumstances in a country holds the key to a more productive outcome. Fortunately we are long past the period of simple recommendations of trade liberalization and laissez-faire policies in the pursuit of outward-oriented development strategies. Governments do have an important role to play in ensuring functioning markets and institutions and in encouraging entrepreneurs and new investments. Certain second-best policies may be justified to address market failures if the risks of rent-seeking are acknowledged and limited in time. I also see an increasing recognition of the thesis that the cost/benefit ratio of certain regulatory WTO obligations may be related to the level of development of countries and that a one-size-fits-all approach is not always appropriate. As Minister for Development Cooperation, I am aware that the investments required to meet resource-intensive WTO obligations in partner countries can compete with other development priorities for scarce funds and limited administrative capacity.

Within the remaining time in the Doha Round or in a post-Doha work programme, WTO members should take a closer look at the available policy instruments and the conditions attached to them. We need to explore how "qualified" SDT rights could better take into account the specific situation in individual countries, without undermining the integrity of the rules-based multilateral trading system. Therefore, I would welcome a move away from the present politicized debate that is now held in binary terms of "graduation" versus "total opt-outs" towards a more problem-oriented discussion of dealing with market imperfections and economic instruments.[33] In this regard, effective technical assistance will be indispensable to assist developing countries to both implement obligations and facilitate economic adjustment in the interim.

Less than full reciprocity in tariff reduction commitments for developing countries remains a litmus test in the Doha Round, as was explicitly formulated in the non-agricultural market access (NAMA) mandate. Having added rules to the mix of tariff negotiations has of course made such an assessment more complicated. In the complex and broad WTO negotiations covering both market access for goods and services and rules, determining the overall balance of reciprocity has become an art rather than a science. Within the context of an overall reasonable asymmetry, every country needs to make this judgement on its own. In the future, developing countries could actually play a very useful role as guardians of market openness and a global level playing field in the WTO. After implementing the Doha Round results, developing countries will still maintain higher tariffs than developed countries.[34] In future trade-offs, some more advanced developing countries could perhaps use the attraction of their growing markets and their tariff-bargaining chips as leverage to resist moves from developed countries to invent new trade barriers or to discipline their policy space for trade-distorting subsidies. Developed countries may by then have abolished most of their tariffs for manufactures (with the exception of many agricultural goods and in particular for sensitive products) but they will still have considerable subsidies at their disposal that will affect competitive conditions and hence trade.

From trade-related technical assistance towards Aid for Trade

The scale and scope of trade-related technical assistance and capacity-building (TACB) have expanded considerably since the WTO came into existence in 1995. TACB expenditures accelerated after 2001, spurred by developed countries' commitments undertaken at the launch of the Doha

Round. TACB covers two core areas: (i) trade policy and regulation, including training and building negotiating capacity of officials and support to implement WTO obligations; (ii) trade development, which includes support services for business, infrastructure and trade promotion. Key principles in TACB strategies are the mainstreaming of trade priority areas into national development strategies, enhanced coordination between agencies and adequate funding.

The WTO Secretariat has played a key role in launching TACB initiatives, such as the Integrated Framework (IF) for the LDCs in 1997 and the broader Aid for Trade initiative in 2005. This has been done in cooperation with other international organizations and bilateral donors.[35] In the IF, the WTO, the World Bank, the IMF, UNCTAD, the International Trade Centre and the UNDP try to coordinate their TACB activities with those of bilateral donors, to support LDC governments in meeting their trade needs. The struggle in ensuring effective TACB is clear – having been established in 1997, revamped in 2002 and further enhanced in 2008. The broader Aid for Trade initiative launched at the Hong Kong Ministerial Conference in 2005 aims to assist developing countries to implement new obligations, take advantage of trade opportunities and cope with certain adjustment costs.

In addition to the core areas of TACB, Aid for Trade aims to help developing countries, particularly LDCs, to build the trade-related supply-side capacity and infrastructure needed to implement and benefit from WTO Agreements and more broadly to expand trade. Since 2007, the WTO has taken the lead in monitoring Aid for Trade in an annual global review of relevant Aid for Trade flows and their impact. There is also a general understanding among developed and developing countries that more Aid for Trade is a complement to and not a substitute for ambitious market access outcomes in relevant areas for developing countries and WTO rules that take account of development needs.

Looking behind the relatively rosy picture of growing Aid for Trade flows and multilateral initiatives, I share much of the analysis of Carolyn Deere.[36] The core problems facing most Aid for Trade are that it is still too donor driven and lacks real local ownership in beneficiary countries. Serious shortcomings in the design, quality and delivery stem from these basic flaws. Various attempts have been made to better align Aid for Trade allocations with the trade and development priorities of recipients, but this process will have to go further and deeper. Aid for Trade donors have committed themselves to apply the agreed principles of effective aid outlined in the Paris Declaration on Aid Effectiveness of March 2005, in particular ownership by the recipients, alignment with their policies and procedures and harmonization by donors. These principles are also core elements of the new Joint EU Aid for Trade Strategy.

On paper, this implies stronger linkages of Aid for Trade to countries' poverty reduction strategies, improved needs assessments, increased predictability, improved donor coordination and more focus on regional approaches where possible. In practice, many donors continue to allocate funding for Aid for Trade according to their own priorities and choosing their preferred implementing agencies. Though the bulk is provided through multilateral channels and intermediary organizations, it still follows a supply-driven and *à la carte* approach. Deere claims that, in the area of trade policy regulation, many donors provide bilateral TACB with the unwritten desire of wanting to influence the interpretation and implementation of WTO rules in recipients' national laws and policies. This restricts the options for development-friendly interpretations of WTO rules and jeopardizes the ability of developing countries to make use of the policy space under the existing rules.

Many LDCs also lack the capacity to articulate their own needs in this area properly. When needs were formulated, evaluations have shown that the capacity to mainstream and implement programmes in poverty reduction strategies has been lacking. At the same time, the possibility to take advantage of the Aid for Trade on offer is often limited by human resource constraints, thus resulting in a classic Catch-22 situation. Weak national ownership is not helped either by unpredictable donor support that favours one-off, stand-alone and short-term Aid for Trade rather than long-term investments in sustainable trade policy formulation and local institutions in developing countries.

How to fix these two problems of Aid for Trade, which – not surprisingly – mirror many of the problems facing development cooperation in general? Deere's analysis points, in line with the Paris Declaration, in the direction of empowering developing countries to build long-term institutional capacity *in situ*, both within government and in society at large. Greater attention should be devoted to strengthening domestic policy-making processes. This involves better coordination among relevant government departments and proper consultation of stakeholders, including the business sector, labour unions, parliaments, nongovernmental organizations and academia.

Deere rightly recommends that the focus of TACB should also be explicitly development oriented in character rather than "neutral". It should strengthen the position of poor countries in the WTO and assist beneficiaries to identify their national interests in implementing existing WTO rules or in negotiations.[37] In addition to this, developing countries should be encouraged and facilitated to participate much more in the world trading system. Aid for Trade should also help countries to build their supply-side capacity and trade-related infrastructure. In order to become more effective and achieve concrete results, donors will have to harmonize their Aid for Trade programmes, further untie them and align with developing countries' poverty reduction strategies. A genuine, concerted effort by donors and multilateral agencies will be necessary to realize this. Going in this direction will require stronger multilateral coordination and administration of Aid for Trade activities and effective ownership in beneficiary countries, while at the same time putting the neutral WTO Secretariat in a monitoring role at arm's length. In the case of the enhanced IF for the LDCs, this approach is now being developed.

Further improvement of the Doha Development Agenda Trade Capacity Building Database (TCBDB) will also be an important step in the right direction of creating greater transparency of donor activities.[38] As a monitoring tool it can be made more effective if donors report more accurately on the country, regional and sectoral aspects of their activities. This should enable a better interaction in the WTO Global Aid for Trade Review between recipient countries and donors. In the multilateral monitoring of the implementation of Aid for Trade commitments, quality and effectiveness should get more attention. Monitoring could also become part of the regular WTO trade policy reviews of individual WTO members and the topic of dedicated collective peer reviews of Aid for Trade in which use should also be made of independent external evaluations.

Dealing with other legitimate policy objectives: Deepening the agenda of the WTO and how?

Focus on (disciplining) internal measures

Governments pursue many legitimate objectives through a broad variety of policies and instruments. In the process of formulating and implementing public policies they are driven by many stakeholders, who often have divergent interests. Whereas domestic regulation is affecting the conditions of competition and hence trade, trade policy and WTO rules have also become part of the broader picture for other policies in areas such as the environment, human rights, animal welfare and labour standards. Claims about the mutual supportiveness of policies, WTO rules being a "chill factor" for domestic regulation and international negotiations on higher standards and spurring a race-to-the bottom to attract investment, and the need for a level playing field because of "unfair" foreign competition, are vying for attention in the public debate in many developed countries.

A core challenge for the WTO, according to the *World Trade Report*,[39] is to distinguish between the implementation of legitimate public policies and protectionism. Internal "behind-the-border" measures related to the fiscal treatment of a good or the regulation of its sale and entry into the market can have a significant impact on goods from third countries. Such measures, for example lifecycle-based technical product regulations aimed at reducing greenhouse gas emissions and waste, try to secure legitimate objectives in environmental policy. Usually they do not intend to discriminate against foreign producers, at least not explicitly. The WTO rightly shows complete deference to national policy-makers when it comes to regulating domestic products and their national production processes. But internal measures can also contain (extraterritorial) elements or conditions that may affect and (de facto) discriminate against foreign products and their suppliers. And then they become a matter for the WTO to scrutinize in order to safeguard predictable and stable market access.

Over the years, GATT and the WTO have become more concerned with and involved in dealing with internal measures that affect the conditions of competition between domestic and foreign goods and services. One trade-related reason was that internal regulatory measures can circumvent bound tariff concessions (for example by subsidizing domestic producers) or hinder market access unnecessarily (through product requirements). The basic WTO provisions on internal measures are GATT Article III (on national treatment of like products in internal taxation and regulation) and the general exceptions in GATT Article XX (which allow WTO members under certain conditions to pursue other public policy objectives with trade measures that deviate from substantive WTO disciplines). Concerns about the lack of specific guidance from these basic provisions and the desire to protect acquired market access rights were the main reasons for negotiating additional, more specific and stringent obligations in the WTO. This has led to specific and detailed provisions in the Agreements on Subsidies, Technical Barriers to Trade (TBT), Sanitary and Phytosanitary (SPS) measures and Agriculture. Many GATT and WTO disputes have revolved around the interpretation of these WTO provisions and their impact on trade and the degree of policy freedom to regulate.

The WTO provisions related to internal measures hinge on the key concept of "like product" and elaborate the basic discipline of avoiding discrimination against imported like products.[40] If products are like, then domestic and imported products should be treated in the same way. If products are not like, they can be treated differently. Even when domestic and foreign products are considered to be like, governments may still treat them differently provided they can justify the different treatment under the (limited) exceptions for other public policies in GATT Article XX. Few measures at the centre of WTO disputes have met these conditions in practice and often for good reason in the individual cases at hand. Over time, thinking about the likeness of products has evolved somewhat as has the interpretation of the exceptions for other public policies in GATT Article XX in WTO jurisprudence. But the determination of whether products are "like" remains basically – in the view of the Appellate Body – a determination about the nature and extent of the competitive relationship between these products in the market. Of course this makes good sense from a trade perspective. Is it the same for other policies?

From product standards to harmonized standards for processing and production methods

In general, the WTO has treated products that are physically the same and that share the same end uses, consumer preferences or tariff classification as like products, irrespective of the production process or method employed. And so national measures by WTO members that did differentiate products on this basis and discriminated against foreign products have been challenged in dispute settlements and mostly disciplined. The TRIPS and SPS agreements did change this approach somewhat by introducing international minimum standards of a production and process methods (PPMs) character. This was done either by direct insertion in the case of TRIPS or by referral to the standards developed by the three international standardizing organizations for SPS matters. Sampson notes that there is a fundamental difference in the way trade policy distinguishes products compared with some other public policies.[41] For example, distinguishing between environmentally friendly and harmful products and the environmental impact of their respective lifecycles is the core business of environmental policy when designing regulations or using subsidies or levies. Does this put the WTO at odds with other policies? Not necessarily, but tensions are growing.

In today's globalized world the relevant question has become whether the manner in which a product has been produced can or should become a legitimate reason to discriminate against *like* foreign products. Pleas can be heard to go beyond product-related PPMs and add extraneous circumstances or policies in the country of origin as conditions for market access, such as the labour conditions or implementing national laws in line with international agreements in other areas. Current examples (in the making) are minimum sustainability criteria of the European Union for biofuels based on meeting minimum savings of greenhouse gas emissions over the whole lifecycle (compared with the fossil reference product)[42] and the protection of bio-diversity, and pleas for import prohibitions on products produced with the worst forms of child labour or on agricultural products that fail EU domestic animal welfare standards.

Increasingly, developed countries attempt to influence (directly or indirectly) the production methods of certain products and/or related public policies in third countries. Compliance with domestic PPM standards, including those not incorporated in the product, could become a condition for foreign products to access the market or qualify for fiscal or regulatory advantages. Even if such national regulation does not formally discriminate on the basis of origin, de facto discrimination against imported products may still occur. This is likely to happen if the domestic regulation imposes a heavier burden on foreign producers than domestic producers in order to meet the PPM standards. This is certainly the case if it requires significant investments and policy changes in the exporting countries while national producers are not or hardly affected. Exporters from developing countries in particular could face extensive costs to adapt production processes and for certification throughout the product chain or run the risk of having their market access denied.

Who could be against compliance with basic labour standards, the prevention of child labour, the promotion of sustainable development and the protection of biodiversity, the environment and animal welfare? In my view these are essential elements of a sustainable future based on the three Ps (people, planet and profit). No one would be against, but of course the real question is how to promote these objectives effectively and determine when the use of trade measures should be allowed. It is sometimes argued that most countries have already undertaken commitments in these areas in other international agreements such as the ILO and conventions on human rights, biological biodiversity and environmental issues. Does that make a convincing case to allow unilateral trade measures to pursue these objectives if such measures have not been explicitly authorized in these agreements? The answer is no, certainly not in a legal sense. In my view, however, societal concerns and values, referred to as non-trade concerns (NTCs), do deserve the WTO's attention – though not necessarily always in the form of negotiating rule change – because of the intrinsic importance of most NTCs. Ignoring them could undermine public support for the WTO and trigger uncontrollable use of unilateral trade measures.

In the context of global governance and the role of the WTO and trade measures therein, more specific questions to take into account are:

- What is the best way to deal with these NTCs, especially when promoting them in third countries and competitiveness concerns seem to dominate?
- How will developing countries be affected if their exports are denied access to the markets of developed countries in an effort to enforce compliance with (unilateral) rules and standards on NTCs, and would that assist in meeting the NTCs or make matters worse?

These are complex and sensitive questions, particularly when one considers that PPM standards are often intimately related to a country's general level of development. The Netherlands' government is eager to examine to what extent it is possible and desirable to address NTCs while ensuring the achievement of the Millennium Development Goals. These general considerations are only a first step in the deliberations on NTCs. There is no international consensus on what NTCs exactly entail, which of them are truly global or cross-border in nature, what trade measures are permitted under current WTO rules, what changes in WTO rules (if any) would be needed or desirable, and what instruments or combination of policies would work best in practice. The approach would probably also vary depending on the NTC.

As regards the current WTO's legal framework, it is uncertain where the grey area lies in the interpretation of the current agreements, how WTO case law may evolve and what the relationship is to other international treaties containing trade-related provisions. Divergent views exist on the room for manoeuvre, the WTO compatibility of various PPM-based instruments addressing NTCs and the need for (upward) harmonization of PPM standards at international level. Nevertheless, demand in developed countries continues to grow for some kind of public intervention on NTCs.

Deepening the agenda in the WTO and cross-linkages between issues?

Dealing with domestic regulation and WTO disciplines and the interface between other public policies and market access can affect the conditions of competition and hence trade. It is also closely linked with the content of the future negotiating agenda of the WTO. After Cancun, the Doha Round was limited mainly to "traditional" market access issues and related regulations. This does not have to be the case for the next round. What should be the appropriate coverage and reach of the WTO and how should the content of the negotiating agenda be established? What issues should be in or out, and, if in, how far should coverage by WTO rules stretch? These questions continue to divide the WTO membership and will not be easily resolved when decisions have to be taken by consensus. In the past, heated discussions have taken place in the WTO over whether to incorporate new policy areas such as intellectual property rights protection, investment, competition, government procurement, environmental issues and labour standards.

I share the pragmatic view on how to move this debate forward expressed in the *World Trade Report 2007*.[43] Ultimately, the scope of the multilateral trading system and its negotiating agenda is the result of a political process that is primarily based on offering a quid pro quo (which can also be outside the WTO), with a reasonable asymmetry of commitments based on the level of development. Attempting to define criteria – such as trade-relatedness or specificity – before deciding whether to add an issue to the WTO agenda and subsequently include it in the single undertaking of a future round can be an interesting exercise.[44] In the end, however, it is unlikely that parties will ever be able to agree on such criteria beforehand.

Governments will always, for different reasons, search for linkages between issues and policies that may be unrelated to considerations of market access and competition. Although such linkages will undoubtedly complicate negotiations in the WTO even more, they could still deliver beneficial outcomes. From the perspective of global governance and enhancing global welfare, such linkages should therefore not be rejected out of hand. Cross-linkages between trade and climate change negotiations, for example, have become very topical and require our urgent attention. If negotiations about internal measures would imply an upward harmonization of PPM-based standards at international level and have serious cost implications for certain parties (often developing countries), then a negotiated outcome could be viable only if adequate compensation for the "losing" parties is agreed as part of the deal. Before launching negotiations on any issue that also has trade and cost implications, having a platform in the WTO to learn and deliberate about the problem extensively could be useful in its own right. Establishing a dedicated working group in the WTO for this purpose should not automatically imply that negotiations will be started down the road. Other actions may be warranted.

The decision to launch international negotiations on a certain type of internal measures is of course separate from the choice of forum.[45] In most cases, international negotiations on these matters should preferably take place in a specialized international (standardizing) organization, such as a multilateral environmental agreement (MEA) for environmental issues. If the problem at stake is global or cross-boundary in nature and trade measures would be needed to deal effectively with the problem, then the WTO should encourage and accommodate balanced and equitable multilateral solutions.

It is high time that WTO members agreed to properly define the relationship of the WTO with other relevant international (standard-setting) bodies that use trade instruments to pursue their objectives. The leading principle in this should be the need to avoid conflict between different bodies of international law, especially if the parties to these agreements and the membership of the WTO are not fully overlapping. In those circumstances, normal conflict rules in international law cannot easily resolve the conflict. The scope of the negotiations on environment in the Doha Round is now oddly limited to how the existing WTO rules apply among the parties to the MEA in question. Some have argued that a conflict between international bodies of law has not occurred yet and therefore the WTO does not need to deal with this matter.

Innovative and balanced proposals on how to structure a mutually supportive relationship between the WTO and MEAs have been put forward in the Committee on Trade and Environment (CTE) and show the way forward.[46] Trade measures taken in pursuance of the objectives of a broad-based MEA and specifically mandated therein could receive a presumption of WTO conformity, for example by reversing the burden of proof in dispute settlement. Such MEAs would preferably contain a combination of instruments, including financial assistance and technology transfer. This approach could be applied in other areas as well. Simultaneously, governments must strengthen these specialized international organizations and stimulate better cooperation between their secretariats and among policy-making departments at home, as I discussed under the coherence issue.

The final question is whether WTO rules need to be changed in order to accommodate NTCs. With the exception of finding a legal accommodation of the multilateral approach mentioned above, first exploring alternative courses of action and the use of mechanisms already available in the WTO would make more sense and certainly be less contentious. One could think of options like interpretations of the existing rules or Ministerial Decisions and Declarations. After careful consideration of the issue, these instruments could create the required legal or policy flexibility if any was still needed.[47] The Ministerial Declaration on TRIPS and Public Health adopted in Doha in 2001 offers a useful model. Negotiating deals in specific sectors, as in the case of fisheries subsidies in the ongoing Doha Round, is also a possibility. The controversial case of biofuels could be a similar candidate that could most benefit from a more coherent international approach in all relevant international organizations, including the WTO. Proponents of NTCs should, however, realize that changes in the fundamental rules such as GATT Articles I, III, XI and XX do not come easily in the WTO, and for good reason.

The special case of climate change

Considering the issue of climate change and some of the more controversial proposals floating around, a conflict between different legal regimes is no longer a theoretical possibility. I refer in particular to the threats to use border tax adjustment measures on imported energy-intensive goods because of alleged competitiveness concerns arising from greenhouse gas (GHG) obligations for domestic producers and to avoid the risk of carbon leakage in energy-intensive sectors. Trade ministers meeting informally in the margins of the United Nations Climate Change Conference in Bali in December 2007 rightly called for a multilateral approach on climate change.[48] They acknowledged the potentially mutually supportive linkages between climate change, trade and development but also recognized the risk of serious pressures on the trading system in the absence of a multilateral approach.[49] This also raises the issue of the responsibility of developed and developing countries with regard to GHG emissions reductions. It underlines the need for a comprehensive and equitable global regime to tackle climate change, avoid carbon leakage from countries with stringent emissions policies to those without and take account of developing countries' concerns.

Various trade issues and WTO rules are very relevant for climate change policies.[50] They may seem to protect developing countries in particular, while some developed countries may perceive these WTO disciplines as burdensome, and all aspects seem to converge in the case of biofuels. In my view there is every reason for the WTO to take up the interface between trade and climate change urgently in the CTE or another dedicated forum.

Relevant legal and policy questions are:

- Which products will be on the list of environmental goods for which tariffs will be abolished in the Doha Round?
- What leeway is there for offsetting border measures on imported energy-intensive goods that compete with products of domestic producers that have to buy emissions allowances or face other environmental costs?
- What does the national treatment obligation of GATT Article III imply for policy freedom on fiscal incentives and regulatory measures (such as blending requirements for transport fuels) if based on the level of carbon emissions over the lifecycle of a product or other PPM-based requirements?
- How do the WTO subsidies disciplines affect possible trade-distorting subsidies for renewable energy, biomass and energy services?
- How do TBT rules for standards, technical regulations, certification and labelling requirements for products relate to PPM-based sustainability criteria for biofuels or other products?
- What are the policy effects of the TRIPS Agreement on technology transfer and is additional flexibility required to facilitate the spread of renewable energy technology and the transition to a low-carbon economy in developing countries?

Conclusions

It is an urgent requirement that the global trading system remains governed by the rule of law. It should continue to contribute to better global governance by offering a stable and predictable environment for world trade and equitable development. The WTO does not always function as efficiently and inclusively as it might, but qualified optimism is justified about the WTO being effective in the end. It is easy to be cynical about the Doha Round owing to yet another missed deadline or a new deadlock over agriculture or NAMA. Notwithstanding the failure to conclude the negotiations in July 2008, a successful and reasonably ambitious and balanced conclusion is within reach and greatly needed for global governance and development.

Most governments remain committed to the multilateral process and continue to work hard to negotiate new agreements. But negotiators will have to overcome their hardwired reluctance to show their cards until others do so first. This brinkmanship makes it hard to estimate the remaining gaps that still have to be overcome. It also hinders a bottom-up and member-driven negotiating process, certainly if the chairs of the negotiating groups are constrained from submitting draft texts to take the final leap. It is for the major players in the G-6 in the WTO (the United States, the European Union, Brazil, India, Australia and Japan) to show leadership, but developing countries will also have to engage more in the negotiations. A fair international trading regime, however, will have to allow for special and differentiated treatment of developing countries and acknowledge the need for and reinforce balanced and sustainable growth of the world economy.

Disagreements about major policy issues or unwillingness to negotiate by give-and-take cannot be solved by procedural improvements, although they will certainly help to enhance the legitimacy of the negotiated outcomes. Over time, transparency and inclusiveness in decision-making have emerged as important institutional challenges. Some progress has been made through organic changes in the form of practical arrangements, technical assistance and changes in behaviour, but more work is needed. Institutional designers should complement their vision and allow for practices to evolve as circumstances change and for binding rules to emerge only after extensive learning and deliberation. If new rules are to apply to all members, then voice really matters. Hence there is a need to keep working on making the procedures more inclusive and to assist developing countries to participate in the process through effective TACB with renewed vigour. Vigilance is called for to ensure a fair process in the endgame.

While the negotiations in Geneva in July 2008 came close to reaching agreement, it is clear that enhancing the promised development dimension of the Doha Round will require specific attention in the final stretch of the negotiations. In my view, priority should be given to three elements: ambitious market access openings for products and services modes of relevance to developing countries; duty- and quota-free trade for the LDCs; and disciplining the policy space of developed countries to use trade-distorting subsidies. At the same time, adequate policy space for the poorer countries should assist them in their growth and poverty reduction policies. We are beyond orthodoxy here and looking for pragmatic solutions. Neither market fundamentalism nor neo-protectionism has worked well, as successful emerging economies have shown in the past.

Moving forward in the SDT debate in the direction of differentiated treatment that is better tailored to the individual circumstances of developing countries is most likely to happen only in a built-in post-Doha work programme. In this area not everything needs to be negotiated in the WTO or should have to lead to (new) rights or obligations. Rather than trying to negotiate contentious rules, it might be easier to achieve flexibility and coherence with the broader WTO objectives by having an open discussion in the underutilized trade policy review mechanism[51] or the Committee on Trade and Development.

The WTO system is part of a much broader international system of emerging global governance that is still far from being perfect or coherent. When it comes to NTCs, I support any initiative that seeks to improve their promotion, whether in the European Union or in developing countries. Scarcity of funds and limited institutional capacity will require priority setting. One member's non-trade concerns may also easily become another member's trade concern. Concerning the future WTO agenda and coverage or cross-linkages between trade and NTC issues, I will make an effort to ensure that Dutch and EU policies on NTCs respect the sovereignty and the priorities of the developing countries and do not revert to (disguised) neo-protectionism. Negotiating specialized international regimes, strengthening existing international organizations, enhancing mutual supportiveness with the WTO through stronger coherence of policies at home, and finally flanking development cooperation policies can take us a long way.

New opportunities emerge in the form of voluntary partnerships with the business sector and stakeholders. Customized multilateral frameworks, as in the case of climate change, are needed that could contain effective trade measures, although preferably as part of a broader package of instruments. However, there is no sense in or justification for unilaterally shutting out products from developing countries solely on the basis of their PPMs if they do not fully accommodate or meet our societal concerns. Not only will this not solve the problems in question; by taking such a drastic step, poor countries would be deprived of the chance to trade and grow towards workable solutions. Only by working together to develop international standards that take account of common but differentiated responsibilities and different circumstances and capacities can we achieve sustainable development on a global scale, reduce poverty and raise the level of labour standards, environmental protection and animal welfare.

Notes

I am the Minister for Development Cooperation of The Netherlands. The findings and conclusions expressed in this chapter are mine and do not necessarily reflect those of the Netherlands' government.

1. Martin Wolf, "What the World Needs from the Multilateral Trading System", in Gary P. Sampson, ed., *The Role of the World Trade Organization in Global Governance*, Tokyo: United Nations University Press, 2001, p. 155.
2. Articles III and V of the WTO Agreement define the functions of the WTO. They include: negotiating trade rules; monitoring the implementation of WTO obligations; administration of WTO agreements; dispute settlement; technical assistance and capacity-building; research; cooperation with relevant international organizations; outreach to civil society.
3. See Sylvia Ostry, *The Post-war International Trading System: Who's on First?* Chicago: Chicago University Press, 1997, and Oxfam, *Rigged Rules and Double Standards: Trade, Globalization, and the Fight against Poverty*, Make Trade Fair campaign, 2002, available at ⟨http://www.maketradefair.com/assets/english/report_english.pdf⟩ (accessed 13 March 2008).
4. WTO, *World Trade Report 2007. Six Decades of Multilateral Cooperation: What Have We Learnt?*, Geneva: WTO, 2007, available at ⟨http://www.wto.org/english/res_e/reser_e/wtr_arc_e.htm⟩ (accessed 28 August 2008), p. iii.
5. Ibid., p. xxv.
6. *A Governance Audit of the WTO: Roundtable Discussion on Making Global Trade Governance Work for Development*, Global Economic Governance Programme, University College, Oxford, available at ⟨http://www.globaleconomicgovernance.org/docs/GEGHEIPublicForum181007.pdf⟩ (accessed 13 March 2008).
7. For an overview of negotiating groups in the WTO, see Robert Wolfe, "Can the Trading System Be Governed? Institutional Implications of the WTO's Suspended Animation", CIGI Working Paper No. 30, Centre for International Governance Innovation, September 2007, p. 47, ⟨http://www.cigionline.org/workingpapers⟩.
8. Ibid., p. 9.
9. For detailed case studies of how trade policy is formulated in certain countries and how various stakeholders are involved, see Mark Halle and Robert Wolfe, eds, *Process Matters: Sustainable Development and Domestic Trade Transparency*, Winnipeg, Canada: International Institute for Sustainable Development, 2007, available at ⟨http://www.iisd.org/pdf/2007/process_matters.pdf⟩ (accessed 13 March 2008).

10. See Arunabha Gosh, "Governing the WTO System: The Monitoring Function", in *A Governance Audit of the WTO*.
11. Pascal Lamy in his Foreword to the *World Trade Report 2007*.
12. WTO, *Dispute Settlement Body – Minutes of Meeting – Held in the Centre William Rappard on 6 November 1998*, WT/DSB/M/50, 14 December 1998, p. 1.
13. Peter Sutherland cited in Gary P. Sampson, *The WTO and Sustainable Development*, Tokyo: United Nations University Press, 2005, p. 298.
14. GATT/WTO, *Ministerial Declaration on the Uruguay Round (Declaration of 20 September 1986)*, Punta del Este.
15. *Declaration on the Contribution of the WTO to Achieving Greater Coherence in Global Economic Policymaking*, adopted by the Trade Negotiations Committee on 15 December 1993; in WTO, *The Results of the Uruguay Round of Multilateral Trade Negotiations: The Legal Texts*, Geneva: WTO Secretariat, 1994, pp. 442–443.
16. Pascal Lamy, "Managing Global Security: The Strategic Importance of Global Trade", speech to the Global Strategic Review Conference, Geneva, 8 September 2007.
17. Marc Auboin, ed., "Fulfilling the Marrakesh Mandate on Coherence: Ten Years of Cooperation between the WTO, IMF and World Bank", WTO Discussion Paper No. 13, Geneva, 2007.
18. Dan Ben-David, Håkan Nordström and Alan Winters, "Trade, Income Disparity and Poverty", WTO Special Study No. 5, Geneva: WTO, 1999.
19. Sampson, *The WTO and Sustainable Development*, Chapter 9.
20. See *World Trade Report 2007*, pp. 288–294 for a complete overview.
21. Rohini Acharya and Micheal Daly, "Selected Issues Concerning the Multilateral Trading System", WTO Discussion Paper No. 7, Geneva, 2004.
22. Robert Hudec, *Developing Countries in the GATT Legal System*, Aldershot, Hampshire: Gower Publishing, 1987.
23. For this six-fold typology of SDT treatment, see Committee on Trade and Development, *Implementation of Special and Differential Treatment Provisions in WTO Agreements and Decisions. Note by Secretariat. Revision 1*, 21 September 2001, WT/COMTD/W/77/Rev.1, available at ⟨http://docsonline.wto.org⟩ (accessed 19 March 2007).
24. *World Trade Report 2007*, pp. 291–292.
25. Dani Rodrik, "Industrial Policy for the 21th Century", Centre for Economic Policy Research, Discussion Paper No. 4767, London, 2004.
26. Sampson, *The WTO and Sustainable Development*, p. 201.
27. P. Kleen and S. Page, "Special and Differential Treatment of Developing Countries in the WTO", Global Development Studies No. 2, Stockholm, Ministry of Foreign Affairs, 2005.
28. Keith Maskus, *Intellectual Property Rights in the Global Economy*, Washington D.C.: Institute for International Economics, 2000.
29. Sampson, *The WTO and Sustainable Development*, p. 220.
30. WTO Ministerial Declaration, adopted on 14 November 2001, WT/MIN(01)/DEC/1, 20 November 2001, para. 44.
31. See, for example, Ha-Joon Chang, *Bad Samaritans: The Myth of Free Trade and the Secret History of Capitalism*, New York: Bloomsbury Express, 2007. He claims that developed countries preach free markets and free trade to poor countries while having relied on heavy-handed protectionist policy instruments in their early development that are now being denied to developing countries. He draws on lessons of history to argue that developing countries must be allowed to integrate with the world economy on their own terms.
32. Wolfe, "Can the Trading System Be Governed?", p. 24.

33. *World Trade Report 2007*, p. 303.
34. Sampson, *The WTO and Sustainable Development*, p. 230.
35. The OECD/WTO database on TACB provides transparency on TACB efforts, promotes coordination and coherence of activities among donors and monitors implementation of commitments undertaken.
36. Carolyn Deere, "Governing the WTO System: The Capacity Building Function", in *A Governance Audit of the WTO*, pp. 14–21.
37. A good example is the legal advice provided by the Advisory Centre on WTO Law (ACWL). Being purely demand driven, it has allowed developing country members of ACWL and LDCs to achieve their policy objectives while respecting their WTO obligations in a development-friendly manner and to participate more effectively in WTO decision-making or negotiations. See Advisory Centre on WTO Law, *Report on Operations 2007*, Geneva, January 2008, available at ⟨http://www.acwl.ch/pdf/Oper_2007.pdf⟩ (accessed 28 August 2008).
38. The WTO and OECD have jointly established the TCBDB to provide information on trade-related technical assistance and capacity-building projects (see ⟨http://tcbdb.wto.org⟩, accessed 19 March 2008). This database uses the OECD Creditor Reporting System (CRS) database, which tracks general official development assistance flows from Development Assistance Committee (DAC) member countries. The OECD CRS uses proxies for Aid for Trade volumes based on the WTO Aid for Trade Task Force definition. CRS profiles can be downloaded by country or agency from the OECD website. See ⟨http://www.oecd.org/document/17/0,3343,en_2649_201185_39843665_1_1_1_1,00.html⟩ (accessed 19 March 2008). The OECD and WTO have also prepared a joint publication: *Aid for Trade at a Glance 2007: Country and Agency Chapters*, OECD and WTO, 2007, available at ⟨http://www.wto.org/english/tratop_e/devel_e/a4t_e/a4t_at_a_glance07_e.pdf⟩ (accessed 08 August 2008)
39. *World Trade Report 2007*, p. xxviii and pp. 342–344.
40. For an in-depth analysis of the like product concept and the relevant WTO jurisprudence, see Peter van den Bossche et al., *Unilateral Measures Addressing Non Trade Concerns*, The Hague: Ministry of Foreign Affairs, 2007, part 1.
41. Sampson, *The WTO and Sustainable Development*, p. 279.
42. See Commission of the European Communities, *Directive of the European Parliament and of the Council on the Promotion of the Use of Energy from Renewable Sources*, COM(2008)19 final, Brussels, 23 January 2008, available at ⟨http://ec.europa.eu/energy/climate_actions/doc/2008_res_directive_en.pdf⟩ (accessed 13 March 2008).
43. *World Trade Report 2007*, Foreword by Pascal Lamy and Chapter 6.
44. Wolfe, "Can the Trading System Be Governed?", pp. 33–34.
45. *World Trade Report 2007*, p. 345.
46. Sampson, *Trade and Sustainable Development*, pp. 138–144.
47. Ibid., p. 285.
48. See the proposals in France for offsetting tariffs on products from countries that are not parties to the Kyoto Protocol. The EU Directive to improve and extend the greenhouse gas emission allowance trading system of the Community (COM (2008)16) and proposals in the US Congress explore the option of requiring importers in some energy-intensive sectors to purchase greenhouse gas emissions allowances to avoid carbon leakage.
49. Chair's Summary of the Trade Ministers' Dialogue on Climate Change Issues, UN Climate Change Conference, Bali, 8–9 December 2007.
50. *Climate, Equity and Global Trade*, Selected Issue Briefs No. 2, Geneva: International Centre for Trade and Sustainable Development, December 2007.
51. Wolfe, "Can the Trading System Be Governed?", p. 37.

Part II
Non-trade-related issues

4

Governing at the trade–environment interface

Daniel C. Esty

Managing international interdependence is a defining challenge of our era. Collective decision-making on issues that transcend national boundaries requires a careful structure of global governance that facilitates cooperation but remains cognizant of the limits of "governing" at the supranational scale.[1] Good governance also requires an ability to manage "issue interdependence" and promote cooperation in one policy arena with sensitivity to competing concerns and values in other domains. For international organizations to be seen as legitimate and authoritative mechanisms of global governance, they must therefore demonstrate a capacity for "inter-issue" management. In this regard, the ongoing ability of the World Trade Organization (WTO) to serve as a cornerstone of the global regime that manages international economic interdependence critically depends on the WTO's success in recognizing and reinforcing environmental protection efforts and other policy goals, while promoting trade liberalization.

In the early 1990s, I wrote a book arguing for the "greening" of the General Agreement on Tariffs and Trade (GATT).[2] In that volume, I made the case for both procedural refinements in how trade policy-making gets done at the global scale and substantive reform of the rules of the international trading system so as to accommodate an emerging set of environmental issues.

Pascal Lamy, Director-General of the World Trade Organization, recently reviewed the agenda that I laid out in *Greening the GATT*.[3] He observed that the WTO has made substantial progress across most, if

The WTO and global governance: Future directions, Sampson (ed),
United Nations University Press, 2008, ISBN 978-92-808-1154-4

not all, of the items that were on my reform agenda. Director-General Lamy's conclusion is largely correct. A substantial amount has been accomplished in restructuring the international trading system to reflect environmental concerns. As a result, the WTO has not only strengthened its ability to manage inter-*national* economic interdependence but also enhanced its capacity to address the inter-*issue* policy challenge of aligning trade liberalization and environmental protection efforts. In doing so, the WTO has greatly strengthened its legitimacy and its role as a central pillar in the architecture of global governance. In this chapter, I review the theory and practice of the WTO's governance efforts at the trade–environment interface – highlighting the importance of inter-issue management capacity to good global governance and drawing some lessons for the WTO and other international institutions.

Theoretical foundations

The original GATT agreement of 1946 did not mention the word "environment". For decades, trade policy-makers did not recognize that their policy domain intersected with the environmental realm. Today, however, trade policy-makers at both the national and global levels understand that the trade–environment link is inescapable and must be managed systematically. The focus on the trade–environment relationship is not really a choice but rather a matter of descriptive reality for those engaged in managing international economic interdependence. Folding environmental sensitivity into the international trading system (as well as building sensitivity to economic and trade concerns into environmental decision-making) has a normative logic as well.

Trade policy, and particularly trade liberalization, inescapably affects the natural world. In particular, freer trade promotes expanded economic activity, which often translates into industrialization, increased pollution and the consumption of natural resources. If environmental regulations are optimized – and all externalities internalized – environmental harm need not accrue. But where regulation is inadequate and externalities are not fully internalized, overexploitation of open-access resources and inefficiently high levels of pollution are likely to result. Trade experts and the WTO itself have come to acknowledge this fact.[4]

Simultaneously, environmental programme and policy choices often affect trade. In some cases, trade and environmental policies become intertwined as a function of ecological realities. A number of environmental challenges are global in scope. From the depleted fisheries in many of the world's oceans, to the need to protect the ozone layer, to the build-up of greenhouse gas emissions that may produce climate change, a number of problems cannot be dealt with on a national basis. Indeed, countries that seek to address worldwide problems unilaterally inevitably find that their own efforts cannot resolve the issue. International cooperation is essential. From the perspective of public goods economics, successful "collective action" requires mechanisms to promote collaboration and to discipline "free riders".

The failure to address environmental harms that spill across national boundaries represents an externality that, if left unaddressed, leads to market failure, reduced gains from trade and diminished social welfare – not to mention environmental degradation. This economic logic has been clear for decades, but the policy implications have only recently been fully understood.[5] All nations that benefit from the international trading system must bear a fair share of the burden of providing global public goods, including environmental protection. Whereas leadership in establishing the requisite policies and instruments must come from environmental authorities, the trading system must support and not undermine these efforts.[6] Where international environmental policies have been agreed upon, the trading system needs to reinforce the obligations that have been spelled out. Similarly, where environmental authorities fail to advance comprehensive rules and programmes, trade officials may have to step into the breach. Indeed, it is increasingly evident that where environmental regulations are deficient – and uninternalized harms persist – the trading system is likely to be called upon to fill the gap, either with rules that spell out what constitutes an inappropriate foundation for competitive advantage or through dispute resolution proceedings.

The presence of national regulatory requirements – health standards, emissions limits, disposal requirements, labelling rules and so on – also shapes trade flows. If improperly structured or inadequately disciplined, environmental rules and regulations may become barriers to open markets. More worrisomely, protectionists often try to advance trade barriers in the guise of pollution control measures or natural resource management plans. The WTO must therefore unmask the disguised barriers to trade – but do so in a manner that does not appear insensitive to legitimate environmental goals.

As globalization marches on and economic interdependence grows, the number of points of policy intersection expands and so does the potential for conflict.[7] In the past two decades, a range of "trade and environment" disputes has emerged. From the infamous Tuna–Dolphin dispute of the early 1990s, the list of prominent cases has grown to include the Venezuelan challenge to the reformulated gasoline regulations promulgated under the 1990 US Clean Air Act, the ongoing US–EU Beef Hormone dispute and Canada's claim against France's ban on asbestos.[8] What is remarkable, however, is that the number of trade and environment disputes has *declined* rather than *increased* as the WTO has made efforts to incorporate environmental thinking into its rules and procedures – as Lamy points out.[9]

Fundamentally, trade and environmental policy friction is inevitable in a world of economic integration.[10] International commerce has to have ground rules that constrain commercial behaviour in the international marketplace and ensure a fair and level playing field for competition. Some of these requirements will relate to environmental matters. Clarifying what constitutes a legitimate basis for competitive advantage – and what is an *unfair* advantage – requires judgement calls and creates a potential for dispute. But clear rules enhance order and predictability – and diminish conflict.[11]

The WTO has become much better at integrating trade and environmental goals, as I discuss in detail below. Nevertheless, the process of working through the tension between environmental protection programmes and trade liberalization efforts will inevitably have to continue. As the push for freer trade extends into new realms, fresh environmental questions will be raised. Evolving environmental regulations also present new potential flashpoints. On the immediate horizon lie issues related to how biotechnology will be regulated and to what degree genetically modified organisms will be permitted in food. The emerging global regime to control greenhouse gases, which will alter the price of fossil fuels and therefore affect the value of hundreds of billions of dollars and euros in industrial assets and existing energy investments, could also have significant competitiveness effects and exacerbate trade–environment tensions. While the full spectrum of trade–environment disputes cannot be foreseen, what is clear is that carefully structured efforts to manage the policy interface – as the WTO is doing – reduces the scope for conflict.

Another reason to take the trade–environment linkage seriously derives from the political economy of trade policy-making. In the United States in particular, successful efforts at trade liberalization in recent years have almost always been accompanied by initiatives to address related environmental questions. Most observers do not believe the North American Free Trade Agreement (NAFTA) would have cleared the US Congress but for the environmental provisions written into the agreement and the substantial environmental side agreement that was negotiated in parallel.[12]

For the WTO to continue to play a leading role in global governance, it must further refine its structure of rules and procedures so as to accommodate environmental values (and other concerns, such as poverty alleviation) within the trading system. The long-term legitimacy and durability of the international trading system will furthermore be enhanced to the extent that international economic policy evolves in ways that intersect constructively with other policy-making realms such as the emerging re-gime of global environmental governance.[13] WTO decisions will not win the degree of popular acceptance that they must have to keep the trade system functioning smoothly unless the organization's decision-making processes are seen to be authoritative, effective and procedurally as well as substantively fair.

In conclusion, it has now become clear that trade and environmental policies cannot be kept on separate tracks. In the intervening years since *Greening the GATT* came out, the debate has shifted from *whether* to in-tegrate trade and environmental policy-making to *how* to do it. In *Green-ing the GATT*, I called for a Green Round of trade negotiations aimed at refining WTO rules and procedures so as to ensure that the international trading system would work to promote both open markets and environ-mental protection. As Pascal Lamy suggests, the WTO has made major strides toward trade–environment policy integration. A good number of the items that I identified as essential to a WTO Green Round have now been adopted in one form or another. So it is perhaps an auspicious time to review the progress on greening the WTO.[14]

The WTO's green record

At the outset, it is worth noting that the collapse of the trading system forecast by some of the diehard supporters of the old closed trade com-munity in the face of pressure for the WTO to take on board environ-mental concerns has not come to pass. On the contrary, the elements of the environmental agenda that the WTO has adopted have helped to strengthen the trading system and have reduced, not increased, the inten-sity and frequency of trade–environment disputes.

Likewise, as Pascal Lamy stresses, the WTO has not undermined envi-ronmental values or policies. The organization has come a long way from the days when "GATTzilla" was condemned by green activists around the world. Though the WTO's record in managing trade and environ-ment tensions deserves ongoing scrutiny, it must be said that the trading system has achieved both procedural and substantive gains in its inter-issue management capacity.

Although the WTO continues to call out nations for environmental politics that disrupt trade, the organization has helped to steer its mem-ber states toward collaborative efforts to respond to environmental problems in a number of cases. It has promoted multilateralism and dem-onstrated that commonly agreed upon standards are much more durable than those asserted unilaterally by one nation or trading bloc. When the United States imposed a ban on shrimp imports from Asian countries whose shrimping practices were seen to be killing endangered sea turtles, the WTO dispute resolution process did not simply reject the US position as GATT-illegal.[15] The dispute panel decision went out of its way to explain what the United States needed to do to stay within the confines of its trade obligations. Thus, although this panel decision might have been seen as a defeat for the environmental community, it actually helped to spur an international dialogue on how to protect endangered sea turtles. In the end, the WTO helped to promote a Memorandum of Understanding on the Conservation and Management of Marine Turtles and Their Habitats of the Indian Ocean and South-East Asia.[16]

Procedural advances

On the procedural front, *Greening the GATT* called for a more transparent trading system. Opening up of the negotiation process to observers from non-governmental organizations (NGOs) and, more generally, creating mechanisms for greater public participation in WTO policy-making, I argued, would enhance the legitimacy of the WTO and improve its functioning as a part of the global governance structure. I also suggested that the undertaking of environmental assessments of trade agreements would promote systematic thinking about the possible environmental impacts of freer trade in advance of a deal being cut. This process would allow for environmental policies to be advanced in parallel with trade liberalization.

Greening the GATT further urged that the dispute resolution procedures be made more open and authoritative, with environmental groups or other NGOs being allowed to witness the taking of evidence in GATT disputes. The "black box" nature of the trading regime could be diminished and public confidence in the policy dictates emanating from the shores of Lake Geneva could be enhanced, I explained, if the judicial functions of the WTO were conducted in public. Moreover, I pushed for mechanisms to permit NGOs to offer opinions on the issues in question, through a process akin to the *amicus curiae* briefs allowed in US courts. I explained that, where pollution or natural resource issues were at the core of a case, dispute panels should have access to environmental experts to guide them toward an outcome that would be both consistent with GATT principles and supportive of environmental protection efforts. Finally, *Greening the GATT* exhorted the WTO to ramp up its environmental staff and become a centre for dialogue around trade–environment issues.

As Lamy has noted, the WTO has made progress on virtually all of these issues. The organization has made significant strides forward in

terms of transparency. New WTO requirements have increased information availability for national governments and the public alike.[17] Furthermore, NGOs and other interested parties now have access to vast
quantities of documents through the heavily visited and information-rich
WTO website.[18]

Public participation in the WTO policy-making process has also considerably increased.[19] Although NGOs do not have access to the GATT
Council or to dispute resolution hearings, the WTO provides numerous
opportunities for dialogue on trade issues. In recent years, for example,
the WTO has hosted a series of public forums that have brought thousands of participants into the trading system and widened the trade policy
dialogue well beyond the usual trade ministers and other trade experts.
In 2007, nearly 2,000 people participated in a series of four WTO open
sessions on climate change and the relationship with trade.[20]

The call for easier access to environmental guidance in the dispute
settlement process has been heeded in part. Some WTO members have
objected, but the WTO's Appellate Body has laid out procedures for
amicus briefs.[21] This opportunity has been taken up by dozens of entities, resulting in increasing submissions from NGOs, most notably in the
ongoing biotech dispute.[22] Consultation with environmental experts and
other technical advisers has also become a WTO norm.[23] Although there
is still more that could be done to open up the dispute settlement process
and to ensure that the "judicial" activities of the WTO are conducted in
the open, real progress has been made.

A number of other procedural advances have facilitated work across
the trade–environment interface. Environmental impact assessments are
now a standard part of trade negotiating procedures in a number of countries. And the WTO itself has developed a substantial in-house environmental expertise and thus enhanced its capacity to provide advice to its
members on the likely pollution implications or natural resource impacts
of trade liberalization.[24]

Substantive steps forward

In *Greening the GATT*, I suggested that the rules of the trading system
needed to accommodate the commitments governments had made to international environmental agreements. I observed that it would be useful
to identify specific treaties or other agreements (as the NAFTA treaty
does) where the parties had undertaken environmental obligations that
should not be overridden by efforts to promote freer trade. I also argued
that the sharp distinction in GATT rules between product standards and
regulations aimed at production processes and methods (PPMs) could not

be sustained. In a world of ecological interdependence, I explained *how* things are made is as important as *what* gets made. I pushed for a reinterpretation of the "necessary" test under GATT Article XX. Requiring governments to adopt the "least trade restrictive" regulatory approach to any particular environmental concern was, I insisted, an inappropriate basis for integrating trade and environmental goals within the trading regime. The hurdle imposed by the "least trade restrictive" language was too high and represented an inappropriate balancing between trade and environmental values. I went on to propose a new balancing test for trade and environmental disputes that would take more seriously the need to reinforce legitimate environmental regulations even in the face of some disruption to trade. I argued for particular attention to the need to accommodate eco-labels within the trading regime and to ensure action on priority issues where trade seemed to be having a deleterious effect on the natural world, highlighting trade impacts on deforestation and declining fisheries.

Although the Doha Round has centred on a development agenda, it has a number of elements that could qualify as constituting a "Green Round". Director-General Lamy argues that the Doha Agenda encompasses nearly all of the substantive points that I suggested should be included in a reconciliation of trade and environmental interests. The Doha negotiating mandate calls for the WTO to pursue freer trade in a fashion that promotes sustainable development.[25] The need for the trading system to respect environmental treaties is expressly part of the Doha Development Agenda. In addition, there is an explicit focus on declining fisheries and the need to end subsidies that lead to overexploitation of the world's oceans.

Specific negotiations have centred furthermore on bringing down tariffs on clean technology goods and services. This emphasis on allowing environmental technologies to move freely across borders is essential to any response to climate change and helpful in many other contexts. Indeed, it is increasingly recognized that the key to reducing greenhouse gas emissions and to progress on a range of other environmental challenges is innovation and technology development.[26] Trade rules have an important role to play in opening world markets and expanding the opportunities available to entrepreneurs who can provide emissions control devices, technology support for energy efficiency, alternative energy sources and perhaps even cost-effective approaches to carbon capture and sequestration.

Progress has also been made in refining the prevailing interpretation of GATT Article XX so that environmental goals and trade liberalization ends can be pursued in parallel. Lamy argues (and I believe he is correct) that the WTO's necessity test has been softened. He points to the 2001 panel decision which ruled that France could continue its ban on the importation of asbestos under an environmental public health exception to the usual GATT rules. He goes on to suggest that the Shrimp/Turtle case clarified the right of GATT member states to impose trade measures in support of international environmental agreements so long as they pursued multilateral negotiations in support of their policy goals first.[27] Again, I believe that Director-General Lamy is correct in his reading of the evolving GATT jurisprudence. His argument is reinforced by Carrie Wofford's careful study which found that professionalization of GATT dispute resolution procedures resulted in substantive improvements in the WTO's ability to balance trade and environmental goals.[28]

There remains, of course, more to be done. The GATT-compatibility of PPM standards still requires some clarification. Moreover, the WTO has not adequately addressed the issue of eco-labels, nor has it fully adopted modern principles of transparency. The emerging global focus on climate change is likely to present particular challenges to the trading system. As countries bear significant costs to reduce their own greenhouse gas emissions, pressure will surely mount to ensure that every country shoulders a fair share of this economic burden. In fact, one of the largest unions in the United States, the International Brotherhood of Electrical Workers, and the largest US electricity utility company, American Electric Power, have put legislation before the US Congress to impose trade penalties on imported goods from countries that are not shouldering their share of the burden of responding to climate change.[29] Such provisions, which the French government has also endorsed, will trigger disputes if invoked.[30] More generally, disputes will arise if countries underperform against global expectations concerning the control of greenhouse gas emissions and seek to seize a competitive advantage in the international marketplace as a result.

Broader institutional reform

Thus far, much of the work to integrate trade and environmental policy-making has been undertaken at the WTO. But responsibility for inter-issue work should not fall solely on the WTO's shoulders. The international environmental regime – and the United Nations Environment Programme (UNEP) in particular – should share this burden. But UNEP has not developed a strong inter-issue management capacity and now seems incapable of playing a major global governance role and fulfilling its mandate as *the* key environmental body for the United Nations. Although UNEP's shortcomings are significant, the weakness of the international environmental regime has broader origins. There are 44 international organizations that officially have environmental programmes. Close to 500 multilateral environmental agreements (many with their own independent secretariats) exist.[31] The international community has carved up the projects, funding and authority of the international environmental regime, leading to fragmented and ineffective global environmental governance. As a result, progress on climate change, biodiversity conservation, declining fisheries, deforestation and other issues requiring international policy cooperation has been slow or non-existent. The international environmental regime is thus poorly positioned to address critical issues, cannot manage across competing goals and values and cannot contribute to resolving trade and environment tensions.

As the weakness of this system was already evident in the 1990s, I called for the creation of a Global Environmental Organization, or GEO, in *Greening the GATT*. That policy proposal has been taken up by a number of governments and opinion leaders.[32] The idea of a United Nations Environment Organization is now under debate.

A more robust global environmental governance structure, constructed out of some of the pieces of the existing system, including UNEP, might facilitate a more systematic international response to challenges of pollution control and natural resources management, relieving pressure on the WTO as the only international body within which trade and environmental tensions are worked out.[33] A GEO could enhance international environmental policy-making and provide a venue for global rule-making on critical supranational issues such as climate change. It might also facilitate data and information exchanges, serve as a technology clearinghouse and manage the flow of resources needed to engage developing countries in global-scale policy efforts. In addition, it would serve as a counterpoint and a counterbalance to the WTO – providing another forum for working through trade–environment issues. A body with greater inter-issue management capacity might be given a greater role in global governance because it would have greater legitimacy than today's UNEP.

Conclusion

Managing interdependence is never easy. But the WTO has emerged as a cornerstone of the modern structure of global governance, in part because it has learned how to reconcile competing policy interests. To provide a solid foundation for international efforts to move toward freer trade and manage issues that intersect with the trade liberalization agenda, the WTO must continue to demonstrate a capacity to manage "inter-issue" tensions. Expectations regarding environmental protection are rising around the world. This will put an additional degree of focus on the WTO's own efforts to accommodate environmental values. But a great deal of progress has been made – and it is clear, that under Director-General Lamy, the commitment to continue the process is strong.

Notes

1. Daniel C. Esty, "Good Governance at the Supranational Scale: Globalizing Administrative Law", *Yale Law Journal*, Vol. 115, No. 7, 2006.
2. Daniel C. Esty, *Greening the GATT: Trade, Environment and the Future*, Washington, DC: Institute for International Economics, 1994.
3. Pascal Lamy, "The 'Greening' of the WTO Has Started", speech at Yale University, 24 October 2007; available at ⟨http://www.wto.org/english/news_e/sppl_e/spp179_e.htm⟩ (accessed 19 February 2008).
4. Hakan Nordstrom and Vaughan Scott, *Trade and Environment: WTO Special Studies 4*, Geneva: World Trade Organization, 1999, available at ⟨http://www.wto.org/english/ tratop_e/envir_e/environment.pdf⟩ (accessed 19 February 2008); Jagdish Bhagwati, "Trade and the Environment: The False Conflict?", in Durwood Zaelke, ed., *Trade and the Environment: Law Economics and Policy*, Washington, DC: Island Press, 1993; Brian R. Copeland and M. Scott Taylor, *Trade and the Environment: Theory and Evidence*, Princeton, NJ: Princeton University Press, 2003.
5. William J. Baumol and Wallace E. Oates, *The Theory of Environmental Policy*, Cambridge: Cambridge University Press, 1988.
6. Esty, *Greening the GATT*.
7. André Dua and Daniel C. Esty, *Sustaining the Asia-Pacific Miracle: Environmental Protection and Economic Integration*, Washington, DC: Institute for International Economics, 1997.
8. GATT Panel Report, *US – Restrictions on Imports of Tuna*, DS21/R-39S/155, 1991; WTO, Appellate Body Report, *United States – Standards for Reformulated and Conventional Gasolines*, WT/DS2/AB/R, 20 May 1996, available at ⟨http://www.wto.org/english/ tratop_e/envir_e/edis07_e.htm⟩ (accessed 19 February 2008); WTO, "Relationship between Trade and Investment", "Interaction between Trade and Competition Policy" and "Transparency in Government Procurement", in Doha WTO Ministerial 2001, *Ministerial Declaration*, WT/MIN(01)/DEC/1, adopted 14 November 2001, paras 20–26, Geneva: WTO, 2001; WTO, Appellate Body Report, *European Communities – Measures Affecting Asbestos and Asbestos-Containing Products*, AB-2000-11, WT/ DS135/AB/R (00-1157), adopted by Dispute Settlement Body, 5 April 2001; WTO, Appellate Body Report, *United States – Import Prohibition of Certain Shrimp and Shrimp Products*, WT/DS58/AB/R, 6 November 1998.
9. WTO, "Relationship between Trade and Investment", "Interaction between Trade and Competition Policy" and "Transparency in Government Procurement", in Doha WTO Ministerial 2001, *Ministerial Declaration*.
10. Daniel C. Esty, "Economic Integration and the Environment", in Norman J. Vig and Regina S. Axelrod, eds, *The Global Environment: Institutions, Law, and Policy*, Washington, DC: CQ Press, 1999; Steve Charnovitz, "The Moral Exception in Trade Policy", *Virginia Journal of International Law*, Vol. 38, 1998.
11. Lon Fuller, *The Morality of Law*, New Haven, CT: Yale University Press, 1964.
12. Carolyn L. Deere and Daniel C. Esty, eds, *Greening the Americas: NAFTA's Lessons for Hemispheric Trade*, Cambridge: MIT Press, 2002.

13. Daniel C. Esty and Maria H. Ivanova, *Global Environmental Governance: Options and Opportunities*, New Haven, CT: Yale School of Forestry & Environmental Studies, 2002.

14. Lamy, "The 'Greening' of the WTO Has Started".

15. WTO, Appellate Body Report, *United States – Import Prohibition of Certain Shrimp and Shrimp Products*.

16. IOSEA [Indian Ocean – South-East Asian] Marine Turtle Memorandum of Understanding Secretariat, *Memorandum of Understanding on the Conservation and Management of Marine Turtles and Their Habitats of the Indian Ocean and South-East Asia*, June 2001, available at ⟨http://www.ioseaturtles.org/Mou/MoU_CMP_combo.pdf⟩ (accessed 19 February 2008).

17. WTO Secretariat, *Trade and Environment at the WTO*, Geneva: WTO, 2004, available at ⟨http://www.wto.org/english/tratop_e/envir_e/envir_wto2004_e.pdf⟩ (accessed 19 February 2008).

18. Elizabeth Smythe and Peter J. Smith, "Legitimacy, Transparency, and Information Technology: The World Trade Organization in an Era of Contentious Trade Politics", *Global Governance*, Vol. 12, No. 1, 2006; Bernard M. Hoekman, and Petros C. Mavroides, "WTO Dispute Settlement, Transparency and Surveillance Source", in Bernard M. Hoekman and Will Martin, eds, *Developing Countries and the WTO: A Pro-Active Agenda*, London: Blackwell, 2001.

19. Robert Wolfe, "Regulatory Transparency, Developing Countries, and the WTO", *World Trade Review*, Vol. 2, No. 2, 2003.

20. Lamy, "The 'Greening' of the WTO Has Started".

21. WTO, "Participation in Dispute Settlement Proceedings", Dispute Settlement System Training Module, Chapter 9, section 9.3: "Amicus Curiae submissions"; available at ⟨http://www.wto.org/english/tratop_e/dispu_e/disp_settlement_cbt_e/c9s3p1_e.htm⟩ (accessed 19 February 2008).

22. Robyn Eckersley, "A Green Public Sphere in the WTO?: The Amicus Curiae Interventions in the Transatlantic Biotech Dispute", *European Journal of International Relations*, Vol. 13, No. 3, 2007.

23. WTO Secretariat, *Trade and Environment at the WTO*.

24. Ibid.; WTO, "Overview of the WTO Secretariat", available at ⟨http://www.wto.org/english/thewto_e/secre_e/intro_e.htm⟩ (accessed 19 February 2008).

25. Richard H. Steinberg, "In the Shadow of Law or Power? Consensus-based Bargaining and Outcomes in the GATT/WTO", *International Organization*, Spring 2002, pp. 339–374.

26. Daniel C. Esty and Andrew S. Winston, *Green to Gold: How Smart Companies Use Environmental Strategy to Innovate, Create Value, and Build Competitive Advantage*, New Haven, CT: Yale University Press, 2006; Claudia H. Deutsch, "Goldman to Encourage Solutions to Environmental Issues", *New York Times*, 22 November 2005.

27. Lamy, "The 'Greening' of the WTO Has Started"; Robert Howse, "The Appellate Body Rulings in the *Shrimp/Turtle Case*: A New Legal Baseline for the Trade and Environment Debate", *Columbia Journal of Environmental Law*, Vol. 27, No. 2, 2002.

28. Carrie Wofford, "A Greener Future at the WTO: The Refinement of WTO Jurisprudence on Environmental Exceptions to GATT", *Harvard Environmental Law Review*, Vol. 24, No. 563, 2000.

29. Michael G. Morris and Edwin D. Hill, "Trade Is the Key to Climate Change", *Energy Daily*, 20 February 2007.

30. "Climate Change: Sarkozy Backs Carbon Tax, EU Levy on Non-Kyoto Imports", Agence France Press, 25 October 2007.

31. Maria H. Ivanova and Jennifer Roy, "The Architecture of Global Environmental Governance: Pros and Cons of Multiplicity", in Lydia Swart and Estelle Perry, eds, *Global Environmental Governance: Perspectives on the Current Debate*, New York: Center for UN Reform Education, 2007.

32. Jacques Chirac, speech to the Conference for Global Ecological Governance, Paris, 2 February 2007, available at ⟨http://www.ambafrance-ng.org/article.php3?id_article=475⟩ (accessed 28 August 2008); Renato Ruggiero, "A Global System for the Next Fifty Years", address to the Royal Institute of International Affairs, London, 30 October 1998, available at ⟨http://www.wto.org/english/news_e/sprr_e/chat_e.htm⟩ (accessed 19 February 2008); "Why Greens Should Love Trade: The Environment Does Need to Be Protected but Not from Trade", *The Economist*, 9 October 1999.

33. Esty, *Greening the GATT*.

5

Promoting policy coherence in the global governance of trade and employment

Juan Somavia

Introduction

Globalization creates the possibility of employment and income opportunities for both developed and developing countries. I use the word "possibility" advisedly. I have long believed that the extent to which this possibility is realized depends on two conditions. First, the possibility depends on the degree to which the policies pursued by the agencies of the multilateral system are coherent with respect to each other. Policies that are not coherent with each other, both within and across agencies, risk cancelling each other out, resulting in waste, the frustrated aspirations of member states and the weakened credibility of the multilateral system itself. In light of the themes of this volume, I will focus in particular in this chapter on coherence between trade policies and labour policies, as well as trade policies and social policies. Of course one could also imagine a coherent set of policies, each well integrated with the other, that nonetheless provide only very limited benefits from globalization. Indeed I will go further. During recent decades, the policies promoting globalization have been extremely coherent but the outcomes have been far from fair. So coherence in itself is not the issue – the issue is coherence around what objectives? Policy coherence is a means to a goal. This brings me to the second condition – that policies also need to make sense in their own right, able to achieve what they are meant to achieve. Both of these conditions then – policy coherence on shared goals and policies that make sense – bear on countries' prospects of realizing the benefits of globalization.

The WTO and global governance: Future directions, Sampson (ed),
United Nations University Press, 2008, ISBN 978-92-808-1154-4

In my view, it is the lack of policy coherence on shared goals and of policies that make sense that motivate concerns about the negative repercussions of globalization in developed and developing countries alike. It is far too easy to create a caricature of these concerns, lumping all voices together as the voice of unthinking anti-globalization. In truth, these concerns are far more challenging and substantive, and it is a grave error to think otherwise. Most of these voices of concern call into question not globalization as such but rather how the policies underlying the liberalization of international financial, product and labour markets are designed and implemented.

For instance, the World Trade Organization's Doha Round of trade negotiations launched in 2001 has been touted as a "development round". But whether Doha meets this objective, enabling a wide range of developing countries to benefit significantly from further integration into global markets, obviously depends on the extent and pace of tariff reductions. It also depends on the lead time given to developing countries to create the capacity and know-how to successfully produce for international markets and to move into goods and services with higher value-added. These concerns have become particularly pointed in the Non-Agricultural Market Access (NAMA) negotiations at the WTO, with the outcome currently very much in flux. Although these negotiations are not explicitly about employment, the underlying concerns are very much about employment and about industrialization and de-industrialization. It is worth bearing in mind that de-industrialization is commonly defined as a declining proportion of manufacturing to total employment. This illustrates how very intertwined are developments in trade and labour, inseparably so, and argues for coherence and coordination in the development of trade and labour policies. That is why the International Labour Organization (ILO) believes that the only viable globalization is a fair globalization in which all countries, rich and poor alike, and workers and employers as well as consumers, equitably share the fruits of globalization.

The challenge of the coherence of trade and labour policies is an old one, of course, part of the histories and indeed pre-histories of the ILO and WTO themselves. Concerns about a "race to the bottom" in conditions of work motivated the debates on international labour legislation during the last wave of globalization beginning in the late nineteenth century and ending with the first Great War, concerns that culminated in the creation of the ILO in the wake of that war. These concerns are reflected in the Preamble to the ILO's Constitution, which states: "The failure of any nation to adopt humane conditions of labour is an obstacle in the way of other nations which desire to improve the conditions in their own countries."

Indeed, central to the original vision of the post-war multilateral system was coherence among the policy spheres of labour, finance and trade. These were meant to be embodied in the ILO, the Bretton Woods institutions and an International Trade Organization, with each of these institutions having overlapping rather than exclusive mandates among these policy spheres. For the ILO, this vision of policy coherence is embodied in the Declaration of Philadelphia of 1944, which states that "it is a responsibility of the International Labour Organization to examine and consider all international economic and financial policies and measures in the light of this fundamental objective", where the fundamental objective is "social justice".[1] Article I of the International Monetary Fund's Articles of Agreement states that one of the purposes of the International Monetary Fund is to "facilitate the expansion and balanced growth of international trade, and to contribute thereby to the promotion and maintenance of high levels of employment and real income and to the development of the productive resources of all members as primary objectives of economic policy".[2]

Provisions for the protection of workers' rights in trade agreements were addressed by the Havana Charter of 1948, which was intended to lead to the creation of an International Trade Organization. Indeed, Article 7 of the Charter is titled "Fair Labour Standards" and states: "The Members recognize that unfair labour conditions, particularly in production for export, create difficulties in international trade, and, accordingly, each Member shall take whatever action may be appropriate and feasible to eliminate such conditions within its territory."[3] Tellingly, the Havana Charter was the product of the United Nations Conference on Trade and Employment and the participants clearly recognized the link between the two spheres when they pledged to work together under the International Trade Organization to "facilitate ... the solution of problems relating to international trade in the fields of employment, economic development, commercial policy, business practices and commodity policy" (Article 1).

Instead of an International Trade Organization, the General Agreement on Tariffs and Trade (GATT) came into force in 1948, supplanted by the World Trade Organization (WTO) in 1994, and neither GATT nor the WTO, we know, address workers' rights in their regulations. At the WTO's Ministerial Conference in Singapore in 1996, however, the participants affirmed their commitment to respecting basic workers' rights and also that the ILO was the appropriate agency in the multilateral system for setting and enforcing international labour standards.

It is the challenges of our current era of globalization that brought a renewed sense of the need for policy coherence in the multilateral system. It is nonetheless useful to bear in mind that, in endeavouring to meet this need, we move towards realizing the original vision of the founders of the post-war multilateral system. It is important to remember that, though policy coherence must be built anew in the multilateral system, we build upon a rich common legacy.

The ILO's response to the challenge of policy coherence is embodied in the Decent Work agenda. Decent Work is a vision for development based on the four pillars of social dialogue, social protection, worker rights and employment and income opportunities, with all four pursued simultaneously, not sequentially. Clearly, globalization represents an employment and income opportunity for both developed and developing countries, for workers and employers alike. In this sense, the Decent Work agenda provides the ILO with a conceptual framework for addressing trade policies and labour and social policies together. But Decent Work is not just for the ILO. Indeed, one of the ILO's recent achievements of which I am most proud is the adoption of the Decent Work objectives by agencies throughout the multilateral system. In this sense, the Decent Work agenda has become a mainstay of the system of global governance. An important new vehicle in this regard is the recent "Toolkit for Mainstreaming Employment and Decent Work", launched under the umbrella of the United Nations System Chief Executives Board for Coordination, which aims to facilitate the work of agencies in the multilateral system in their pursuit of the objectives of decent work and employment, as well as provide assistance to member countries and their constituents.[4]

It is my belief that the adoption of the Decent Work agenda in the multilateral system can provide a foundation for meeting the two necessary conditions I laid out at the outset for countries to best reap the gains that globalization can offer. It is this story that I would like to tell next. I shall follow this with a discussion of a recent collaborative effort between the WTO and the ILO, a joint study addressing research on the relationship between trade and employment. I discuss this in some depth, as I believe it can set a useful precedent for future collaboration between the WTO and the ILO and perhaps a model for greater policy coherence within the multilateral system as a whole.

Decent work in the multilateral system

The ILO has undergone several substantial shifts in its orientation over its long history of defending and promoting the values for which it stands. Designed in 1919 to address the challenges presented by the first pre-1914 era of globalization and the profound social and labour tensions that came with it, the ILO had to come to terms with a global depression, a retreat into economic protectionism, the rise of ideologies that rejected its fundamental democratic values and World War II.[5] It survived and was reinvigorated by the Declaration of Philadelphia in 1944 as a key part of a new international architecture for peace and development and with the clear intention of constituting a balance to the Bretton Woods institutions. But that vision was distorted by the Cold War. Nevertheless, even while it was in the frontline of the battle of ideas about ways to organize economic and social development, the ILO was able to innovate and respond to the ending of colonialism and a huge expansion in its membership from independent developing countries. A new era began around 1990 with the end of the Cold War. The ILO played a significant role in the eventual crumbling of the totalitarian control over workers' organizations and enterprises that underlay the division of Europe, as in the strong support to Solidarność in Poland, as well as in the solidarity with the struggle to end apartheid in South Africa and other international situations – such as the support to democratic trade unions in Chile under the Pinochet dictatorship.

The term "globalization" came into use at this time and spread rapidly to describe how, in the wake of the breakdown of political blocs, the opening of trade and financial markets to international competition and foreign investment, together with the rapid spread of radical technological changes, has dramatically transformed social and economic relations within and among countries.

A strong signal of the change in the environment for the ILO's work came in 1995 with the successful holding of the World Summit for Social Development in Copenhagen. While I was Ambassador of Chile to the United Nations, I proposed the idea of a World Social Summit and was later honoured to be elected President of its Preparatory Committee. It was a major personal experience because the odds were clearly against its success. It was also an opportunity to work closely with the workers' and employers' groups of the ILO. Such a global conference on social development, attended by around 120 heads of state and government, could not have been held 10 years earlier and it reached consensus on a programme of 10 commitments to address poverty, unemployment and social exclusion. By the mid-1990s, however, it was becoming clear that the benefits and opportunities of globalization were unequally shared and that many people were seriously concerned. The Social Summit is key to understanding the role of the ILO today and in the future. It addressed the major social issues raised by the Declaration of Philadelphia in the contemporary setting of globalization. It logically concluded that, to implement its 10 commitments, the ILO normative tripartite system should be strengthened.

As a consequence, the ILO's role and broad mandate were reinforced in the Copenhagen Declaration and Programme of Action of the World

Summit for Social Development, which included the commitment "to promote the goal of full employment as a basic priority of our economic and social policies, and to enable all men and women to attain secure and sustainable livelihoods through freely chosen productive employment and work".[6] The Social Summit was the first high-level pronouncement that absolute poverty should be eradicated, not merely alleviated. That consensus became the basis of the Millennium Development Goal on Poverty Reduction. But the Millennium Development Goals (MDGs) failed to link employment creation and poverty reduction and, as events later proved, highlighted the ILO's key role – by omission.

Amongst the issues contained in the Copenhagen Declaration to which I paid particular attention was the commitment to pursue "the goal of ensuring quality jobs, and safeguard the basic rights and interests of workers and to this end, freely promote respect for relevant International Labour Organization conventions, including those on the prohibition of forced and child labour, the freedom of association, the right to organize and bargain collectively, and the principle of non-discrimination".[7] Reinforcing the ILO's standard-setting function appeared essential at a time when deregulation was presented as the magic wand that would empower markets to solve prevailing economic and social ills.

The 1998 ILO Declaration on Fundamental Principles and Rights at Work built a new ILO instrument on this consensus and created a new means of action for the organization. It has furthermore proved to be an attractive reference point for many public and private bodies engaged in building a social floor to global development. In the words of its Preamble, the Declaration asserts, "in seeking to maintain the link between social progress and economic growth, the guarantee of fundamental principles and rights at work is of particular significance in that it enables the persons concerned, to claim freely and on the basis of equality of opportunity, their fair share of the wealth which they have helped to generate, and to achieve fully their human potential".[8]

In the following year, 1999, the concept of Decent Work was launched in my Report to the International Labour Conference. It identified and addressed three interlinked challenges for the ILO: "to refocus its programme, to restate its message in the idiom of contemporary needs, and to mobilize external partnerships for resources and expertise". It further specified that:

> the primary goal of the ILO today is to promote opportunities for women and men to obtain decent and productive work, in conditions of freedom, equity, security and human dignity. This is the main purpose of the Organization today. Decent work is the converging focus of all its four strategic objectives: the promotion of rights at work; employment; social protection; and social dialogue. It must guide its policies and define its international role in the near future.[9]

The establishment of the World Commission on the Social Dimension of Globalization in 2001 and its subsequent report, *A Fair Globalization: Creating Opportunities for All*, was a major milestone in engaging a wider interest in the ILO.[10] The fact that the tripartite ILO was ready to sponsor the exercise of bringing together a high-level group of "non-like-minded" personalities from a wide variety of cultures and interests to seek a way forward that would command broad support was itself important. The fact that they were able to agree on a comprehensive package of proposals, which included the global goal of Decent Work as a common aspiration for people all over the world, further reinforced the re-emergence of the ILO as a leading agency in an evolving architecture for the governance of globalization.

The work of the World Commission was immediately acknowledged in the 2004 United Nations General Assembly Resolution 59/57 which, *inter alia*, took note of its report "as a contribution to the international dialogue towards a fully inclusive and equitable globalization" and requested the Secretary-General to take it into account "in his comprehensive report for the high-level review of 2005 at the sixtieth session of the General Assembly, within the follow-up to the outcome of the Millennium Summit of the United Nations".[11] The 2005 World Summit Outcome included the following paragraph:

> We strongly support fair globalization and resolve to make the goals of full and productive employment and decent work for all, including for women and young people, a central objective of our relevant national and international policies as well as our national development strategies, including poverty reduction strategies, as part of our efforts to achieve the Millennium Development Goals. These measures should also encompass the elimination of the worst forms of child labour, as defined in International Labour Organization Convention No. 182, and forced labour. We also resolve to ensure full respect for the fundamental principles and rights at work.[12]

This strong endorsement of the ILO's Decent Work agenda has led to further important steps in the United Nations intergovernmental and inter-agency process. In July 2006, the ministerial segment of the United Nations Economic and Social Council (ECOSOC) focused on the theme of "Creating an environment at the national and international levels conducive to generating full and productive employment and decent work for all, and its impact on sustainable development". The ECOSOC Ministerial Declaration further endorsed Decent Work as a central development goal and gave specific guidance on coordination arrangements for its effective implementation by the United Nations system and other multilateral organizations. It also identified a number of concrete steps aimed at furthering implementation of the 2005 United Nations Summit commitment to make the goal of full and productive employment a central objective of national and international policies and at systematically monitoring progress.[13]

This effort to foster a coherent system-wide follow-up to the 2005 Summit gained added significance as the drive to improve the effectiveness of the United Nations system as a whole gathered momentum in 2006.[14] The ECOSOC Ministerial Declaration has enabled the ILO to push for a coherent system-wide effort to promote Decent Work for all, by calling on the whole multilateral system and donor agencies to mainstream the Decent Work agenda in their policies, programmes and activities, for the achievement of the MDGs and the wider, internationally agreed, development goals. The ministers also requested the ILO, in collaboration with all relevant parties, to develop time-bound action programmes in the 2015 time-frame foreseen for the Millennium Summit and the MDG reviews. As a result, mainstreaming Decent Work is emerging on the agenda of several United Nations and other bodies charged with coordinating follow-up action on the MDGs. The ILO has also worked closely with partner agencies under the umbrella of the Chief Executives Board, chaired by the Secretary-General, to prepare and launch a toolkit to assist in the mainstreaming of Decent Work as a system-wide goal that is vital to accelerating progress towards the MDGs.[15] The toolkit is designed to be a "lens" that agencies can look through to see how their policies, strategies, programmes and activities are interlinked with employment and decent work outcomes and how they can enhance these outcomes by taking full account of the implications of their policies, strategies, programmes and activities for employment and decent work during the design stage and while advising and assisting countries and constituents with regard to their adoption and implementation.

Parallel to the recognition within the United Nations system, several other international and regional high-level meetings have backed the Decent Work agenda. Following the African Union Extraordinary Summit (Ouagadougou, September 2004), the Fourth Summit of the Americas (Mar del Plata, November 2005) and the report of the Asian Development Bank (2005), the Decent Work agenda received strong support from European and Latin American heads of state and government at the fourth European Union, Latin America and Caribbean (EU–LAC) Business Summit (Vienna, May 2006) and from European and Asian heads of state and government at the Sixth Asia–Europe Meeting at the level of heads of state (Helsinki, September 2006). The European Commission has also adopted several communications on Decent Work as a goal of both its external and internal policies. As well as the backing of intergovernmental bodies, the ILO's Decent Work agenda has received a positive response at diverse gatherings of non-state actors such as the World Economic Forum and the World Social Forum. The Programme of the new International Trade Union Confederation (ITUC), adopted at its founding Congress in Vienna in 2006, states: "Congress expresses support for the ILO's Decent Work Agenda – the application of international labour standards, policies for full employment, social protection, and social dialogue – which has increased the organisation's standing and visibility, and calls on the ITUC to participate fully in its concrete implementation."[16] The Decent Work agenda has now been universally endorsed at the highest political level, both globally and regionally. At the civil society level, a campaign for "Decent Work for a Decent Living" has been launched by a number of non-governmental organizations in cooperation with the ITUC.

These trends connect with ILO efforts towards the implementation of Decent Work Country Programmes (DWCPs), which are the main instrument for cooperation with member states, and the ILO's specific contribution to international development frameworks, such as the United Nations Development Assistance Framework, poverty reduction strategies, national MDG strategies and other integrated development plans. These country programmes, which reflect an articulation between the normative, policy and operational dimensions of the Decent Work agenda, are the main vehicle for ILO engagement with the "Delivering as One" objective in the United Nations reform, calling for greater coordination at the country level. A particular emphasis is placed on ensuring that the ILO's national tripartite constituency is closely involved in the preparation of DWCPs and the integration of DWCPs into comprehensive development strategies.[17]

Let me conclude this overview of the ILO and particularly of the Decent Work agenda in the multilateral system. I have argued that Decent Work has provided a response to the challenge of globalization by combining policy coherence with policies that make sense, in which the four strategic objectives of social dialogue, social protection, worker rights and employment and income opportunities are pursued simultaneously. Globalization offers employment and income opportunities and there is a real sense in which decent work provides a framework for integrating trade policies and labour and social policies. Though the Decent Work agenda has roots in the World Summit for Social Development of 1995, it was taken up as the ILO's vision of development in 1999. Since then, the ILO has made considerable headway in incorporating the Decent Work agenda into the objectives of agencies throughout the multilateral system, providing a basis for greater policy coherence in global governance.

Trade and employment: Towards greater policy coherence

It has long been recognized that trade policies have a significant impact on the level and structure of employment, on wages and wage differentials, and on labour market institutions and policies. At the same time, labour and social policies influence the outcomes of trade policies in terms of the growth of output and employment and the distribution of income. There is, however, a less clear understanding of how the interaction between trade and labour market policies unfolds in a particular setting and how policies in the two domains can be designed in a more coherent and consistent manner that would allow countries to reap the benefits of trade and to achieve good labour market outcomes at the same time.

When Pascal Lamy and I met shortly after he took up his position as the Director-General of the WTO, we agreed that examining these links between trade and labour market policy could serve as a useful input to the policy-making process in both domains. We subsequently requested our respective staff to prepare a study on trade and employment, which was published in early 2007.[18] As a joint undertaking by the WTO Secretariat and the International Labour Office, the study aims to provide an impartial view of what can be said, and with what degree of confidence, on the relationship between trade and employment. It provides a thorough and objective review of the academic literature, both theoretical and empirical. Since a number of important policy conclusions relevant to both the ILO and the WTO emerge from this work, the following two sections will go into the findings of the study in some detail and outline some of the policy implications.

Trade and the dynamics of job destruction and job creation

As trade theory has long predicted, trade should lead to a greater division of labour between countries. The standard argument for greater trade openness is that this will lead to a re-shuffling of resources in line with comparative advantage, thus creating gains from trade that are to everybody's advantage. In order for this to happen, highly productive producers will expand their production and conquer foreign markets, while other firms will not be able to withstand competition from imports and will reduce their output or close down. As the joint study argues, "trade liberalization is expected to trigger a restructuring of economic activity that takes the form of company closures and job losses in some parts of the economy and start-ups of new firms, investment in increased production and vacancy announcements in other parts of the economy".[19] This view was also backed by a study for the Financial Services Forum, which concluded:

> The aggregate gains from global engagement, large though they are, are not evenly shared and do not directly benefit every worker, firm, and community. The many constituent forces of global engagement have also fostered economic changes that have pressured the well-being of many workers. These pressures are both short-term and long-term, and they often are concentrated in particular groups of workers, firms, and communities.[20]

Therefore, trade liberalization is generally associated with both job destruction and job creation. The net employment effect may be positive or negative in the short run, depending on country-specific factors such as the functioning of the labour and product markets. In the long run, however, economic theory predicts that the efficiency gains caused by trade liberalization lead to positive overall employment effects, in terms of quantity of jobs, wages earned or a combination of both. But even when average wages actually rise, this does not mean that all workers are better off since an average increase can mask adverse distributional change and affect parts of the labour force negatively.

Employment, inequality and the limits of traditional trade theory

Although trade theory offers some insights into these relocation processes, the joint study points out three important phenomena where the empirical trends and traditional trade theory are at odds with each other – and all three of them have major implications for trade and labour market policies. The conventional assumption was that the reshuffling process triggered by trade liberalization would take place across sectors. According to theory, labour-intensive sectors should shrink in developed countries and skill- and/or capital-intensive industries should expand, while developing countries should – in line with their relative abundance of unskilled labour – see growth in labour-intensive sectors. Such a process would hurt low-skilled workers in industrialized countries and lead to rising inequality, whereas increased demand for labour in developing countries should first and foremost benefit unskilled workers, with a positive impact on inequality. The empirical evidence initially appeared to confirm these predictions; in particular, inequality decreased in a number of East Asian economies as they became more open to trade. At the same time, the wages of low-skilled workers in a number of developed countries fell further behind those for skilled workers (i.e. the skill premium increased). In other developed countries, decreasing demand for low-skilled workers manifested itself in rising unemployment for this group. However, the overall picture has now changed in three important aspects.

First, despite the integration of developing countries such as China and India into the global trading system, industrialized countries trade, above all, with other industrialized countries. However, traditional trade theory had so far focused on trade between developed and developing countries and has very little to offer in terms of predicting the employment effects of this kind of trade. Thus, we need to turn to a newer body of literature that has examined such trade flows and, worryingly, concluded that they, too, can increase the wage inequality between low-skilled and high-skilled labour. Another implication of increased trade between industrialized countries is that it may increase the sensitivity of labour demand to wage changes. Moreover, the mere possibility to relocate production can be used as a credible threat to weaken workers' resistance to wage reductions. This structural shift in bargaining power can have repercussions for the functional distribution of income between capital and labour, tilting it towards the former, and thus further contribute to greater income inequality. In addition, the possibility to relocate production might explain why workers in industrialized countries perceive a loss of job security as countries liberalize.

The second phenomenon emphasized in the joint study is that, contrary to the expectations of traditional trade theory, greater wage differentials between low-skilled and high-skilled workers have also been observed in developing countries during trade liberalization, notably in Latin America. A number of factors have been advanced in the literature to explain this increase in skill premiums, including the timing of trade liberalization, the tariff schedules in place before trade liberalization and trade-induced technological change. More research on this clearly needs to be done, in particular to explain the interaction between trade, foreign direct investment and technological change and their consequences for wage inequality and the functional distribution of income between capital and labour.

The third unexpected outcome of trade liberalization is that substantial reshuffling of employment has taken place within sectors rather than between sectors, as traditional trade theory would lead us to expect. One possible explanation is that trade liberalization has enabled the most productive firms in each sector to expand, regardless of whether they are import-competing or not. On the other hand, trade destroys firms in all sectors that are unable to withstand the increased competitive pressure. Thus we can observe that, within the same sector, some firms expand while others are closing down and lay off workers. This could be seen as good news because it should be easier to re-employ these workers within the same sector. However, it also means that trade liberalization can affect jobs within virtually all sectors, and not just in import-competing sectors. This makes targeted interventions more difficult and, as the joint study argues, hard to justify.

Promoting equity to achieve a fair globalization

In sum, traditional trade theory appears to have downplayed some important implications of trade liberalization that can be observed in many – though not all – countries: greater inequality that results from increased skill premiums and/or a shift from labour to capital incomes, and a loss of employment security in industrialized countries. Both are of course important consequences that, if left unaddressed, create opposition to globalization and can make it politically and socially unsustainable. I would therefore argue that labour and social policies are required in order to redistribute some of the gains from trade from winners to losers. However, as the authors of the joint study recognize, policy-makers may be confronted with a trade-off between equity and efficiency, although this need not necessarily be a very steep one. But, even where a trade-off exists, it should not be a pretext to lose sight of the equity objective. As I have argued above, attaining greater equity and providing social protection in times of insecurity were two of the fundamental objectives that lay behind the foundation of the ILO almost 90 years ago. That they remain as valid and urgent as always becomes ever more clear as the current era of globalization unfolds, and achieving a "fair globalization" has thus become one of the ILO's central objectives.[21]

Having outlined these meta-trends of increasing inequality and insecurity, it is important to highlight another argument brought forward by the joint study – that the consequences of trade liberalization are highly dependent on context and that country-specific factors such as labour market policies, macroeconomic policies and skills endowment will all affect the way that a country can adapt to greater trade openness. The study therefore argues that "one of the general conclusions that can be drawn from the literature is that the employment effects of trade have differed significantly across countries".[22] This implies that a one-size-fits-all approach to trade liberalization is ill equipped to take account of these country-specific factors: it will not allow countries to reap the full benefits of trade liberalization and, I would argue, it can at times be detrimental to employment outcomes. Therefore, each country will have to find ways to best address the challenges posed by trade liberalization. Social dialogue between workers, employers and governments can be an effective way to find such well-adapted solutions that take the needs of each side into account.

Policy responses to trade opening and the Decent Work agenda

In what follows, I would like to outline some examples that illustrate how social and labour market policies can make trade liberalization more successful. I start by discussing social dialogue as a process to find well-adapted solutions, then highlight the importance of social security systems and active labour market policies, and finally turn to mechanisms for redistribution and policies for education and vocational training. I focus on these aspects because they all relate to the Decent Work agenda and therefore fall within the ILO's mandate and area of expertise. Coherent action in these policy areas not only will contribute towards making Decent Work a reality for women and men around the world and thus make globalization more fair and sustainable, but also makes good economic sense. However, policy coherence cannot mean that social and labour market policies should be subordinated to the imperative of trade liberalization. Quite to the contrary – and I will return to this point later – it means that trade policy itself needs to be designed with its social ramifications in mind. After all, the stated objective of trade liberalization is to enhance welfare – and this is not an abstract goal but can be achieved only by improving the lives of working women and men and their families.

Freedom of association and social dialogue

I have already highlighted the importance of social dialogue in formulating policies that can address the challenges posed by trade liberalization. For this to be effective and meaningful, workers and employers alike must be able to organize freely and without interference from the state. Respect for freedom of association and the right to bargain collectively, one of the fundamental principles and rights at work, is now supported by a broad global consensus and forms a cornerstone of the ILO's Decent Work agenda. Nevertheless, there has been debate about the economic effects of these rights, and some developing countries have expressed concerns that the full exercise of these rights could have a negative impact on their economic competitiveness. However, as the joint study concludes, there has been little empirical support for this view in the economic literature. On the contrary, the evidence suggests that there is, for example, a strong relationship between these rights and higher total manufacturing exports. In my view, this finding does not come as a surprise since we have long known about the importance of sound democratic institutions and the rule of law for economic development; – and freedom of association and the right to bargain collectively are clearly one of the most important elements of these, with a direct impact on the way an economy works. As a process right, it is also invaluable to promote broad social support for economic reforms and to advance a more equitable distribution of the burdens and benefits from trade liberalization.

Providing social security and facilitating the transition between jobs

As we have seen above, trade liberalization will trigger a reshuffling of resources within and between sectors, – and it is indeed this process of reallocating resources from inefficient to more efficient use that is supposed to generate the positive long-term effect from trade liberalization. However, labour is not just a resource, it is people. The ILO has long understood that labour is not a commodity. Workers depend on the income from their work and therefore value security and insurance over adverse professional events such as the loss of their job. Job security legislation and unemployment benefits are tools that can meet this demand for insurance and provide a buffer against the most negative consequences of job losses. Given that retrenchments often affect men and women differently, such provisions also have an important gender dimension. Having social security and job protection systems in place is thus an important prerequisite when implementing trade liberalization, and I would argue that they can be designed without incurring a major cost in terms of efficiency losses. The joint study supports this view and concludes that, while "there are reasons to believe that a trade-off exists between efficiency and insurance,... this trade-off does not need to be very steep if insurance policies are designed appropriately".[23]

Efficiency and equity are clearly compatible goals when it comes to policies that facilitate the transition between jobs: they aim to give workers a new source of employment and at the same time ensure that labour does not lie idle. In particular, active labour market policies attempt to facilitate re-employment by providing retraining or by assisting workers to relocate geographically. Most industrialized countries make broad use of such active labour market policies and they are increasingly being seen as a preferable alternative to passive income support for the unemployed. Whereas some middle-income countries have begun to strengthen social protection systems and increasingly make use of active labour market policies, this is not the case in many low-income countries, mainly owing to resource constraints. The possibility of introducing such policies for a limited duration, and specifically targeting those negatively affected by trade reform, has been discussed in the literature and has recently been raised in the context of the "Aid for Trade" debate. Strengthening the capacity of developing countries to design and implement such programmes could, indeed, enable them to cope better with the social impact of economic reforms as well as help to increase popular support for the reforms themselves.

Redistribution policies to address inequality

As the joint study argues, it is also increasingly recognized that it is important for policy-makers to ensure that the benefits of global economic integration are sufficiently widely shared in order to maintain or obtain public support for trade opening. Increases in the skill premium or in income inequality represent a particularly serious challenge for developing countries with limited experience in the design of redistribution policies and the necessary financial and administrative capacities. Yet, again, there are indications that the trade-off between equity and efficiency need not be great and that win–win strategies exist where policies that are good for equity are also good for growth.

Education and training policies for pro-poor growth

One such policy with simultaneous benefits for equity and growth is to provide wider access to education. As the joint study has brought out, good education policies are pivotal to equip countries to deal with economic and technological change – whether educed by trade opening or other factors. The same holds true on the level of an individual worker: good education enhances an individual's capacity to deal with change, an important aspect in a globalized world that expects individuals to adapt constantly to new situations. However, the joint study also makes it clear that it has become increasingly hard to predict the set of skills needed for future employment, and that education systems will need to be sufficiently flexible in order to respond to economic changes. Moreover, the dynamic requirements on individual skills make it clear that education cannot be a once-off process that ends when a person leaves school or university. Rather, it underscores the need for comprehensive vocational training systems and for continued on-the-job training – two tools to foster individual employability and overall economic efficiency that the ILO has long promoted.

Other policies and Aid for Trade

Although strong institutions for social dialogue can help to design appropriate policies to accompany trade opening in areas such as social security, redistribution and education, these policies by themselves – important as they are – are clearly not sufficient to make trade liberalization successful. The joint study argues rightly that how successful developing economies are in the creation of more and/or better jobs depends above all on the supply response of the economy to trade liberalization. Developing countries, in particular, face a number of bottlenecks that include inadequate finance, physical infrastructure, tele-communication, information and human capital. The international community can play a vital role to help developing countries to overcome such supply constraints, an idea that is increasingly reflected in the debate on Aid for Trade. However, even with broad international support, it will take many years to overcome some of the bottlenecks – which limits the potential benefits of a rapid opening to trade. This may explain why the expected benefits of rapid trade liberalization have often failed to materialize and why their overall outcome has often been disappointing. The pace and scope of trade reform itself are thus important, and countries should determine them according to the supply bottlenecks present in the economy and adapt reform to the existing social and labour market conditions.

Conclusions: Integrating social and economic policy – a challenge for global governance

In my view, what emerges strongly from this discussion is that trade policies and labour and social policies do interact and that greater policy coherence in the two domains can help to ensure that trade reforms have significantly positive effects on both growth and employment. This has two fundamental implications.

First, countries that have well-designed social and labour market policies in place when undergoing trade liberalization will be in a better position to reap its benefits and to cope with possible adverse effects. We at the ILO, through our Decent Work Country Programmes, help our member countries to build sound labour market institutions and to formulate policies in dialogue with the social partners, namely workers and employers. The discussion has shown the importance of adequate social protection for displaced workers, but I would want to argue that we cannot stop there. In my view, what is needed is a comprehensive and coherent package of labour market policies with the dual goal of creating social equity and improving economic efficiency. Although there can be a trade-off between these two goals, this need not be a steep one – and there is significant scope for win–win solutions. For example, facilitating the transfer of labour between and within sectors will be in the interest of workers and reduce inequality, but it will also contribute to efficient resource allocation – as can education and vocational training. Likewise, the full exercise of the fundamental right to freedom of association can be equity-enhancing by improving the bargaining power of workers, but functioning social dialogue can also increase efficiency by identifying ways to improve productivity, maintaining social stability and facilitating negotiated solutions that are in the interest of both workers and employers.

Here, the Decent Work Agenda we pursue at the ILO, with its objective to promote opportunities for women and men to obtain decent and productive work in conditions of freedom, equity, security and human dignity, has a lot to offer in terms of practical tools and well-adaptable solutions. Decent Work provides not only a goal, however, but also a framework for policy coherence within and among the agencies of the multilateral system, particularly regarding coherence between trade policies and labour and social policies.

However, as one member of the ILO's Governing Body put it when we debated the joint study in March 2007, poorly designed trade policies cannot be made right by well-designed labour market policies. What this implies is that trade policy needs to be designed and implemented in a manner that takes account of adjustment problems in the labour market. This should be done with the aim not only to make trade reform economically beneficial but also to ensure that the benefits are widely shared by workers. All too often, today's segmented approach results in the opposite outcome – namely that the economic gains from trade reform fall short of expectations and yet the social cost they cause is considerable. However, we need to be careful to avoid generalizations, since, as argued by the joint study, the impact of trade on employment and wages will vary with country-specific characteristics. What follows from this is that countries will have to adapt steps towards greater trade openness to their specific situation, e.g. through appropriate sequencing and timing, to maximize the long-term benefits from free trade and to avoid adverse, unintended social consequences. The ILO is working to develop techniques of impact assessment that could help countries to anticipate and thus prepare for the changes that intensified competition brings. This is of particular importance for countries at early stages of development, which generally lack adequate social protection mechanisms.

Under the current special and differential treatment provisions, developing countries are generally granted longer grace periods to comply with agreements and commitments, and developing countries also receive support to strengthen their capacity to conform to WTO agreements and to handle disputes. In addition, there are numerous special provisions for the least developed countries. As the World Commission on the Social Dimension of Globalization argued in its report *A Fair Globalization: Creating Opportunities for All*:

Uniform rules for unequal partners can only produce unequal outcomes. Given the vast differences in levels of development, we believe that there is a need for affirmative action in favour of countries that are latecomers and do not have the same capabilities as those which developed earlier. It is possible to have a set of multilateral rules in which the obligations of countries are a function of their level or stage of development. A simple starting point would be to allow flexibility to these countries for joining in, or opting out of proposed disciplines or new issues in the WTO to permit greater policy space for them to pursue national development policies.[24]

Improving the interaction between trade policies and policies to promote Decent Work requires both sufficient policy space to put in place country-specific strategies and increased capacity to design and implement such strategies. Enhanced collaboration between the ILO and the WTO, respecting each organization's specific mandates and expertise and within a broader multilateral framework for improved policy coherence, is a practical way of improving governance and achieving the shared goal of sustainable development.

I believe that the Decent Work agenda has given us an opportunity to look at the positive interaction between trade and social policies, and to do so by moving away from the certainty of some that trade is always good and the certainty of others that, that if trade is stopped, overall social conditions will improve. Neither is true. The joint study on trade and employment by the ILO and WTO secretariats concluded that trade liberalization produces both job destruction and job creation. In the short run the effects of liberalization may be positive or negative, depending on factors such as the functioning of a labour and product market as well as the pace, depth and sequencing of market openings, the fairness of international rules and the existence or not of social protection measures to weather the adjustment needs.

In the long run, if the necessary policy balances are there, more open markets are likely, on average, to generate more jobs, better wages or a combination of both. But such averages will, we know, hide impacts that affect some working women and men negatively and sometimes very negatively. I believe that the tripartite ILO is today well placed to develop a balanced approach to trade and employment issues that respects the interests of developed and developing countries and those of workers and employers in all regions – and to do so away from imposed conditionalities but with a clear commitment to the values of all strategic objectives in the Decent Work agenda. Furthermore, we can do this in cooperation with the WTO and other interested international organizations. The basis is an integrated approach that recognizes the need for fair trade rules, sustainable enterprises and appropriate employment and social policies to deal with the downsizing. This will give greater security to workers, families and communities and greater opportunities for all countries to share in the benefits of trade.

Notes

1. "Declaration Concerning the Aims and Purposes of the International Labour Organization" [Declaration of Philadelphia], Annex to the ILO's Constitution, 10 May 1944; available at ⟨http://www.ilo.org/ilolex/english/constq.htm⟩ (accessed 7 January 2008).
2. IMF, *Articles of Agreement of the International Monetary Fund*, adopted at the United Nations Monetary and Financial Conference, Bretton Woods, New Hampshire, 22 July 1944, entered into force 27 December 1945; available at ⟨http://www.imf.org/external/pubs/ft/aa/aa01.htm⟩ (accessed 7 January 2008).
3. *Havana Charter for an International Trade Organization*, Final Act of the United Nations Conference on Trade and Employment held at Havana, Cuba, 21 November 1947 to 24 March 1948, Interim Commission for the International Trade Organization, New York, April 1948, p. 17; available at ⟨http://www.wto.org/english/docs_e/legal_e/havana_e.pdf⟩ (accessed 7 January 2008).
4. *Toolkit for Mainstreaming Employment and Decent Work*, Geneva: International Labour Office, 2007; available at ⟨http://www.ilo.org/public/english/bureau/dgo/selecdoc/2007/toolkit.pdf⟩ (accessed 7 January 2008).
5. Antony Alcock, *History of the International Labour Organisation*, London: Macmillan Press, 1971.
6. United Nations, *Report of the World Summit for Social Development (Copenhagen, 6–12 March 1995). Annex I: Copenhagen Declaration on Social Development*, UN Doc. A/CONF.166/9, 19 April 1995, p. 14; available at ⟨http://www.un.org/documents/ga/conf166/aconf166-9.htm⟩ (accessed 28 August 2008).
7. Ibid., p. 15.
8. *ILO Declaration on Fundamental Principles and Rights at Work*, 86th Session, Geneva, June 1998, at ⟨http://www.ilo.org/dyn/declaris/DeclarationWeb.IndexPage⟩ (accessed 8 January 2008).
9. ILO, *Report of the Director-General: Decent Work*, International Labour Conference, 87th Session, Geneva: International Labour Office, 1999, p. 3, italics in original.
10. World Commission on the Social Dimension of Globalization, *A Fair Globalization: Creating Opportunities for All*, Geneva: International Labour Office, 2004.
11. United Nations General Assembly, fifty-ninth session, 2 December 2004, Resolution 59/57: *A Fair Globalization: Creating Opportunities for All – Report of the World Commission on the Social Dimension of Globalization*, UN Doc. A/Res/59/57, 30 March 2005.
12. United Nations General Assembly, sixtieth session, 16 September 2005, Resolution 60/1: *2005 World Summit Outcome*, UN Doc. A/Res/60/1, 24 October 2005, para. 47.
13. United Nations Economic and Social Council (ECOSOC), *Draft Ministerial Declaration of the High-Level Segment Submitted by the President of the Council on the Basis of Informal Consultations*, UN Doc. E/2006/L.8, 5 July 2006. For a detailed summary and analysis of the Declaration, see ILO Governing Body, 297th session, Geneva, November 2006, Working Party on the Social Dimension of Globalization, at ⟨http://www.ilo.org/public/english/standards/relm/gb/docs/gb297/pdf/sdg-1.pdf⟩ (accessed 8 January 2008).
14. The publication in 2006 of the report of the UN Secretary-General's High-level Panel on UN System-wide Coherence in the Areas of Development, Humanitarian Assistance,

and the Environment, entitled *Delivering as One*, has further stimulated these consider-ations; available at ⟨http://www.un.org/events/panel/⟩ (accessed 8 January 2008).

15. *Toolkit for Mainstreaming Employment and Decent Work*.
16. *Programme of the ITUC*, November 2006, para. 47, at ⟨http://www.ituc-csi.org/IMG/pdf/ Programme_of_the_ITUC.pdf⟩ (accessed 8 January 2008).
17. For an overview of several significant developments in the ILO's work within the multi-lateral system, see ILO Governing Body, *The ILO in an Evolving Multilateral System: An Overview*, 298th session, Geneva, March 2007, at ⟨http://www.ilo.org/public/english/ standards/relm/gb/docs/gb298/pdf/gb-4-2.pdf⟩ (accessed 8 January 2008).
18. Marion Jansen and Eddy Lee, *Trade and Employment: Challenges for Policy Research*, a joint study of the International Labour Office and the Secretariat of the World Trade Organization, Geneva: ILO and WTO, 2007; available at ⟨http://www.ilo.org/wcmsp5/ groups/public/---dgreports/---dcomm/---webdev/documents/publication/wcms_081742. pdf⟩ (accessed 8 January 2008).
19. Ibid., p. 2.
20. Grant Aldonas, Robert Z. Lawrence and Matthew Slaughter, "Succeeding in the Global Economy", Financial Services Forum policy research paper, Washington, June 2007.
21. ILO, *A Fair Globalization: The Role of the ILO*, Report of the Director-General on the World Commission on the Social Dimension of Globalization to the International La-bour Conference, 92nd Session, Geneva: International Labour Office, 2004.
22. Jansen and Lee, *Trade and Employment*, p. 6.
23. Ibid., p. 8.
24. World Commission on the Social Dimension of Globalization, *A Fair Globalization*, p. 85.

6

Placing human rights in the Geneva consensus

Louise Arbour and Shervin Majlessi

The new world order after the Second World War envisaged among other things the creation of a new human rights mechanism and a new world trading system. Soon after the end of the war, and almost simultaneously, a Universal Declaration of Human Rights (UDHR) and the Havana Charter for an International Trade Organization were adopted. The human rights system was later complemented by a series of treaties and treaty bodies as well as the Special Procedures of the Commission on Human Rights (now replaced by the Human Rights Council). The Havana Charter, however, never entered into force, and instead the General Agreement on Tariffs and Trade (GATT) acted as a de facto organization *ad interim*.

The end of the Cold War provided for an opportunity to revamp the human rights machinery and to complete the world trade project, leading respectively to the Vienna Declaration and Programme of Action and the Marrakesh Agreement Establishing the World Trade Organization. Again, however, these simultaneous evolutions happened on parallel tracks.

Since the publication of the precursor of the current volume,[1] the link between trade, development and human rights has been treated extensively in academic circles and beyond. Nonetheless, among both the human rights community and trade practitioners these linkages are still not immediately obvious.

However, the current Director-General of the WTO, Pascal Lamy, has shown greater openness to the inclusion of social and development issues

The WTO and global governance: Future directions, Sampson (ed),
United Nations University Press, 2008, ISBN 978-92-808-1154-4

on the trade agenda, especially through his proposal for a new "Geneva consensus" (as opposed to the more market fundamentalist "Washington consensus"): "a belief that trade opening does work for development, on the condition that the imbalances it creates, both domestically and internationally, are properly addressed."[2] To address global problems, including the social impact of economic policies, he then proposed a system of global governance.[3]

In discussing the role of the WTO in global governance, this chapter will focus on the position of human rights in global governance and the linkage between the human rights, trade and development agendas, by placing the question of human rights within the framework of the Geneva consensus. In order to illustrate the relevance of human rights to the proposed Geneva consensus, we shall first elaborate on the linkage between trade and human rights, especially in the areas of trade in agriculture, services, investment and intellectual property, as well as questions of non-discrimination in trade and human rights and of trade and development. We will then address the role of human rights in the context of the three elements that Lamy proposes for a system of global governance: common values, legitimate actors and a system of arbitrating the values.[4] The conclusion will reiterate that, whereas the multilateral trading system provides a legal framework for the economic aspects of the liberalization of trade, human rights norms and standards provide a legal framework for addressing the social dimensions of trade liberalization. Coherence among global actors is the key to reconciling these frameworks.

Trade and human rights – opportunities and risks

There is a link between trade, development and human rights. Trade can help guarantee the enjoyment of human rights by improving opportunities for economic growth, job creation and the diffusion of technology and capital and can contribute to development and the eradication of poverty. Trade can, however, also threaten human rights in some situations.

In response to mandates from the Commission on Human Rights and the Sub-Commission on the Promotion and Protection of Human Rights, the High Commissioner for Human Rights prepared six reports that cover different aspects of the linkage between trade and human rights. This chapter draws on these reports to outline briefly the potential impact of trade liberalization in different sectors on various human rights.

Trade liberalization in agriculture

The International Covenant on Economic, Social and Cultural Rights (ICESCR) specifically identifies the need to ensure that international trade promotes the right to food. Article 11(2) states: "[t]he States Parties to the present Covenant, recognizing the fundamental right of everyone to be free from hunger, shall take, individually and through international co-operation, the measures, including specific programmes, which are needed ... taking into account the problems of both food-importing and food-exporting countries, to ensure an equitable distribution of world food supplies in relation to need."[5]

Liberalization of trade in agricultural products can create export opportunities in agricultural exporting countries, augment domestic supplies of food, optimize the use of world resources, increase transparency and accountability in international trade in agriculture, and promote growth and development.[6] However, the liberalization of agricultural trade can also have a negative impact on human rights. For example, small farmers might not have the capacity to grow sufficient export crops and might even experience greater competition for resources, including land, thus marginalizing them from the potential benefits of trade. Similarly, greater export opportunities might lead to the reallocation of land and other resources away from domestic food production, with possible adverse consequences for household food security. Without the introduction of appropriate safeguards and transitional measures, trade rules and policies could have adverse effects on the right to food, workers' rights of small farmers and the rural poor. On the other hand, agricultural subsidies in developed countries can also have an impact on the human rights of the rural poor in developing countries. According to the *Human Development Report 2005*, "[m]ore than two-thirds of all people surviving on less than $1 a day live and work in rural areas either as smallholder farmers or as agricultural labourers. Unfair trade practices systematically undermine the livelihoods of these people." The report cites as an example the price distortions caused by US subsidies that have a direct impact on cotton producers in poor countries, because these subsidies lower world prices by 9–13 per cent.[7]

In principle, in addition to subjecting international agricultural trade to a rule-based and more transparent system, the WTO's Agreement on Agriculture includes special and differential treatment provisions for developing countries.[8] However, the Agreement on Agriculture currently does not make a distinction between different types of agriculture, such as commercial agriculture or subsistence agriculture, or between different players, from low-income and resource-poor farmers on the one hand to national and international agribusiness on the other. The results of a study by the Food and Agriculture Organization (FAO) suggest that, "particularly for countries at earlier levels of development, trade reform can be damaging to food security in the short to medium term if it is introduced without a policy package designed to offset the negative effects of liberalization."[9] Furthermore, according to the Organisation for Economic Co-operation and Development (OECD), since the Uruguay Round, governments in OECD countries have continued to maintain relatively high levels of support and protection to agriculture.[10]

At the outset of the Doha Round of negotiations, WTO member states agreed that differential treatment for developing countries should be an integral part of all elements of the ongoing negotiations in order to enable them to take into account their development needs, including food security and rural development.[11] Such commitments can be seen as potential means of operationalizing the international cooperation commitments under the ICESCR and the Declaration on the Right to Development.[12] With the fate of Doha Round still in the balance, similar commitments have to be extended to future rounds of negotiations within the WTO in order to ensure the flexibility necessary for states to liberalize agricultural trade, while at the same time respecting, protecting and fulfilling human rights.

The liberalization of trade in services

In a general sense, the more efficient supply of services in any sector can promote economic growth and development, and therefore could provide the economic means needed to promote human rights.[13] Liberalization of trade in services can promote economic performance, provide a means for countries to capitalize on competitive strengths, offer lower prices to consumers in areas such as telecoms, promote faster innovations, and encourage technology transfer. However, without adequate governmental regulation and proper assessment of its effects, the liberalization of trade in services can also have undesirable effects and can threaten universal access by the poor to essential services. The liberalization of trade in services can affect human rights, such as the right to health (including the right to water) and the right to education, in various ways, depending on a range of issues, not least the type of services being supplied, the mode of service delivery, the development level of the country and its internal infrastructure, the regulatory environment and the level of existing services prior to liberalization. The case of the privatization of the water supply in Cochabamba, Bolivia, illustrates this point. After a private consortium obtained a concession to mange the water supply, the increase in user charges led to public protest and eventually the contract had to be cancelled.[14] Different service sectors require different policies and time-frames for liberalization and some areas are better left under governmental authority.

Two parts of the General Agreement on Trade in Services (GATS) are particularly relevant to human rights. First, the "general obligations and disciplines" include: the principle of non-discrimination ("most-favoured-nation treatment"); the promotion of transparency in relation to laws and regulations that affect trade in services; assurances that regulations affecting trade in services are applied in a reasonable, objective and impartial manner; a safeguard to protect countries facing serious balance of payment difficulties; provisions to increase developing country participation in world trade by strengthening their domestic services capacity (through technology transfer, improving their access to information and opening up markets in sectors relevant to developing country exports); and also exceptions to the application of GATS in order to protect public morals, as well as human, animal and plant life.[15] Second, GATS sets out specific "market access" and "national treatment" obligations that apply only to those service sectors (ranging from transport to health and education) identified and scheduled by each member state.[16]

At the same time, from a human rights perspective, all people are entitled without discrimination to certain levels of health care, education, drinking water supply and other basic services, and these entitlements should be protected in the processes of liberalization and privatization. States, therefore, hold responsibilities, both nationally and internationally, to guarantee minimum standards of affordable access to service supply and should not leave the concerns of human welfare solely to market forces.[17]

Consequently, regulators need to be conscious of ensuring that liberalization policies take into account state responsibilities to respect, protect and fulfil human rights. Human rights law does not place obligations on states to be the sole provider of essential services; however, states must ensure non-discriminatory and equitable service supply and guarantee the availability, accessibility, acceptability and adaptability of essential services (such as health, education or water), including their supply, especially to the poor, vulnerable and marginalized. To do so requires constant monitoring of policies and targeted action by independent regulators.

Investment

Even though the issue of investment was dropped from the Doha Round agenda in 2004, foreign direct investment (FDI) and its effect on the enjoyment of human rights is particularly important as a trade and human

rights issue and is likely to be raised again in future WTO and other multilateral or bilateral negotiations.[18]

The fact that investment can promote trade, growth and development
through upgrading national infrastructures, introducing new technologies
and providing employment opportunities suggests at first glance a potential correlation between investment and the enjoyment of human rights,
particularly economic, social and cultural rights and the right to development.[19] The United Nations Conference on Trade and Development
(UNCTAD) has noted that investment has generated significant employment in certain economic sectors, and there is evidence to suggest that
increases in investment have had positive effects on the participation of
women in paid employment.[20] Investment can, however, also have unde-
sired effects where there is insufficient regulation to protect human rights.

Whereas the objective of ensuring efficient *international* production by
lowering barriers to investment might be what drives investors, governments generally seek higher levels of investment in order to pursue *national* development objectives. Meeting these two goals might sometimes
require compromise. From a human rights perspective, it is important to
balance these objectives, with a view not only to attracting investment
and promoting national development but also to achieving economic, social, cultural and political development in which all human rights and
fundamental freedoms can be fully realized.

The relationship between human rights and investment depends on a
range of variables – the country and sector in question, the type of investment, the motivations of the investors and the responsibility of the government. Investment liberalization can modify the balance among those
variables by strengthening investors' rights and affecting to an extent the
policy choices that governments have to direct investment. On the one
hand, this potentially increases the available resources needed to promote and protect human rights. On the other hand, strengthening investors' rights alone could skew the balance of rights and obligations in
favour of investors' interests over those of states, individuals and communities. In the past, there has been concern that governments have lowered environmental and human rights standards – including labour and
health standards, freedom of expression and freedom of association – to
attract investment (known as the "race-to-the-bottom"). An extreme example is the temptation for transnational pharmaceutical companies to
relocate their research and development to less developed countries
where they can flout employment and social protection policies, including
ethical and medical standards, that exist in developed countries. For instance, the number of clinical research organizations has increased considerably in India during recent years and India has adopted guidelines
on "good clinical practices" that govern clinical trials of pharmaceutical

products and include "consent by the patients". However, some observers have questioned the meaning of consent from patients who are
illiterate and might not adequately understand the true risks involved in
the trials.[21]

From a human rights perspective, therefore, complementary measures
are needed to ensure an appropriate balance of rights and obligations
between states and towards investors, bearing in mind states' responsibilities under human rights law. As states undertake multilateral or bilateral
negotiations to achieve progressively higher levels of investment liberalization through implementation of investment agreements, it is important
to remember that states also have concurrent responsibilities under international law to promote and protect human rights. In this context, balancing investors' rights with investors' obligations, and ongoing efforts
to promote corporate social responsibility should be explicitly acknowledged in investment agreements.[22]

Intellectual property

Intellectual property protection – particularly patent protection – should
lead to more investment in innovation, including in pharmaceutical research, which is necessary for the promotion of the right to health.[23] At
the same time, it may result in an overly commercial approach to innovation and a concentration of control over the dissemination of drugs and
other technology in the hands of relatively few corporations, and it may
have an impact on the protection of indigenous knowledge. In so doing,
the protection of intellectual property might lose sight of its overall developmental objectives, namely the incentivization of innovation with a
view to developing new technology that will benefit society as a whole.
In particular, highly priced drugs could become unaffordable for poor
people and have negative implications for the enjoyment of the right to
health and other human rights.[24] The case of the 1997 amendment to
the Medicines and Related Substances Act of 1965 in South Africa illustrates this point. In that instance the government encouraged pharmacists
to substitute costly patented drugs with cheaper generic equivalents in an
attempt to ensure the supply of more affordable drugs in the face of the
rising AIDS crisis. The amendment was challenged in court by the Pharmaceutical Manufacturers Association and 39 drug companies on several
grounds, including that it violated South Africa's obligations under the
WTO's Agreement on Trade-Related Aspects of Intellectual Property
(TRIPS); in response, the government invoked its positive duty to fulfil
the right to health.[25]

From a human rights perspective, the ICESCR identifies a need to balance the protection of both public and private interests in intellectual

property and binds states to design intellectual property systems that strike a balance between promoting general public interests in accessing new knowledge as easily as possible and protecting the interests of authors and inventors in such knowledge.[26]

TRIPS provides some room for achieving this balance. First, members may take measures to protect issues relevant to the ICESCR, in particular health care, nutrition and the environment. Second, in relation to patents, members may authorize third parties to work the patent without the authorization of the patent holder, subject to certain limitations ("compulsory licensing"). Third, TRIPS encourages international cooperation and developed country members are obliged to provide incentives to their enterprises and institutions to promote and encourage technology transfer to least developed countries.[27] However, although the Agreement identifies the need to balance rights with obligations, it gives no guidance on how to achieve this balance.

The WTO Doha Declaration on the TRIPS Agreement and Public Health (2001) strengthens the right of countries to use compulsory licensing for importing generic drugs and promoting public health and has to be interpreted in a spirit that reflects this commitment.[28] States must monitor the implementation of TRIPS to ensure that the right balance is achieved between the interests of the general public and those of the authors, while taking into account the cultural and other rights of indigenous and local communities. Developed countries should also be encouraged to establish clear incentives to promote technology transfer and the supply of affordable drugs to developing countries.

Non-discrimination in trade and in human rights

In treating the subject of trade and human rights it is essential to outline the difference in meaning and implications of the principle of non-discrimination under each discipline.[29]

It is important to highlight the fact that the goals of the two principles are, in many ways, quite different. The human rights principle of non-discrimination, rooted in the Charter of the United Nations and the UDHR, is intrinsically linked with the principle of equality. As two sides of the same coin, non-discrimination and equality provide the foundations for the free and equal enjoyment of human rights. The equality referred to is not restricted to formal equality but extends to achieving substantive equality, which creates an obligation for states to take positive measures to redress the structural biases that lead to discrimination.[30] Nonetheless, it is important to note that this principle does not require guaranteeing equality of outcomes and does not purport to remove entirely the incentives according to which markets function.

The trade principle of non-discrimination is primarily directed towards reducing trade protectionism and improving international competitive conditions rather than achieving substantive equality. For example, the trade principle of "national treatment" does not prohibit discrimination against nationals even if the national provider of a "like" product or service might be in a weaker position comparatively.[31] But treating unequals as equals is problematic for the promotion and protection of human rights and could result in the institutionalization of discrimination against the poor and marginalized. For example, non-discriminative application of trade rules that do not take into account the need to alleviate rural poverty can increase the vulnerability of small farmers and rural poor.

Accordingly, even where the net social benefit from trade liberalization favours the majority in a certain country, the principle of non-discrimination under human rights law requires action to protect the human rights of those who do not benefit. It has to be noted that the WTO does allow certain exceptions to the principle of non-discrimination, generally to protect public morals and human, animal or plant life or health, or to allow developed countries to implement generalized preferences in favour of developing country imports (known as "the generalized system of preferences").[32]

Trade and the right to development

Although the basis and notion of the right to development has been subject to much debate, and is not like other legally binding human rights embodied in an international treaty, at the World Conference on Human Rights in 1993 a consensus emerged where the right to development was recognized "as a universal and inalienable right and an integral part of fundamental human rights."[33] According to the Declaration on the Right to Development, states have a duty to formulate appropriate national development polices that aim at the constant improvement of the well-being of the entire population.[34] The right to development is a right to a particular process of equitable development in which all fundamental freedoms and human rights (economic, social, cultural, civil and political) can be realized.[35] Accordingly, states and the international community have a responsibility in this area that goes beyond the theory of comparative advantage played out at the international level. As Robert Howse pointed out in his 2004 study commissioned by the High Commissioner for Human Rights, "in the context of trade liberalization the right to development conveys a set of quite definite, and powerful normative messages, and ... mainstreaming the right into the WTO actually yields a very concrete agenda for transformation of practice and even structure".[36]

The "Doha Development Agenda" of the WTO, which placed development issues and the interests of developing countries at the heart of the WTO's work, and the WTO work programme on Aid for Trade, which comprises aid that finances trade-related technical assistance, trade-related infrastructure and aid to develop productive capacity, are important steps in addressing the imbalances created by trade liberalization. Whatever the result of the current round of trade negotiations, the WTO must keep its focus on development in accordance with its stated objectives.[37] However, the organization's approach to the question of development should be broadened to take into account the human rights considerations outlined above.

Human rights and the Geneva consensus

WTO agreements contain no reference to human rights. Several WTO agreements contain general exception clauses, some of which are closely linked to specific human rights (ban on the use of prison labour, protection of privacy), and some of which could be applicable to a broader range of human rights concerns (allowing states to take measures for the protection of public morals, protection of human, animal and plant life or health, and protection of public order).[38] The preamble of the WTO Agreement also refers to the objectives of "raising standards of living" and "sustainable development".

In recent years, however, there has been increasing recognition that "globalization needs to be humanized" and that "we must take care of the victims of globalization".[39] Importantly, Pascal Lamy has demonstrated greater openness to the inclusion of social and development issues on the trade agenda, in particular through proposing a Geneva consensus. It is also very encouraging that, in elaborating on the notion of sustainable development in the preamble of the WTO agreement, Lamy states that "by definition sustainable development calls for the consideration of fundamental values other than those of market opening to include, for instance, the protection of the environment, *human rights* and other social values".[40] To address global problems, including the social impact of economic policies, he then proposes a system of global governance "to enhance and promote the interdependence of our world" comprising three elements: "*common values, actors with sufficient legitimacy*, and *mechanisms of governance* that are truly effective and can arbitrate values and interests in a legitimate way."[41]

As demonstrated in the previous section, some of the imbalance that is created by trade agreements could be addressed by giving due weight to human rights considerations. At the same time, as we shall elaborate in the next sections, the human rights system is and should be part of the three elements of the global governance system that Lamy has proposed to address the social impact of economic policies.

Human rights as common values

In his quest for a system of global governance, Lamy calls for "common values" that "may allow us to define the common goods or benefits that we would like to promote and defend collectively on a global scale" and that go "further than the UN Charter of Rights which is 60 years old".[42]

The Universal Declaration of Human Rights and other human rights instruments derive from a range of cultures, philosophical and religious traditions and value systems and give expression to the human rights obligations of states. During the past 60 years, the UDHR and other human rights instruments and the work of the UN human rights treaty bodies have furthered the quest for collective and common values of the international community.

Furthermore, many provisions in international human rights treaties are now recognized as rules of customary international law, which means that they are generally recognized among states as obligatory and are thus binding on all states, regardless of whether they have signed or ratified the relevant human rights treaty. As demonstrated in Table 6.1,[43] all members of the WTO have ratified at least one human rights instrument, 126 have ratified the ICESCR, and all but one have ratified the Convention on the Rights of the Child.[44]

While under the International Covenant on Civil and Political Rights (ICCPR) states have obligations to "protect and ensure" the human rights of their own population, under the ICESCR states have obligations to "respect, protect and fulfil" the economic, social, and cultural rights and to take steps, individually and through international assistance and cooperation, to achieve progressively the full realization of these rights. In the field of economic, social and cultural rights:

(a) the obligation to respect requires states to refrain from interfering with the enjoyment of economic, social and cultural rights;
(b) the obligation to protect requires states to prevent violations of such rights by third parties;
(c) the obligation to fulfil requires states to take appropriate legislative, administrative, budgetary, judicial and other measures towards the full realization of such rights.

WTO members should therefore bear in mind their concurrent obligations to promote and protect human rights when negotiating and implementing international rules on trade liberalization, recognizing the

Table 6.1 The status of ratification of seven of nine core human rights treaties by WTO members, as of 27 July 2007

	ICESCR	ICCPR	ICERD	CEDAW	CAT	CRC	ICMW
Albania	*	*	*	*	*	*	*
Angola	*	*		*		*	
Antigua and Barbuda			*	*	*	*	
Argentina	*	*	*	*	*	*	*
Armenia	*	*	*	*	*	*	
Australia	*	*	*	*	*	*	
Austria	*	*	*	*	*	*	
Bahrain		*	*	*	*	*	
Bangladesh	*	*	*	*	*	*	S
Barbados	*	*	*	*		*	
Belgium	*	*	*	*	*	*	
Belize	S	*	*	*	*	*	*
Benin	*	*	*	*	*	*	S
Bolivia	*	*	*	*	*	*	*
Botswana		*	*	*	*	*	
Brazil	*	*	*	*	*	*	
Brunei Darussalam				*		*	
Bulgaria	*	*	*	*	*	*	
Burkina Faso	*	*	*	*	*	*	*
Burundi	*	*	*	*	*	*	
Cambodia	*	*	*	*	*	*	S
Cameroon	*	*	*	*	*	*	
Canada	*	*	*	*	*	*	
Central African Republic	*	*	*	*		*	
Chad	*	*	*	*	*	*	
Chile	*	*	*	*	*	*	*
China	*	S	*	*	*	*	
Colombia	*	*	*	*	*	*	*
Congo	*	*	*	*	*	*	
Costa Rica	*	*	*	*	*	*	
Cote d'Ivoire	*	*	*	*	*	*	
Croatia	*	*	*	*	*	*	
Cuba			*	*	*	*	
Cyprus	*	*	*	*	*	*	
Czech Republic	*	*	*	*	*	*	
Democratic Republic of the Congo	*	*	*	*	*	*	
Denmark	*	*	*	*	*	*	
Djibouti	*	*	S	*	*	*	
Dominica	*	*		*		*	
Dominican Republic	*	*	*	*	S	*	
Ecuador	*	*	*	*	*	*	*
Egypt	*	*	*	*	*	*	*
El Salvador	*	*	*	*	*	*	*

Table 6.1 (cont.)

	ICESCR	ICCPR	ICERD	CEDAW	CAT	CRC	ICMW
Estonia	*	*	*	*	*	*	
Fiji			*	*		*	
Finland	*	*	*	*	*	*	
France	*	*	*	*	*	*	
Gabon	*	*	*	*	*	*	S
Gambia	*	*	*	*	*	*	
Georgia	*	*	*	*	*	*	
Germany	*	*	*	*	*	*	
Ghana	*	*	*	*	*	*	*
Greece	*	*	*	*	*	*	
Grenada	*	*	S	*		*	
Guatemala	*	*	*	*	*	*	*
Guinea	*	*	*	*	*	*	*
Guinea-Bissau	*	S	S	*	S	*	S
Guyana	*	*	*	*	*	*	S
Haiti		*	*	*		*	
Honduras	*	*	*	*	*	*	*
Hungary	*	*	*	*	*	*	
Iceland	*	*	*	*	*	*	
India	*	*	*	*	S	*	
Indonesia	*	*	*	*	*	*	S
Ireland	*	*	*	*	*	*	
Israel	*	*	*	*	*	*	
Italy	*	*	*	*	*	*	
Jamaica	*	*	*	*		*	
Japan	*	*	*	*	*	*	
Jordan	*	*	*	*	*	*	
Kenya	*	*	*	*	*	*	
Kiribati					*	*	
Kyrgyzstan	*	*	*	*	*	*	*
Latvia	*	*	*	*	*	*	
Lesotho	*	*	*	*	*	*	*
Liechtenstein	*	*	*	*	*	*	
Lithuania	*	*	*	*	*	*	
Luxembourg	*	*	*	*	*	*	
Madagascar	*	*	*	*	*	*	
Malawi	*	*	*	*	*	*	
Malaysia					*	*	
Maldives	*	*	*	*	*	*	
Mali	*	*	*	*	*	*	*
Malta	*	*	*	*	*	*	
Mauritania	*	*	*	*	*	*	*
Mauritius	*	*	*	*	*	*	
Mexico	*	*	*	*	*	*	*

Table 6.1 (cont.)

	ICESCR	ICCPR	ICERD	CEDAW	CAT	CRC	ICMW
Mongolia	*	*	*	*	*	*	
Morocco	*	*	*	*	*	*	*
Mozambique		*	*	*	*	*	
Myanmar					*	*	
Namibia	*	*	*	*	*	*	
Nepal	*	*	*	*	*	*	
Netherlands	*	*	*	*	*	*	
New Zealand	*	*	*	*	*	*	
Nicaragua	*	*	*	*	*	*	*
Niger	*	*	*	*	*	*	
Nigeria	*	*	*	*	*	*	
Norway	*	*	*	*	*	*	
Oman				*	*	*	
Pakistan	S			*	*		*
Panama	*	*	*	*	*	*	
Papua New Guinea			*	*		*	
Paraguay	*	*	*	*	*	*	S
Peru	*	*	*	*	*	*	*
Philippines	*	*	*	*	*	*	*
Poland	*	*	*	*	*	*	
Portugal	*	*	*	*	*	*	
Qatar			*		*	*	
Republic of Korea	*	*	*	*	*	*	
Republic of Moldova	*	*	*	*	*	*	
Romania	*	*	*	*	*	*	
Rwanda	*	*	*	*		*	
Saint Kitts and Nevis				*	*	*	
Saint Lucia				*	*	*	
Saint Vincent and the Grenadines	*	*	*	*	*	*	
Saudi Arabia			*	*	*	*	
Senegal	*	*	*	*	*	*	*
Sierra Leone	*	*	*	*	*	*	S
Singapore					*	*	
Slovakia	*	*	*	*	*	*	
Slovenia	*	*	*	*	*	*	
Solomon Islands	*		*	*		*	
South Africa	S	*	*	*	*	*	
Spain	*	*	*	*	*	*	
Sri Lanka	*	*	*	*	*	*	*
Suriname	*	*	*	*		*	
Swaziland	*	*	*	*	*	*	
Sweden	*	*	*	*	*	*	
Switzerland	*	*	*	*	*	*	
Thailand	*	*	*	*		*	

Table 6.1 (cont.)

	ICESCR	ICCPR	ICERD	CEDAW	CAT	CRC	ICMW
The Former Yugoslav Republic of Macedonia	*	*	*	*	*	*	
Togo	*	*	*	*	*	*	S
Tonga			*			*	
Trinidad and Tobago	*	*	*	*		*	
Tunisia	*	*	*	*	*	*	
Turkey	*	*	*	*	*	*	*
Uganda	*	*	*	*	*	*	*
United Arab Emirates			*	*		*	
United Kingdom of Great Britain and Northern Ireland	*	*	*	*	*	*	
United Republic of Tanzania	*	*	*	*		*	
United States of America	S	*	*	S	*	S	
Uruguay	*	*	*	*	*	*	*
Venezuela (Bolivarian Republic of)	*	*	*	*	*	*	
Viet Nam	*	*	*	*		*	
Zambia	*	*	*	*	*	*	
Zimbabwe	*	*	*	*		*	

Notes: * signifies ratification and "S" signifies signature of a convention. Signatories to a convention are bound by international law to refrain from acts that would defeat the object and purpose of the convention. The table excludes Hong Kong, Macao and the European Union, which are customs territories and are covered by the obligations of China (Hong Kong and Macao) and the member states of the European Union. The Separate Customs Territory of Taiwan, Penghu, Kinmen and Matsu (referred to in the WTO as "Chinese Taipei") is also not included.

declaration made at the World Conference on Human Rights in Vienna that human rights are "the first responsibility of Governments".[45]

To ensure observance of their human right obligations, states must assess the potential and real impact of trade policy and law in order to avoid implementation of any retrogressive measure that reduces the enjoyment of human rights. Accordingly it will be important to integrate human rights standards more explicitly in Poverty and Social Impact Assessment (PSIA) for trade-related policy measures.

Principle of participation and its application in the context of globalization

As the second element of a system of global governance, Lamy rightly focuses on "actors who have sufficient legitimacy to get public opinion interested in the debate".[46] But it could equally be suggested that at a broader level the *public* itself needs to be involved, based on the principle of participation.[47]

The principle of participation is expressed through the recognition of political rights and the right to participate in the conduct of public affairs in the UDHR and the ICCPR, in the context of combating discrimination against women in the Convention on the Elimination of All Forms of Discrimination against Women (CEDAW) and, in the area of racial discrimination, in the International Convention on the Elimination of All Forms of Racial Discrimination (ICERD), which prohibits racial discrimination in connection with participation in political and public life.[48] Furthermore, the Human Rights Committee has interpreted the right to take part in the conduct of public affairs broadly, noting that the conduct of public affairs covers "all aspects of public administration, and the formulation and implementation of policy at the international, national, regional and local levels".[49]

Accordingly, the question of participation in the context of globalization can be examined at three levels. The first level is the respect for participatory rights nationally. The second level of participation concerns the participation of states, as the primary human rights duty bearers and subjects of international law, at the global level. The third level concerns the direct participation of individuals and groups at the international level in global institutions. The last is also important because decisions affecting people locally are increasingly being taken globally.

At the national level, participation in national policy-setting in areas such as poverty reduction and trade reform needs to be strengthened. Not only would this be a means of promoting wider enjoyment of participatory rights nationally; it could also help promote a broader consensus on often controversial policies related to trade, finance and development. Strengthened enforceability of economic, social and cultural rights and providing appropriate means of redress in the case of clear violations of these rights will also empower stakeholders to exercise their rights and challenge trade policies that might lead to violation of their rights at national levels.

At the international level, there is a need to consider ways to strengthen the participation of poorer countries in decision-making processes, for instance by enhancing their capacity through technical cooperation. Furthermore, opportunities for direct participation of individuals and groups in the conduct of public international affairs need to be enhanced.[50]

To this end, the role of parliaments at the national and international levels – for instance through global parliamentary networks – can be strengthened and the participation of civil society in institutions such as the WTO can be increased. The WTO's Trade Policy Review Mechanism, through which WTO members undertake periodic peer review of the trade policies of individual members against the background of their wider economic and developmental needs, policies and objectives, could benefit from wider participation by different stakeholders. Also of relevance in the context of the WTO are proposals for the participation of local authorities as key partners in development work, specifically because very often the work of local authorities has the most direct influence on the lives of citizens in areas such as water and sanitation, education and health services.[51]

The experiences of the United Nations system or international financial institutions can provide guidance on modes of participation at the international level. The World Bank accountability mechanism, for instance, includes the Inspection Panel, which investigates complaints from groups of affected people in relation to World Bank loans; and the tripartite system of the International Labour Organization (ILO) enables workers' and employers' organizations to participate in the decision-making system of the ILO. Within the Human Rights system, participation of non-governmental organizations (NGOs) in the Human Rights Council and their contribution to the monitoring system of human rights treaties as well as human rights special procedures can be replicated in the world trading system. Within the United Nations as well as the WTO it is acknowledged that participation of NGOs needs to be further enhanced in the light of developments in recent decades.[52]

However, the increasing engagement of civil society groups can also burden the already loaded agendas of intergovernmental decision-making structures and decrease their efficiency. It is thus important to note that participation has to be effective and subject to reasonable and objective limitations in order to avoid over-burdening the system. To that end, the responsibilities and accountability, as well as the legitimacy, of civil society groups need to be addressed.

Arbitrating the values: What role for trade and human rights mechanisms?

The third element of a system of global governance from Lamy's point of view is a mechanism to "arbitrate values and interests in a legitimate way".[53] In the context of trade and human rights, what exactly is the conflict to be arbitrated?

Certain elements of human rights require time, resources and planning to realize, depending on the particular conditions existing in the country in question. Nonetheless, states have undertaken to move as expeditiously as possible towards the realization of those elements. At the same time, trade rules envisage a process of legal and policy development towards achieving progressively higher levels of liberalization. Although these two processes need not move in opposite or conflicting directions, the adoption of any deliberately retrogressive measure in the liberalization process that reduces the extent to which any human right is protected in principle constitutes a violation of human rights.

The WTO mechanisms that are entrusted with the task of implementation and interpretation of the rules and settlement of disputes involving human rights considerations and obligations of states should ensure that these two processes – progressive realization of socio-economic rights and progressive trade liberalization – can be implemented simultaneously and coherently. This requires, at a very minimum, that the states' international trade commitments not be interpreted so as to undermine the fulfilment of their international human rights law obligations.[54]

Lamy has also acknowledged that "the WTO is a sophisticated system for rules making and for ensuring their enforcement. But this does not mean that the WTO is hegemonic and does not take into account other international norms and other international organisations. On the contrary, the WTO is not more important than other international organisations and WTO norms do not necessarily supersede or trump other international norms."[55] As we outlined in previous sections, the norms and standards of human rights provide the legal framework for the protection of the social dimensions of trade liberalization as a complement to trade rules.

In the trade policy community, trade expansion is often viewed as an end in itself and is used to measure the success of these policies; a view that in turn can be reflected in the methodologies, agenda and review mechanisms of the organization. In order to ensure the sustainability of trade law and policy from a human rights and development perspective, WTO bodies and mechanisms, including the Trade Policy Review Mechanism and the Dispute Settlement System, should adopt a methodology and view that examine trade law and policy comprehensively, focusing not only on economic growth, markets or economic development but also on health systems, education, water supply, food security, labour, political processes and so on.

The country-specific recommendations of the human rights treaty bodies (e.g. the Committee on Economic, Social and Cultural Rights, CESCR, or CEDAW), the special procedures (e.g. reports of the Special Rapporteur on the right to food, or the Special Rapporteur on the right of everyone to the enjoyment of the highest attainable standard of physical and mental health, or the Special Representative of the Secretary-General on human rights and transnational corporations and other business enterprises), and the Universal Periodic Reviews at the new Human Rights Council can be taken into consideration in arbitrating conflicts between trade rules and human rights obligations. For example, issues related to trade and economic policy have already been raised in the CESCR, where the Committee has strongly recommended "that the State party's obligations under the Covenant should be taken into account in all aspects of its negotiations with the international financial institutions to ensure that the enjoyment of economic, social and cultural rights, particularly by the most disadvantaged and marginalized groups, are not undermined".[56] Similarly, the Special Rapporteur on the right of everyone to the enjoyment of the highest attainable standard of physical and mental health recommended that. "[i]f a State chooses to engage in trade liberalization in those areas that impact upon the right to health, then it should select the form, pacing and consequences of liberalization that is most conducive to the progressive realization of the right to health for all, including those living in poverty and other disadvantaged groups".[57] The exact modalities of raising human rights in trade policy forums, and their potential interaction with human rights bodies, are open to further study and deliberation.

Conclusion: Coherence among global governance actors

WTO member states have committed themselves to conducting their relations in the field of trade and economic endeavour with a view to raising standards of living, ensuring full employment and expanding the production of and trade in goods and services while allowing for the optimal use of the world's resources in accordance with the objective of sustainable development.[58] They have also committed themselves to international cooperation and assistance to promote human rights as a set of common global values and to create a social and international order through which all human rights and fundamental freedoms can be fully realized.[59]

Effective implementation of these economic obligations in line with universal human rights values and obligations requires coherence at national, international and institutional levels, between and within states and with the effective participation of different stakeholders. In particular, the dialogue between human rights, trade, finance and environmental practitioners needs to be improved and more concerted consultation in this respect should be conducted.

At the *national level*, improved consultation between social sector and trade/finance ministries and greater dialogue with civil society are encouraged. Within civil society groups, dialogue between trade and human rights organizations at the national and international levels has to be promoted. States, in implementing and reviewing trade rules, are encouraged to consider the most appropriate mechanisms that both promote and protect human rights and are minimally trade distorting.

At the *international level*, delegates to the WTO and delegates representing the same country at the Human Rights Council should be encouraged to conduct consultations, specifically on the links between human rights and trade and on particular ways to ensure coherence in policy and rule-making.

At the *institutional level*, the pertinent bodies could consider appropriate means of promoting institutional dialogue between, for example, the WTO General Council and the Human Rights Council and between treaty bodies and the WTO Appellate Body, as well as with the civil society. The issue of the direct role of the WTO in the interpretation and enforcement of the human rights obligations of member states is open to debate. However, as Pascal Lamy has acknowledged: "The challenge to humanise globalization necessarily involves other actors in the international scene: IMF/WB and the United Nations family."[60] Within the WTO it is also important that the methodology and conceptual tools used in trade policy review and technical assistance functions take into account the overlap with development and human rights issues or involve other relevant organizations and stakeholders.

At all levels, in order to ensure the adoption of the most appropriate policies and regulations in line with human rights obligations, assessments of the potential and actual impact of trade policies are fundamental. States can raise the question of such impact assessment studies in the process of review of trade agreements and in future rounds of negotiations. However, developing countries often do not have the capacity or infrastructure either to undertake assessments or to develop and implement the most appropriate regulations. This is a fitting area for developed countries to fulfil their obligations and provide international cooperation and assistance.

WTO members should therefore bear in mind their concurrent human rights obligations, and the larger members, particularly developed countries, should negotiate in ways that enable poorer countries to maintain the maximum flexibility to develop policies to meet their commitments to the progressive realization of human rights. It is also important that countries currently negotiating accession to the WTO benefit from the full special and differential treatment open to developing countries and are able to avail themselves of the flexibility provided for in many WTO agreements. Countries involved in accession talks should ensure that such preferences are not negotiated away.

Finally, as in other areas of international cooperation, it is important to ensure that multilateral efforts to regulate international trade bear fruit.

Cohesion among international actors who interact in different forums is best ensured in a multilateral setting. A return to bilateral and regional trade agreements, as recently pointed out by UNCTAD, "is a risky departure from multilateralism" that may limit policy-makers' options to carry out their development strategies and thus adversely affect human rights.[61]

The WTO has already made a very important contribution to enhancing multilateralism and a rule-oriented international trading system. The challenge facing the international community is the development of a system of trade liberalization that benefits everyone, leaving no individual, group or state behind in the process of globalization. The WTO, through coordination with other global governance actors, clearly has a crucial role to play in the development of such a system.

Notes

1. Gary P. Sampson, ed., *The Role of the WTO in Global Governance*, Tokyo: United Nations University Press, 2000.
2. Message from Pascal Lamy to the GARNET Network of Excellence (Global Governance, Regionalisation & Regulation: The Role of the EU); at ⟨http://www.garnet-eu.org/index.php?id=197⟩ (accessed 5 July 2007).
3. Pascal Lamy, "Humanising Globalization", speech in Santiago de Chile delivered on 30 January 2006; available at ⟨http://www.wto.org/english/news_e/sppl_e/sppl16_e.htm⟩ (accessed 21 May 2007).
4. Ibid.
5. *International Covenant on Economic, Social and Cultural Rights*, Adopted and opened for signature, ratification and accession by General Assembly resolution 2200A (XXI) of 16 December 1966, entry into force 3 January 1976; at ⟨http://www.unhchr.ch/html/menu3/b/a_cescr.htm⟩ (accessed 14 January 2008).
6. For further detail, see *Globalization and Its Impact on the Full Enjoyment of Human Rights*, Report of the United Nations High Commissioner for Human Rights submitted in accordance with Commission on Human Rights resolution 2001/32, 15 January 2002, UN Doc. E/CN.4/2002/54.
7. United Nations Development Programme (UNDP), *Human Development Report 2005. International Cooperation at a Crossroads: Aid, Trade and Security in an Unequal World*, New York: United Nations, pp. 129 and 131.
8. *Agreement Establishing the World Trade Organization, Annex 1A: Agreement on Agriculture*, Articles 6, 9(4) and 15. see ⟨http://www.wto.org/english/docs_e/legal_e/14-ag_01_e.htm⟩ (accessed 14 January 2008).
9. FAO, *Trade Reforms and Food Security: Country Case Studies and Synthesis*, Rome, 2006, p. 75. The Programme of Action adopted at the Third United Nations Conference on Least Developed Countries (LDCs) held in Brussels in May 2001 noted that agriculture is the pivotal sector in LDCs, underpinning food security, foreign exchange earnings, industrial and rural development, and employment generation. The LDC Conference encouraged continuing the process of trade liberalization to expand the sources of food supply. In this context, the Programme of Action calls for coherent action by the United Nations and other organizations as an essential element in policy reform

directed to transforming trade into a powerful engine for growth and poverty eradication in LDCs. *Programme of Action for the Least Development Countries adopted by
the Third United Nations Conference on Least Developed Countries*, Brussels, 14–20
May 2001, UN Doc. A/CONF.191/11, paras. 57, 62, and 65.

10. OECD, *Tackling Trade in Agriculture*, Policy Brief, November 2005, at ⟨http://
www.oecd.org/dataoecd/34/45/35686834.pdf⟩ (accessed 10 July 2007).

11. WTO, *Ministerial Declaration*, Ministerial Conference, Fourth Session, Doha, 10–14
November 2001, adopted on 14 November 2001, WT/MIN(01)/DEC/1, 20 November
2001, para. 13.

12. *International Covenant on Economic, Social and Cultural Rights*, Article 2; United
Nations General Assembly, *Declaration on the Right to Development*, 4 December
1986, UN Doc. A/RES/41/128, Article 4, at ⟨http://www.un.org/documents/ga/res/41/
a41r128.htm⟩ (accessed 14 January 2008).

13. For further detail, see *Liberalization of Trade in Services and Human Rights*, Report
of the High Commissioner for Human Rights submitted in accordance with Sub-
Commission on the Promotion and Protection of Human Rights resolution 2001/4, 25
June 2002, UN Doc. E/CN.4/Sub.2/2002/9.

14. United Nations Conference on Trade and Development (UNCTAD), *World Investment
Report 2004: The Shift towards Services*, New York and Geneva: United Nations, 2004,
p. 63.

15. *Agreement Establishing the World Trade Organization, Annex 1B: General Agreement
on Trade in Services* (GATS), generally Part II, and Articles II and IV; available at
⟨http://www.wto.org/english/docs_e/legal_e/26-gats.pdf⟩ (accessed 14 January 2008).

16. GATS, generally Part III, and Articles XVI and XXI.

17. *See* Universal Declaration of Human Rights, *Articles 22 and 25*, available at ⟨http://
www.unhchr.ch/udhr/lang/eng.htm⟩ (accessed 14 January 2008); International Covenant
on Economic, Social and Cultural Rights, *Articles 2, 12, 13, 14*; Convention on the
Rights of the Child, *Adopted and opened for signature, ratification and accession by
General Assembly resolution 44/25 of 20 November 1989 entry into force 2 September
1990, Articles 28 and 29*, available at ⟨http://www.unhchr.ch/html/menu3/b/k2crc.htm⟩
(accessed 14 January 2008); Declaration on the Right to Development, *Articles 2 and 4*.

18. WTO, *Doha Work Programme: Decision Adopted by the General Council on 1
August 2004*, WT/L/579, at ⟨http://www.wto.org/english/tratop_e/dda_e/draft_text_gc_
dg_31july04_e.htm⟩ (accessed 15 July 2007).

19. For further detail see *Human Rights, Trade and Investment*, Report of the High Com-
missioner for Human Rights submitted in accordance with Sub-Commission on the
Promotion and Protection of Human Rights resolution 2002/11, 2 July 2003, UN Doc.
E/CN.4/Sub.2/2003/9.

20. UNCTAD, *Foreign Direct Investment and Development*, UNCTAD Series on issues in
international investment agreements, New York and Geneva: United Nations, 1999,
p. 41; N. Cagatay, *Trade, Gender and Poverty*, New York: United Nations Development
Programme, October 2001, pp. 20–21.

21. UNCTAD, *World Investment Report 2005: Transnational Corporations and the Interna-
tionalization of R&D*, New York and Geneva: United Nations, 2005, pp. 192–193.

22. The Secretary-General's Global Compact, launched in 1999, provides a platform for encouraging and promoting good corporate practices and learning experiences in the areas
of human rights, labour and the environment and the basis for a structured dialogue between the United Nations, business, labour and civil society on improving corporate
practices. The work of the Special Representative of the Secretary-General on the issue
of human rights and transnational corporations and other business enterprises, John

Ruggie, is also relevant in this area. See the report entitled *Business and Human Rights: Mapping International Standards of Responsibility and Accountability for Corporate Acts*, 19 February 2007, UN Doc. A/HRC/4/35.

23. For further detail see *The Impact of the Agreement on Trade-Related Aspects of Intellectual Property Rights (TRIPS) on Human Rights*, Report of the High Commissioner for Human Rights submitted in accordance with Sub-Commission on the Promotion and Protection of Human Rights resolution 2000/7, 27 June 2001, UN Doc. E/CN.4/Sub.2/2001/13.

24. See, UNDP, *Human Development Report 2005*, pp. 135–136. For example, estimates by the government of Costa Rica suggest that its pharmaceutical budget would have to rise fivefold to maintain universal coverage without access to generic drugs.

25. World Bank, *World Development Report 2006: Equity and Development*, Washington DC: World Bank and Oxford University Press, 2005, p. 215.

26. *International Covenant on Economic, Social and Cultural Rights*, Article 15; see also *Universal Declaration of Human Rights*, Article 27.

27. *Agreement Establishing the World Trade Organization, Annex 1C: Agreement on Trade-Related Aspects of Intellectual Property* (TRIPS), Articles 8, 27, 31, 66 and 67, available at ⟨http://www.wto.org/english/docs_e/legal_e/27-trips.pdf⟩ (accessed 14 January 2008).

28. WTO Doha Ministerial 2001, *Declaration on the TRIPS Agreement and Public Health*, adopted on 14 November 2001, WT/MIN(01)/DEC/2, 20 November 2001, available at ⟨http://www.wto.org/english/thewto_e/minist_e/min01_e/mindecl_trips_e.htm⟩ (accessed 12 March 2008) and the subsequent *Implementation of the WTO General Council Decision on Paragraph 6 of the Declaration on the TRIPS Agreement and Public Health*, WT/L/540 and Corr.1, 1 September 2003, available at ⟨http://www.wto.org/english/tratop_e/trips_e/implem_para6_e.htm⟩ (accessed 12 March 2008). See also UNDP, *Human Development Report 2005*, p. 135.

29. For further detail see *Analytical Study of the High Commissioner for Human Rights on the Fundamental Principle of Non-Discrimination in the Context of Globalization*, Report of the High Commissioner for Human Rights submitted in accordance with Commission for Human Rights resolution 2002/28, 15 January 2004, UN Doc. E/CN.4/2004/40.

30. See, e.g., *Universal Declaration of Human Rights*, Article 1; Office of the High Commissioner for Human Rights, *International Covenant on Civil and Political Rights*, Adopted and opened for signature, ratification and accession by General Assembly resolution 2200A (XXI) of 16 December 1966, entry into force 23 March 1976, Articles 3 and 26; *International Covenant on International Covenant on Economic, Social and Cultural Rights*, Article 3; and Human Rights Committee, General Comment No. 18, "Non-discrimination", 1989, para. 7.

31. See, e.g., General Agreement on Tariffs and Trade (GATT 1947), Article I; GATS, Article II; and TRIPS, Article 4.

32. GATT, Article XX; GATS, Article XXV; GATT, "Differential and More Favourable Treatment, Reciprocity and Fuller Participation of Developing Countries", Decision of 28 November 1979, L/4903 (known as "the Enabling Clause"); and various special and differential treatment provisions in WTO Agreements and Decisions.

33. United Nations, World Conference on Human Rights, *Vienna Declaration and Programme of Action*, Vienna, adopted by the World Conference on Human Rights on 25 June 1993, UN Doc. A/CONF.157/23, paras 10 and 72.

34. *Declaration on the Right to Development*, Article 2.

35. *Vienna Declaration and Programme of Action*, paras 10 and 11; Commission on Human Rights, *Report of the Independent Expert on the Question of Human Rights and Extreme Poverty: Arjun Sengupta*, UN Doc. E/CN.4/2005/49, paras 33–34.

36. Robert Howse, "Mainstreaming the Right to Development into International Trade Law and Policy at the World Trade Organization", study commissioned by the High Commissioner for Human Rights, UN Doc. E/CN.4/Sub.2/2004/17, 9 June 2004, para. 6.

37. States recognize in the Preamble to the WTO Agreement that "their relations in the field of trade and economic endeavour should be conducted with a view to raising standards of living, ensuring full employment and a large and steadily growing volume of real income and effective demand, and expanding the production of and trade in goods and services, while allowing for the optimal use of the world's resources in accordance with the objective of sustainable development, seeking both to protect and preserve the environment and to enhance the means for doing so in a manner consistent with their respective needs and concerns at different levels of economic development"; *Marrakesh Agreement Establishing the World Trade Organization*, 15 April 1994, available at ⟨http://www.wto.org/english/docs_e/legal_e/04-wto_e.htm⟩ (accessed 14 January 2008).

38. GATT, Article XX; GATS, Article XIV; *Agreement Establishing the World Trade Organization. Annex 4(b): Agreement on Government Procurement*, Article XXIII, available at ⟨http://www.wto.org/english/docs_e/legal_e/gpr-94_e.pdf⟩ (accessed 14 January 2008); TRIPS, Article 27. See also the OHCHR publication *Human Rights and World Trade Agreements – Using General Exception Clauses to Protect Human Rights*, New York and Geneva: United Nations, 2005.

39. Lamy, "Humanising Globalization".

40. Pascal Lamy, "Towards Global Governance?", Master of Public Affairs inaugural lecture at the Institut d'Etudes Politiques de Paris, 21 October 2005, emphasis added.

41. Lamy, "Humanising Globalization", emphasis added.

42. Ibid.

43. The table reflects the status of ratification of seven of nine core human rights treaties by WTO members as of 27 July 2007: International Covenant on Economic, Social and Cultural Rights (ICESCR), International Covenant on Civil and Political Rights (ICCPR), International Convention on the Elimination of All Forms of Racial Discrimination (ICERD), Convention on the Elimination of All Forms of Discrimination against Women (CEDAW), Convention Against Torture and Other Cruel Inhuman or Degrading Treatment or Punishment (CAT), Convention on the Rights of the Child (CRC), International Convention on the Protection of the Rights of All Migrant Workers and Members of Their Families (ICMW). The Convention for the Protection of All Persons from Enforced Disappearance (CED) and the Convention on the Rights of Persons with Disabilities (CPD) have not yet entered into force.

44. An additional four WTO members have signed but not ratified the ICESCR (Belize, Pakistan, South Africa and the United States).

45. *Vienna Declaration and Programme of Action*, Part I, para. 1.

46. Lamy, "Humanising Globalization".

47. For further detail, see *Analytical Study of the High Commissioner for Human Rights on the Fundamental Principle of Participation and Its Application in the Context of Globalization*, Report of the High Commissioner for Human Rights submitted in accordance with Commission for Human Rights resolution 2004/24, 23 December 2004, UN Doc. E/CN.4/2005/41.

48. *Universal Declaration of Human Rights*, Article 21; *International Covenant on Civil and Political Rights*, Article 25; *Convention on the Elimination of All Forms of Discrimination against Women*, adopted and opened for signature, ratification and accession by General Assembly resolution 34/180 of 18 December 1979, entry into force 3 September 1981, UN Doc. A/Res/34/180, Articles 7 and 14, available at ⟨http://www.un.org/documents/ga/res/34/a34res180.pdf⟩ (accessed 14 January 2008); *International Convention on the Elimination of All Forms of Racial Discrimination*, Adopted and opened for

signature and ratification by General Assembly resolution 2106 (XX) of 21 December 1965, entry into force 4 January 1969, Article 5.

49. Human Rights Committee, "The Right to Participate in Public Affairs, Voting Rights and the Right of Equal Access to Public Service (Article 25)", General Comment No. 25, UN Doc. CCPR/C/21/Rev.1/Add.7, 1996, para. 5; Committee on the Elimination of Discrimination against Women, "Article 7 (Political And Public Life) and Article 8 (International Level)", General Recommendation No. 23, 16th session, 1997, para. 35.

50. *WTO Ministerial 2001: Ministerial Declaration* takes note of the issue of participation in para. 10.

51. See United Nations General Assembly, *Report of the Secretary-General in Response to the Report of the Panel of Eminent Persons on United Nations–Civil Society Relations*, 13 September 2004, UN Doc. A/59/354, para. 18.

52. Ibid. See also P. Sutherland et al., *The Future of the WTO: Addressing Institutional Challenges in the New Millennium*, Report by the Consultative Board to the Director-General Supachai Panitchpakdi, Geneva: WTO, 2004, pp. 46–48, and United Nations General Assembly, *We the Peoples: Civil Society, the United Nations and Global Governance: Report of the Panel of Eminent Persons on United Nations–Civil Society Relations*, 11 June 2004, UN Doc. A/58/817 and Corr. 1.

53. Lamy, "Humanising Globalization".

54. The Appellate Body of the WTO has already taken note of non-WTO legal norms in different WTO disputes – for example, in interpreting "exhaustible natural resources" or in recognizing that certain species were endangered in the *Shrimp/Turtle* case.

55. Pascal Lamy, "The WTO in the Archipelago of Global Governance", speech at the Institute of International Studies, Geneva, 14 March 2006, at ⟨http://www.wto.org/english/news_e/sppl_e/sppl20_e.htm⟩ (accessed 21 May 2007).

56. United Nations Economic and Social Council, Committee on Economic, Social and Cultural Rights, Thirtieth Session, *Consideration of Reports Submitted by States Parties under Articles 16 and 17 of the Covenant. Concluding Observations of the Committee on Economic, Social and Cultural Rights: Brazil*, 26 June 2003, UN Doc. E/C.12/1/Add.87, para. 43

57. United Nations Economic and Social Council, Commission on Human Rights, Sixtieth Session, *The Right of Everyone to the Enjoyment of the Highest Attainable Standard of Physical and Mental Health: Report of the Special Rapporteur, Paul Hunt. Addendum: Mission to the World Trade Organization*, 1 March 2004, UN Doc. E/CN.4/2004/49/Add.1, para. 80

58. *Marrakesh Agreement Establishing the World Trade Organization*, Preamble.

59. Charter of the United Nations, Articles 55 and 56; *International Covenant on Economic, Social and Cultural Rights*, Article 2(1); *Universal Declaration of Human Rights*, Article 28.

60. Lamy, "Humanising Globalization"; Gary Sampson, in *The WTO and Sustainable Development* (Tokyo: United Nations University Press, 2005) elaborates on "Coherence and Sustainable Development" and how greater coherence between the WTO and Bretton Woods institutions is achieved, and presents policy proposals on a greater degree of coherence between the WTO and other international institutions that could be extended to the area of human rights.

61. UNCTAD press release, "Developing Countries Face Difficult Choices in Their Relations with Developed Countries", 5 September 2007, UNCTAD/PRESS/PR/2007/025, at ⟨http://www.unctad.org/Templates/webflyer.asp?docid=8948&intItemID=1634&lang=1⟩, (accessed 15 January 2008). See also UNCTAD, *Trade and Development Report 2007*, New York and Geneva: United Nations.

7

Pharmaceutical patents and access to medicines

Celso Amorim

Despite significant improvements in the quality of life achieved in recent decades, a considerable portion of the global population is still left to its own devices when it comes to access to health. Although medical treatment of many diseases is currently available, a large divide remains between those who can and those who cannot afford it. We cannot defeat poverty and inequality without giving people a real opportunity to take care of their health.

The existence of patents for pharmaceutical products and processes influences the extent to which access to medicines is provided. As private, market-oriented instruments whose objects relate to public health, patents on medicines create an inescapable tension between the societal interest that the largest number of people has access to pharmaceutical achievements and the private interest in holding the temporary exclusivity to market the product.

The patent system was originally predicated on a balance between the fairness of rewarding innovators and society's interest in disseminating the fruits of scientific and technological advancements. On the one hand, patents arguably work as one of the important incentives for research and development (R&D) activities, because they enable R&D investment to be recouped and reinvested in future scientific activities. On the other hand, patents are frequently the instrument of anticompetitive practices, and R&D activities are concentrated in a handful of developed countries. Medical research more often than not overlooks the health needs of the vast majority of the world's population.

The WTO and global governance: Future directions, Sampson (ed),
United Nations University Press, 2008, ISBN 978-92-808-1154-4

I believe the recent experience with multilateral rules on patent law has taught countries about the importance of patent protection but also where to draw the line. The international community has realized that there is a point where limits should be imposed on patent protection, especially when health and human life are involved.

In the early 1990s, developing countries were lured into adopting stringent patent protection as a means to usher in technological development. By and large, the promises that increased patent protection would attract greater investment in innovation, in particular medical R&D, have not materialized. Yet developing countries had already committed to high standards of patent protection in the Agreement on Trade-Related Aspects of Intellectual Property Rights (TRIPS), adopted as part of the Uruguay Round of trade negotiations. Among these commitments, the obligation to provide for patent protection of pharmaceutical products and processes meant a great departure from the preceding regime established by the Paris Convention on Industrial Property.

In the case of Brazil, aside from implementing the obligations set out in the TRIPS Agreement, some TRIPS-plus provisions were also incorporated into legislation in the belief that investment in pharmaceutical R&D would increase. More than 10 years after the adoption of the TRIPS Agreement, pharmaceutical investment in R&D in Brazil by private companies, especially multinational corporations, is still modest and Brazil is confronted with ever-increasing demands for tighter patent protection.

Thanks to developing countries' strenuous negotiating efforts, the TRIPS Agreement incorporates flexibilities that support the implementation of policies aimed at ensuring access to medicines. These issues are elaborated below.

The TRIPS framework

The signing of the TRIPS Agreement raised the discussion on intellectual property to a different level. The fact that the Agreement was adopted as a result of negotiations within the framework of a trade pact – the General Agreement on Trade and Tariffs (GATT) – signalled a new approach that was to be taken on matters related to intellectual property: the TRIPS Agreement not only increased the level of obligations of all areas of intellectual property protection, but also linked it to other items on the international trade agenda.

In fact, the Agreement was part of a wider trade-off in the Uruguay Round whereby issues of interest to developed countries were intertwined with those of interest to developing countries in order purportedly to distribute gains evenly. Despite the initial reluctance of developing countries to move intellectual property discussions from the framework of the World Intellectual Property Organization (WIPO) to the GATT/ WTO, a mix of possible gains in the negotiating package, such as the mandatory dispute settlement mechanism, along with a great deal of pressure from developed countries, finally led developing countries to accept a new international instrument on intellectual property.

The TRIPS Agreement has significantly strengthened intellectual property protection by, for example, requiring the patentability of products and processes "in all fields of technology". This provision has forced many countries to include pharmaceutical products and processes within the scope of patentable subject matter when in many cases this had not been foreseen by national legislation. Before TRIPS, countries were not obliged to provide for the patent protection of pharmaceutical products and processes.

The TRIPS Agreement contains flexibilities that ensure a certain balance between rights and obligations and allow developing countries some leeway to implement the Agreement's commitments in line with their national circumstances and legal systems. It is worth recalling also that, in implementing such commitments, countries may adopt measures necessary to promote the public interest in sectors of vital importance to their socio-economic and technological development, such as public health and nutrition. Another important safeguard enshrined in the TRIPS Agreement is the possibility to resort to compulsory licensing of patents in special circumstances, such as the failure to make use of a patent. For countries that did not recognize the patenting of pharmaceutical products and processes before TRIPS, a transitional period was established that permitted patent protection not to be incorporated into national legislation until 2005. It is relevant to note that the importance of some of these flexibilities had not been fully perceived during the negotiations. Their value became more evident over time, especially through the use of the WTO dispute settlement procedure as well as experience with the implementation of TRIPS.

Soon after the TRIPS Agreement entered into force, developed countries began to exert pressure with the purpose of challenging the legal use of the flexibilities permitted by the Agreement. In this context, I should mention the lawsuit filed in South Africa in 1998 by a group of pharmaceutical companies against the South African government, because of its decision to facilitate the acquisition of cheaper AIDS medicines. International public attention was drawn to the effects on access to medicines created by the TRIPS Agreement and the suit was eventually withdrawn in the face of a worldwide protest against the pharmaceutical companies' attitude.

A second example of the attempt to undermine the flexibilities of the Agreement was the panel requested in the WTO against a provision in the Canadian legislation that permitted pharmaceutical products to be manufactured by a generic producer within the patent term of protection, with the sole purpose of submission for marketing approval (the "Bolar" exception). In view of the importance of such a provision to ensure the quick entry into the market of the generic version of a medicine right after expiry of the patent, the panel acknowledged its compatibility with the TRIPS Agreement. Although the case evidently did not involve developing countries, its importance lies in the fact that a public health flexibility was at stake, one that was eventually upheld by the panel.

Brazil was also the subject of legal action when one aspect concerning the working of a patent in its industrial property legislation was challenged in a WTO panel requested in 2001 by the United States. Ironically, the US Patent Code contains a provision similar to the one whose examination was requested to the panel. After Brazil decided to request consultations challenging the legislation of the United States, a mutually satisfactory outcome was achieved and both dispute settlement procedures were terminated.

The fact that the WTO was increasingly meddling in issues that went beyond the sphere of trade, when millions of people were left unprotected in terms of their health needs, gave rise to a significant change in the way world public opinion perceived the WTO in general, and the relation between intellectual property and health in particular. As Ambassador in Geneva, I witnessed how public opinion began to put trade issues in perspective, especially when it came to those matters affecting access to medicines. This was due in part to the involvement of nongovernmental organizations (NGOs) such as Oxfam and Médecins sans Frontières. To a certain extent, this change signalled that the prevailing view during the Uruguay Round – that trade liberalization would bring development – had shifted to one more prone to address social concerns and development needs. Civil society, represented by the NGOs, certainly played a crucial role in this change.

All these events drew attention to the complexity and wide-ranging effects of the commitments enshrined in the TRIPS Agreement and how they might negatively affect access to medicines.

With a view to halting the trend of erosion of TRIPS flexibilities, and the probability that access to medicines be hindered, developing countries felt the need to reaffirm that public health concerns hold priority over trade issues. This move led to the Doha Declaration on TRIPS and Public Health, adopted during the WTO Ministerial Conference in Doha in 2001. Albeit with great difficulty, developing countries have managed to ensure that their interests in public health be addressed.

The Declaration recognizes that "the TRIPS Agreement does not and should not prevent members from taking measures to protect public health" and, in particular, that countries enjoy "the right to grant compulsory licences and the freedom to determine the grounds upon which such licences are granted".[1] The Doha Declaration goes beyond the mere reaffirmation of provisions inscribed in TRIPS. It acknowledges that health issues have precedence vis-à-vis patents and that countries enjoy the policy space to adopt measures aimed at ensuring access to medicines. This had fundamental consequences for negotiation of the Development Round as a whole. To date, it is one of the few results of the Round that is clearly recognizable as "development friendly".

Another relevant result of the Doha Declaration was the mandate to establish a mechanism to enable countries with insufficient or no manufacturing capacities in the pharmaceutical sector to take advantage of measures such as compulsory licences. Since many countries have no national capacity to manufacture medicines, a compulsory licence for national production would be of little avail. Discussions on the matter led in 2006 to the first amendment to the TRIPS Agreement ever adopted, whereby special conditions were stipulated to facilitate the export of medicines to countries lacking manufacturing capacities. The mechanism set out by the amendment is an important one and should bring about tangible results in the future, irrespective of the need to subject it to a reality check.

All things considered, the TRIPS Agreement seems to have established some balance, however limited, between rights and obligations relating to patents. As indicated, despite the considerable changes the Agreement engendered in the multilateral patent regime, some safeguards have been acknowledged that have proven relevant in our decade-long experience with the implementation of TRIPS provisions.

It is also worth noting that the UN Commission on Human Rights approved a resolution in 2001, on Brazil's initiative, stating that access to medication in the context of pandemics such as HIV/AIDS is a fundamental element in progressively achieving the full realization of the right to health.

Pharmaceutical patent protection in Brazil

The Brazilian constitution explicitly recognizes the primacy of human rights as one of the guiding principles of Brazil's international relations. With respect to the interplay between public health and intellectual property, it should be underscored that the constitution considers that intellectual property protection must be in accordance with the social interest and the technological development of the country.

Brazil's patent legislation has always been in line with its international obligations. Before the entry into force of the TRIPS Agreement, the issue was governed by the provisions of the Paris Convention of 1883[2] and by successive amendments thereto, which allowed countries the possibility to exclude pharmaceutical products and processes from the scope of patentable subject matter. Accordingly, pharmaceutical products remained excluded from patentability until the 1996 Industrial Property Act was adopted in Brazil.

Many changes were made in Brazilian patent legislation by that new Act, inspired mainly by the desire to promote and attract foreign direct investment in the medical field. Therefore, although the TRIPS Agreement allowed countries to postpone patent protection for pharmaceuticals until 2005, this protection had been available in Brazil since the entry into force of the Act, in 1997. Brazil has not fully used the special transitional period provided for by the TRIPS Agreement, as other developing countries have.

In addition, Brazil decided to implement a TRIPS-plus regime of "pipeline patents" that sparked retroactive-like effects to validate patent applications filed in third countries that were themselves within the public domain in Brazil. This represented a major unilateral concession on the part of Brazil to foreign pharmaceutical companies as a confidence-building measure aimed at augmenting the investment stock in medical research in and transfer of technology to the country. As a consequence, over 1,000 pipeline patent applications have been accepted in Brazil.

Despite the considerable overhaul of Brazilian patent legislation, the effects in terms of research and development of new drugs are very modest, to say the least. According to data from the Brazilian pharmaceutical industry, the trade balance in the sector shows a significant deficit: exports in 2005 totalled US$473 million whereas imports reached over US$2 billion.[3] These figures indicate that the adoption of high standards of patent protection for pharmaceutical products has served mainly as a mechanism to ensure the concentration of high-value-added pharmaceutical activities in a small number of countries. Irrespective of their "high-standard" legislation, most developing countries still need to import the medicines they need, not always at affordable prices.

This seems to be confirmed by statistics from the Organisation for Economic Co-operation and Development (OECD), which show that business expenditure on pharmaceutical R&D in the United States (36.5 per cent), the European Union (EU-15, 39 per cent) and Japan (14.8 per cent) accounted for around 90 per cent of global investment in this activity.[4] Whereas pharmaceutical R&D investment in Brazil was estimated at

US$129 million for 2006,[5] the pharmaceutical industry in the United States had invested US$51.8 billion in 2005.[6]

A good example of how the concentration of R&D activities affects the provision of medicines in developing countries is the Brazilian National AIDS Programme. As a virtually unparalleled public policy, the Brazilian legislation has since 1996 mandated the provision of universal, free-of-charge treatment for people living with HIV/AIDS in Brazil. The success achieved by this AIDS Programme is mostly due to the adoption of preventive measures that keep the evolution of the infection at manageable rates and that so far have been able to cope with the budgetary constraints on the functioning of the Programme. These measures include not only awareness-raising campaigns but also the pharmacological treatment itself. By virtue of the legal duty freely to provide AIDS medicines, the Brazilian government is one of the major individual buyers of anti-retrovirals in the world. The AIDS Programme has fortunately refuted the sombre figures projected in the early 1990s by the World Bank according to which Brazil would show a dismal record of 1.2 million people infected with AIDS by the year 2000. In contrast, the number of HIV-positive patients was 600,000 in 2000 and it has been kept at a manageable level since then.

In order to maintain a programme that is saving hundreds of thousands of lives by ensuring access to medicines for HIV-infected patients free of cost, the main challenge Brazil faces is how to absorb the costs of a growing number of imported anti-retrovirals within the context of permanent budgetary constraints. Therefore, in its dialogue with the companies that supply the Programme, the Brazilian government is constantly concerned with safeguarding the sustainability of access to medicines. It has always favoured reaching mutually satisfactory outcomes in the price negotiations with the companies that supply its AIDS Programme. In recent years, successful results were achieved in such negotiations with two US laboratories and one French one.

Yet recently Brazil was confronted with a situation in which, after a series of negotiations, no reasonable proposal on the price of an anti-retroviral drug was presented by a supplying company. The conditions tabled by the company would have endangered the sustainability of the AIDS Programme and therefore the decision was taken to grant a public, non-commercial use compulsory licence on the patents relating to this medicine. The decision represented a measure of last resort taken in compliance with the provisions of Brazil's national legislation and a remedy fully backed by the international intellectual property regime. The compulsory licence adopted did not revoke the rights of the patent-holder because the measure was circumscribed to public, non-commercial use and the company will be awarded royalties.

It is also important to stress that vigorous measures have been put in place to curb piracy in Brazil. The country's record on intellectual property enforcement has gained international recognition for the manner in which the complexity of piracy has been dealt with.

The overall assessment of patent protection for pharmaceuticals in Brazil is that the high level of protection ensured by Brazilian legislation has had limited effect in terms of promoting and attracting medical R&D, let alone improving access to medicines in the country. Nonetheless, Brazil is continuing to pursue measures aimed at streamlining the R&D environment with a view to fostering innovation that could lead to improvement in the quality of life of its population. It is in this spirit that Brazil adopted the 2004 Innovation Act, which represents an important paradigm shift in the way R&D is carried out and viewed in Brazil.

New trends in international pharmaceutical patent protection

As stated above, the protection currently provided by the TRIPS Agreement and incorporated into Brazilian legislation strikes some balance between the rights of pharmaceutical patent-holders and the public interest in having access to medicines. Nevertheless, since the entry into force of the TRIPS Agreement, developed countries have been pushing for a new international agenda on patent law in multilateral and regional settings. It is an agenda that may lead to the adoption of international rules that compromise the balance between rights and obligations contained in that Agreement and risk diminishing the public space for the implementation of policies aimed at ensuring access to medicines.

The most serious threat to access to medicines seems to emerge from free trade agreements signed on a bilateral basis between some developed countries and developing countries. A cursory glance at these agreements reveals the existence of provisions that attempt to bring patent protection beyond the standard set by TRIPS, for example by ensuring de facto extended protection to expired patents via the granting of exclusive rights over undisclosed test data. These provisions make it harder for producers of generic versions of medicines to enter the market after patent expiry and represent a serious blow to access to medicines, in particular in developing countries, since generic medicines are responsible for ensuring access to medicines at affordable prices.

At the same time, a TRIPS-plus agenda has been pushed in the WIPO since soon after the signing of TRIPS. In fact, negotiations on substantive patent law harmonization may lead to the erosion of some important TRIPS flexibilities. Although the negotiations on patent law harmonization have come to a halt in recent years, the international community should be aware of the risks such an exercise might entail in terms of access to medicines.

Fortunately, the TRIPS-plus agenda has been countered by another patent agenda seeking to preserve the safeguards and flexibilities that are important for access to medicines. The WTO's Doha Declaration is one example of this agenda. In the United Nations, the Millennium Development Goals adopted in 2000 also provide a substantial basis to support the claims of countries that have concerns about the impact that too-stringent patent protection might have on access to medicines. In 2006, the UN General Assembly adopted a Political Declaration during the Follow-up meeting on the Declaration of Commitment on HIV/ AIDS; this reaffirms the importance of the Doha Declaration on the TRIPS Agreement and Public Health.[7]

Efforts have been made to incorporate the discussion on the effects of pharmaceutical patents on public health into the agenda of the World Health Organization (WHO). As intellectual-property-related aspects of pharmaceutical patents have for long been the object of attention of the WTO and WIPO, the need was perceived to view the issue also from the perspective of public health and access to medicines. Hence the establishment, in 2006, of a Working Group within the WHO to deal with the relation of pharmaceutical patents, innovation and public health. The group is mandated to examine, *inter alia*, measures to allow countries to take full advantage of the TRIPS public health flexibilities.

Brazil has been actively engaged in pursuing an agenda for the WHO in which countries treat patents on medicines from a public health perspective and take full advantage of the flexibilities they are entitled to use. Following the convening of a group of experts on intellectual property and health, whose final work highlighted many risks in the TRIPS-plus patent negotiations,[8] an intergovernmental group has been dealing with this matter with a view to mandating the WHO to carry out measures with the purpose of improving access to medicines, especially for poor countries.

Conclusions

Patents are one of the important instruments that prompt innovation. According to common wisdom, they are the outcome of a social contract in which temporary exclusive rights are conferred upon the inventor as a reward for his achievement. In exchange, before the patent term of protection has elapsed, the information relating to the patent is disclosed to the public, who can benefit from it in order to move knowledge further. Additionally, after the expiry of the patent term of protection, the patented subject matter falls into the public domain. This is the rationale that justifies the granting of a patent.

When we consider patents on pharmaceuticals, the maintenance of this delicate balance becomes even more serious. If the balance is lost, we risk undermining important social goals such as access to medicines.

Given the enormous number of people who lack access to medicines that are available to the happy few, it is quite clear that access to health continues to be a critical problem that needs to be addressed at an international level. Experience reveals that this is a problem whose solution requires the preservation of patent flexibilities. Patent rights certainly play a significant role in bringing new medicines to the market, but they cannot limit people's access to available treatment. As stated by Brazil's President Lula, health should prevail over trade.

Although developing countries are still making strong efforts to cope with the onerous commitments they agreed to in the TRIPS Agreement, flexibilities provided therein give them important leeway to implement public health policies that help ensure sound and fair competition between pharmaceutical and generic companies, which, in turn, leads to more affordable medicines. On the other hand, the patent agenda being pushed bilaterally and multilaterally to increase patent protection represents a dangerous threat to the balance inscribed in the TRIPS Agreement as far as access to medicines is concerned. We risk aggravating the concentration of R&D activities in a couple of developed countries, ruling out R&D on diseases that affect developing countries more directly and turning generic producers into outlaws.

Although the importance of patents should be recognized, it is self-evident that the patent system alone did not respond satisfactorily to the challenge of making medicines available to those in need. Furthermore, because patents are market-driven tools, they have left unaddressed the diseases that predominantly affect developing countries, such as malaria.

Alternative means to fund research and access to medicines are now available – such as the International Drug Purchase Facility of the United Nations (UNITAID) and the International Finance Facility for Immunisation (IFFIm) – and might prove to be very effective. The international community should harness initiatives such as these because they might be able to bypass the perceived shortcomings of the patent system.

Notes

1. *Doha WTO Ministerial 2001: TRIPS. Declaration on the TRIPS Agreement and Public Health*, adopted on 14 November 2001, WT/MIN(01)/DEC/2, 20 November 2001,

paras 4 and 5(b); available at ⟨http://www.wto.org/english/thewto_e/minist_e/min01_e/mindecl_e.htm⟩ (accessed 15 January 2008).
2. Brazil is one of the founding members of the Paris Convention.
3. Federação Brasileira da Indústria Farmacêutica, *A Indústria Farmacêutica no Brasil*, Brasília, 2006, p. 7.
4. OECD, *Main Science and Technology Indicators*, 2006/2.
5. Federação Brasileira da Indústria Farmacêutica, *A Indústria Farmacêutica no Brasil*, p. 7.
6. Accenture, *The Pursuit of High Performance through Research and Development: Understanding Pharmaceutical Research and Development Cost Drivers*, 2007; available at ⟨http://www.phrma.org/files/Accenture%20R&D%20Report-2007.pdf⟩ (accessed 15 January 2008).
7. United Nations General Assembly, *Political Declaration on HIV/AIDS*, adopted 2 June 2006, UN Doc. A/RES/60/262, 15 June 2006.
8. See WHO, *Public Health, Innovation and Intellectual Property Rights: Report of the Commission on Intellectual Property Rights, Innovation and Public Health*, Geneva, 2006.

Part III

The importance of development

8

The WTO, global governance and development

Supachai Panitchpakdi

Introduction

"Trade is not an end in itself, but a means to growth and development."[1] This fundamental truth should be borne in mind when considering the role of the World Trade Organization (WTO) and multilateral trading rules in the overall web of norms and institutions underpinning globalization, liberalization and international economic cooperation for development in an interdependent world. If the multilateral trade regime is to be credible and legitimate, and to promote economic governance for development, it must reflect the trade, development and financial interests and needs of all its members, especially developing countries, allowing them to maximize the gains and minimize the costs of their participation in international trade.[2]

The WTO's central concern with growth and development is underlined in the Preamble to the Agreement Establishing the World Trade Organization. Herein the parties to the Agreement refer to objectives relating to economic growth, expansion of the production of and trade in goods and services, and sustainable development; recognize the need for positive efforts to ensure that developing countries, especially least developed countries (LDCs), secure a share in the growth in international trade commensurate with their economic development needs; indicate their desire to contribute to these objectives by entering into trade liberalization agreements; and resolve "therefore to develop an integrated, more viable and durable multilateral trading system".[3] The WTO Agreements make

The WTO and global governance: Future directions, Sampson (ed),
United Nations University Press, 2008, ISBN 978-92-808-1154-4

numerous references to concerns and principles with a bearing upon development, such as "the promotion of technological innovation and ... the transfer and dissemination of technology ... in a manner conducive to social and economic welfare".[4] The Agreements contain some 155 provisions dealing with special and differential treatment (SDT) for developing countries, including exemptions from the general disciplines, lesser reduction commitments in tariffs and agricultural subsidies, longer implementation periods, favourable procedural rules and technical assistance. As affirmed in the WTO Doha Ministerial Declaration, these provisions are "an integral part of the WTO Agreements".[5]

International trade can be a powerful engine of economic growth, development and poverty eradication, as was universally recognized for example in the United Nations Millennium Declaration, the WTO Doha Ministerial Declaration, the São Paulo Consensus of UNCTAD XI and the 2005 World Summit Outcome.[6] By attracting domestic and foreign investment, catalysing entrepreneurship and stimulating production, increased trade continues to provide many developmental benefits. By generating resources for development, trade creates jobs, raises levels of consumer welfare and national income, and increases access of the poor to essential services.

However, the fragile state of play relating to the current international trade performance and to the Doha Round of multilateral trade negotiations leaves no room for complacency. This chapter discusses areas in which the WTO and the multilateral trading system, especially through the Doha Round, can work to improve effective global economic governance for development. First I highlight major trends in international trade and development. Then I discuss some key emerging systemic issues of the trading system that influence trade governance and how these broad trade, development and governance issues might be addressed in the WTO and in the end-game of the Doha Round negotiations. In the final section I explain the role of the United Nations Conference on Trade and Development (UNCTAD) in contributing to addressing these challenges facing the multilateral trading system and in mobilizing international solidarity to move forward in this area.

International trade and development

A "second generation" of trade-driven globalization is emerging, a distinctive characteristic of which is economic multi-polarity, with the South playing a significant role. In 2006, developing countries' per capita income rose by over 5 per cent and their share in world output expanded to 23 per cent, following steady growth in the world economy since 2002 with a 5.4 per cent expansion in 2006. World merchandise exports increased by 14.8 per cent in 2006, to US$12 trillion, and developing countries increased their share to about 36.8 per cent. Global services exports grew by 9.7 per cent to US$2.7 trillion, with the developing countries' share increasing to 24.5 per cent. Some emerging economies, in particular, experienced a substantial expansion in their trade performance. Moreover, trade between developing countries expanded rapidly. In 2006, South–South trade represented 17 per cent of world merchandise exports, or over 46 per cent of developing countries' exports, out of which 82 per cent was intra-regional, while inter-regional trade increased to 18 per cent.

A key factor fuelling the recent boom of the global economy and the strong trade performance of developing countries is the rise in commodity prices for metals, minerals and oil, with an attendant increase in production, processing and trade in commodities to meet rising demand in emerging economies in particular. There are good prospects of better prices and stable demand growth for some time, thus commodity-dependent developing countries will be able to generate sufficient finance to invest in their development and poverty reduction programmes, depending upon both the international environment and their ability to undertake the necessary institutional changes.

The growth in international trade, partially led by the commodity trade boom, has been a powerful engine of development. During the period 2000–2005, export growth accounted for over 60 per cent of GDP growth for developing countries and over 40 per cent for LDCs, as compared with 30 per cent for developed countries.[7]

However, the current economic, trade and welfare improvements are subject to risks arising from such factors as the continuing build-up of global current account imbalances, the impact of higher energy prices, new protectionist reactions in developed economies in response to the rise of the South and fears of low-wage labour mobility and migration. Also, certain countries and certain segments of the population within countries are being left out of the current boom and are indeed often adversely affected by its consequences. The performance of non-oil-exporting developing countries for example, is significantly worse than that of developing countries in the aggregate. In addition, many countries that have benefited from economic growth in recent years have not managed to translate this effectively into the human development objectives embodied in the Millennium Development Goals.[8] For example, despite recent recovery, the proportion of people living in extreme poverty in sub-Saharan Africa remains very high, decreasing only from 46.8 per cent in 1990 to 41.1 per cent in 2004.[9]

Moreover, the current commodity price boom is yet to take firm root. Harnessing it for development is an urgent matter for developing countries and the international community that will entail a comprehensive agenda, such as the Global Initiative on Commodities launched at the first pre-event (in Brasilia, May 2007) of the Twelfth Ministerial Conference of UNCTAD (UNCTAD XII).[10] The commodity problematique is far from being resolved into a dynamic source of revenue, growth and development. Commodity prices have declined or remained stagnant for some agricultural commodities. The commodities sector is beset by persistent supply/demand imbalances in world commodity markets, owing (in varying degrees across commodities) partly to trade-distorting domestic support and export subsidies in certain industrialized countries. This displaces developing country exporters on world markets and depresses world prices (e.g. for cotton). Another factor has been pressures on low-income commodity-producing countries to increase export volumes, even in the face of declining world prices, so as to expand or maintain the level of foreign exchange earnings and thereby sustain debt servicing requirements and meet fiscal revenue needs. As more than 90 developing countries still derive more than 50 per cent of their export earnings from low value-added primary commodities, they would be hard hit if (as has happened in the past) the current hike in commodity prices is substantially reversed.

The question therefore arises of whether and how the international trading system and the governing institutions and disciplines could be reshaped so as to sustain the current expansion of trade and its changing geography, but also to better address the continuing spectre of worsening poverty and underdevelopment in some countries.

Systemic issues of the multilateral trading system, the WTO and the Doha Round

WTO and global economic governance issues for development must be considered in the light of emerging issues with systemic implications for the multilateral trading system. The benchmark must be the commitment of all UN member states to an open, transparent, predictable, non-discriminatory and equitable multilateral and financial trading system, as captured in the UN Millennium Declaration and further expounded in the Millennium Development Goals. A key opportunity available to realize such ambitions is the Doha Round of multilateral trade negotiations. There is thus an urgent need to bring the six-year-long Doha Round to a

successful conclusion expeditiously and to deliver on its core development agenda. The credibility and viability of the multilateral trading system, its development orientation and the WTO itself as the guardian of
the system are at stake. At the same time it must be noted that, in terms
of overall global governance, the multilateral trading system is only one
pillar. Other pillars relate to the governance of monetary and financial
cooperation. Further improvement of trade governance alone will not
suffice to enhance an enabling global environment for sustained growth
and development. Equally important is the need to strengthen the different elements of global economic governance and achieve greater coherence among these elements.

Market access and policy space vis-à-vis multilateral trade negotiations and agreements

The multilateral trade regime overseen by the WTO contributes to the
removal of trade barriers and to greater certainty and predictability in international trade rules, because it provides a framework for negotiations
of trade liberalization and for an orderly, rules-based system of international trade, with appropriate checks and balances, arbitration of inter-
state trade disputes and determination of the sanctions to be applied.
This regime has been under increasing pressure to expand the number
of areas liberalized and regulated by multilateral disciplines and to move
towards the establishment of a harmonized regulatory framework for
trade in agriculture, manufacturing and services as well as trade-related
aspects of intellectual property rights. Simultaneously, it faces the vital
challenge of making the WTO Agreements more "development-
friendly" to fulfil the promise made in the Doha Ministerial Declaration
to place the needs and interests of developing countries at the heart of
the Doha Work Programme.[11]

Eight rounds of multilateral trade negotiations under the General
Agreement on Tariffs and Trade (GATT) have promoted the lowering
of tariff barriers and the formulation of common trade disciplines to
govern multilateral trade, making trade relations more secure and predictable. At the same time, such liberalization and trade governance
have tended to favour the commercial interests of the more powerful
and well-organized countries with adept trade negotiators and financial
resources. They have moved faster in most cases in areas reflecting
the developed countries' agenda (as well as their national laws and practices), liberalizing areas of export interest to the developed countries
while providing flexibility or exemptions of one form or another in the
areas of their defensive interests such as agriculture, textiles and clothing,
contingency protection measures and rules of origin.

Areas of trade governance and liberalization of interest to developing countries saw limited progress or were eroded. Reform and liberalization of agriculture and of services, sectors of interest to developing countries, were launched and remain to be adequately accomplished. Moreover, most-favoured-nation (MFN) liberalization and opening of markets also further eroded the trade preferences available to developing countries.

Possibly more serious in terms of development impact, the ability and scope of developing countries to use national policies to pursue trade and development goals were increasingly reduced as the WTO embraced and legislated deeper "behind the border" trade regulations. These rules and commitments, which in *legal* terms are equally binding for all countries, might in *economic* terms impose more binding constraints on developing than on developed countries because of the differences in their respective structural features and levels of industrial development. They limit the possibility for developing countries to have recourse to certain development policies in areas such as subsidies, balance of payment measures, infant industry support, trade-related aspects of investment measures (TRIMS), and trade-related aspects of intellectual property rights (TRIPS). These rules make it more difficult for developing countries to create the competitive supply capacity needed to take advantage of improved export opportunities. Further, SDT provisions were transformed into "best endeavour" clauses and were assigned arbitrarily defined time-limited exemptions (most of which have expired, apart from those applicable to LDCs). For developing countries, this has implied that their policy autonomy has been reduced and their regulatory regimes have become subject to scrutiny by the multilateral trading system. This affects and reduces their regulatory autonomy, including for public policy purposes, and hence their flexibility to pursue their development objectives.

The "Single Undertaking" concept of the Uruguay Round also bound all countries to the entirety of liberalization commitments and rules as negotiated and agreed. While effectively eliminating the problem of "free riders" who benefited from trade concessions without offering reciprocal concessions, for many developing countries – which often were only inactive participants in the round owing to limited financial and human resources – there is a perception that the WTO Agreements were imposed on them through the Single Undertaking without their having been given the opportunity to participate meaningfully in their design and in understanding their potential trade and development impact.

Such feelings have been compounded by the "implementation problems" and associated adjustment costs many developing countries have faced in applying the Uruguay Round Agreements, and for which no solution could be found within the WTO system of rights and obligations despite best endeavour (and thus non-operational) clauses relating, for example, to the provision of technical assistance to meet standards relating to Sanitary and Phytosanitary measures (SPS) and Technical Barriers to Trade (TBT). Factors that have hampered them from integrating successfully into the multilateral trading system and benefiting more fully from trade liberalization include financial vulnerability, supply-capacity constraints, trade infrastructure deficits, narrow export potential, restricted access to technology, and weak information networks and distribution channels.

Against this backdrop, several key considerations for economic governance and the WTO emerge, particularly in the context of the Doha Round, which is a key opportunity to correct such imbalances. Removing existing asymmetries and enhancing the equity and development orientation of the multilateral trading system will require breakthroughs in a number of areas of the Doha negotiations. Firstly, substantially reducing and removing trade-distorting agricultural subsidies, with a particular focus on cotton, are indispensable for levelling the playing field for fair competition in agricultural trade. Another key area in this regard relates to facilitating the temporary movement of persons – through the "Movement of natural persons (Mode 4)" under the General Agreement on Trade in Services (GATS) – to supply services at all skills levels. The sheer size of the services economy enhances the potential for significant gains both direct (such as remittances) and indirect (brain gain and knowledge and skill transfer) accruing to both sending and receiving countries. It has been estimated, for example, that, if developed countries increased their quota for the entry of workers from developing countries by 3 per cent, the welfare gains could amount to US$156 billion a year (most of which would accrue to developing countries).[12] Given the increasing opportunities for labour integration and mobility in a context of demographic change, a positive outcome of the Doha negotiations on Mode 4 would thus substantially enhance the WTO's contribution to making globalization more inclusive. The provision of duty-free and quota-free treatment to all LDCs for all their products on a lasting basis, which was agreed at the Sixth WTO Ministerial Conference but which remains to be implemented fully, is a further important component.

Secondly, "development" must be explicitly mainstreamed into the multilateral trading system of rights and obligations, including by way of reinvigorating and strengthening the concept of SDT. It signifies an adequate degree of policy flexibility for economic governance that would allow developing countries (with a wide diversity of levels of development) effectively to manage their domestic economic policies in the light of national development and public policy objectives, within the multilateral framework of rights and obligations. This translates into such measures as the following:

- More operational, effective and mandatory special and differential treatment and less than full reciprocity. The SDT concept and the instruments devised for its implementation deserve substantial revision. Attention should move beyond the traditional SDT provisions of market access (such as preferences), exceptions to the rules, transition periods and technical assistance towards various "pro-development" policies such as flexibility in the use of incentives for competitiveness, support to research and technology, or financing for building supply capacity.
- Measures to preserve tariff revenue; promote domestic nascent industries and pre-empt de-industrialization; preserve long-standing trade preferences; safeguard food security, livelihood security and rural development; provide for the use of policies and measures to foster commodity sector production, diversification and competitiveness; ensure universal access to essential and infrastructural services. Such provisions would allow scope within national policies to appropriately pace and sequence market opening as well as institutional and regulatory reform and, where possible, to introduce needed flanking measures that will ensure that reform and liberalization are institutionally, economically, socially and environmentally sustainable.
- Taking into account in the negotiations and reflected in the outcomes the specific trade, financial and development situations, needs or criteria relating to developing countries, individually or collectively, that have become salient for development. These include most notably issues of interest to LDCs, small and vulnerable economies, recently acceded members, or individual countries facing special circumstances, such as preference-dependent or commodity-dependent countries.

In the current Doha Round, however, efforts to better mainstream development into the architecture of the WTO and expeditiously operationalize SDT provisions, including through addressing implementation-related issues and concerns, have had limited success despite much negotiation. The road ahead towards concluding the Doha Round must not leave behind the key development issues that were supposed to have been resolved at the beginning of the round. It must be appreciated that, unless its development ambition is fully realized, the Doha Round is unlikely to bring major improvements in the overall export opportunities of all countries, including developing countries, and improvement in trade governance. Estimates of the aggregate gains that can be expected to result from a successful conclusion of the round in terms of exports and income for developing countries are relatively modest, and the rise in total developing country exports will be distributed unequally across countries.

Thirdly, development solidarity is required from the international community for developing countries for undertaking adjustment and meeting implementation costs, building trade-related infrastructure, and supplying capacity-building for taking advantage of trade opportunities. There is emerging consensus on the close linkage between trade rules and adjustment concerns. This is evident, for example, from the modalities adopted in the Doha Round for trade facilitation wherein it is explicitly provided that developing countries can implement commitments only to the extent that financial and investment support is forthcoming from the international community. Implementation-related issues, especially those relating to SDT as noted above, need to be resolved in the Doha negotiations. Beyond the negotiations, the Aid for Trade initiative launched at the WTO Hong Kong Ministerial Conference in December 2005 is an essential complement to trade liberalization and a key aspect of better global economic governance. If it provides for additional aid for trade, it could play an important role in helping developing countries realize sustained gains from trade.

Universality of the WTO

To become effective in promoting global economic governance, the WTO must have universal membership. The universality of WTO membership is essential for the legitimacy and governance of the trading system. The accession of 29 developing countries and countries with economies in transition is thus a systemic priority. However, it is crucial for WTO members to ensure fair and equitable terms of accession commensurate with the acceding country's trade, financial and development needs and provision of increased support in all stages of the accession negotiations. This should particularly apply to LDCs. Continued and increased assistance should be provided to acceding countries to carefully assess the implications of accession and to prepare effectively for negotiations and post-accession adjustment.

Regional trade agreements and the WTO

Global economic governance and the role therein of the WTO are being tested by the abundance of regional trade agreements (RTAs) – totalling 214 as of 2006 and with the prospect of 400 agreements by 2010.[13] It is a particularly remarkable feature of international trade today that, notwithstanding the WTO, trade between RTA partners accounted for nearly 45 per cent of global merchandise trade in 2006 and, according to

UNCTAD estimates, was set to reach 50 per cent during 2007. Thus international trade is substantially and increasingly governed by agreements concluded among selected members of an RTA, in comparison with trade under MFN conditions governed by the WTO.

Given the growing number, membership and trade coverage of RTAs, their impact on the international trading system will be significant. An inward-looking approach by RTAs must be avoided as it will hamper trade with third parties and undermine the multilateral trading system. North–North RTAs have greater systemic implications given the sheer volume of trade involved among the parties. North–South RTAs are on the rise, the most comprehensive of which in terms of trade and country coverage include the proposed economic partnership agreements presently negotiated between the African, Caribbean and Pacific (ACP) Group of States and the European Union. While it is true that North–South RTAs may offer important gains in terms of market access and higher foreign direct investment, they may induce developing country members to make deeper commitments (than in the WTO) and might also limit national policy space to pursue development options, which can play an important role in the medium- and long-term growth of competitive industries.[14] The extension of multilateral and regional trade rules to behind-the-border policies could together rule out the use of the very policy measures that were instrumental in the development of today's mature economies and late industrializers.

South–South RTAs, by contrast, are often more effective vehicles of regional cooperation and integration among developing countries in support of the development of member countries. Strengthened regional cooperation among developing countries can help accelerate industrialization and structural change and ease integration into the global economy, particularly when trade liberalization is complemented by active regional cooperation in other areas (such as monetary and financial arrangements, infrastructure, knowledge-generation projects, industrial development or employment). Effective cooperation on these fronts could not only enhance developing countries' output growth and trading capacities but also strengthen their influence on global economic governance. The Global System of Trade Preferences among Developing Countries (GSTP) and its ongoing third round of negotiations, once successfully concluded, could be a significant catalyst to further strengthening, deepening and widening South–South trade.

For improved governance of the trading system in support of development, there are at least three priorities. The first is for a successful conclusion to the Doha Round so that the agreement of multilateral rights and obligations emanating from the round can serve as a bulwark and guarantee against further erosion of the multilateral system through

RTAs. The second is to provide the WTO with clear, improved and effective compliance regimes and disciplines to monitor and ensure the compatibility of RTAs with WTO principles. This is needed because the current system embodied in GATT Article XXIV provisions is largely ineffective. A positive step forward in this regard, as a result of Doha agenda negotiations, has been the provisional operationalization of the transparency mechanism for notification and review of RTAs. At the same time, in view of the development-enhancing aspects of South–South RTAs and the need for policy space by developing countries in North–South RTAs, WTO disciplines on RTAs should provide explicit and effective SDT to developing countries. The third priority is for continuous monitoring and assessment of the evolution and development impact of RTAs through intergovernmental policy dialogues to identify policies and measures needed to ensure the consistency of RTAs with the multilateral trading system in improving trade governance and promoting development.

Non-tariff barriers inhibiting market entry

Although market access conditions for all countries have improved through reductions in tariff barriers, the deployment and use of non-tariff barriers (NTBs) have increased and can prevent effective market entry even when market access is fully guaranteed. Such NTBs have involved heavy compliance costs and adversely affected developing country exports in particular, especially when the standards adopted are higher than international standards.

LDCs have been especially affected, because two-thirds of their exports go to developed countries and their major exports (such as agricultural, fish and wood products, and textiles and clothing) come under the purview of phytosanitary measures or restrictive rules of origin requirements. Other burdensome NTBs have included technical regulations and standards and customs and administrative procedures.

Environmental, health and food safety requirements in particular have become more stringent and complex – a trend set to continue given concerns about food safety, energy efficiency and climate change. Many such requirements are now imposed by the private sector, coexisting and interacting with mandatory governmental requirements. Private standards are widely believed to be outside WTO disciplines and thus pose challenges in terms of justifiability, transparency, discrimination and equivalence.

In view of the multiplying and constantly changing NTBs and their impact on exports and development prospects, efforts to address them are urgently needed. Disciplining NTBs will become a major aspect of trade governance in the years ahead. Several approaches can be taken both within the WTO, through the Doha negotiations, and beyond in other international forums. These might include the following:

- Expedite the ongoing work in the non-agricultural market access negotiations to identify NTBs and elaborate ways to remove them.
- Identify, classify and catalogue NTBs with a view to discipline them. In this regard, UNCTAD has launched a multi-agency initiative to institute a systematic approach to addressing NTBs.
- Expand the multi-agency Standards, Trade and Development Facility, lodged in the WTO. It is a valuable initiative to help developing countries build up facilities to meet international standards, and resources for the facility should be increased.
- Improve the transparency of the standard-setting process by governments and by the private sector. At the bilateral and regional levels, dialogues should be undertaken to avoid NTBs constituting major barriers to market entry.
- Regulatory cooperation (i.e. mutual recognition and harmonization or equivalence of national standards relating to technical barriers to trade, SPS and development-friendly rules of origin) could be undertaken between developing countries and their major trading partners.

Growing consumer demand for environmentally preferable products, while creating new environmental norms, may provide new competitive opportunities for those producers and countries that can produce in more environmentally friendly ways.

Competition in liberalized and globalized markets

In the context of global governance, trading rules cannot be considered in isolation from the rules applicable to enterprise behaviour and to market structures. As governmental barriers to trade have decreased, these have sometimes been replaced by firms' anti-competitive practices (such as cartels or abuses of dominance).

Globalization and technological change have contributed to the establishment of global production and distribution chains, as well as of network-based industries (such as in the computer software sector). This has been accompanied by a trend towards mergers within some sectors in the commodities area (such as in the oil and gas, food, coffee, wheat, or metals and minerals sectors), in manufacturing (such as in automobiles or some electronics and computer subsectors), and in some service sectors (e.g. telecommunications or financial services). In the mining sector, for instance, there was a dramatic rise in the number and value of mergers and acquisitions in 2005 and 2006 (compared with those recorded over the previous decade) – reaching a transaction value of around US$60 billion by the third quarter of 2006.[15] There is a danger that such trends have concentrated market power in the hands of a few global enterprises and reduced competition in the markets involved – for instance, in the agricultural export and import markets of LDCs.

To the extent that developing country imports are subject to anti-competitive practices, the importing country will be penalized by higher import prices. For example, UNCTAD estimates that developing econo-mies were overcharged between US$12.5 billion and US$25.0 billion for several products that were the subject of international cartels during the 1990–1995 period.[16] Moreover, export gains expected to arise from eased market access conditions for developing country products would be curtailed if private anti-competitive practices are in place.

Thus, a crucial aspect of global economic governance for development in the light of globalization and liberalization is the control of anti-competitive practices. Developing countries must be assisted to formu-late, implement and enforce competition policies and legislation to address such practices, particularly those with a cross-border character.

UNCTAD's contribution

The challenge for trade negotiators, policy-makers and law-makers is how to promote inclusive development and preserve the main features of the current favourable economic and trade scenario beyond a cyclical backlash. It is therefore essential that the current economic gains be used in the service of continued and sustainable trade growth and develop-ment and that new ways be found to share the gains from globalization equitably. This requires a strong effort to enhance the WTO's contribu-tion to trade growth within a broader quest for better global governance for inclusive development.

It is clear that the multilateral trading system and the WTO will retain their value beyond the outcome of the Doha process. The current WTO agreements and rules, as well as a well-functioning dispute resolution mechanism, ensure the economic relevance and importance of the WTO in a globalized world economy. The WTO is also becoming increasingly universal in its membership. Efforts and leadership need to be exercised to ensure a balanced and successful conclusion of the Doha Round that does not lead to the lowering of ambitions for the development dimen-sion. Development should be fully and effectively integrated into the core areas of market access negotiations, where most of the commercial benefits would arise, and into the requisite flexibilities to provide suffi-cient policy space to developing countries in support of their future economic and social development. It is the shared responsibility of all countries, and especially the major players, to demonstrate political will and flexibility to facilitate the conclusion of the negotiations.

There is also a need for a fundamental reassessment and renewal of the system of global governance and coherence in a manner that sufficiently reflects new realities such as the rise of the South and regionalization trends. Some issues open for debate include: what should be the objectives of governance, including what should be the optimal weighting and mix of values and objectives related to efficiency and market competition, on the one hand, and equity and development solidarity, on the other; what should be governed, and how far, or left to market outcomes; how best to achieve coherence in the governance of interrelated issues such as trade and finance and across different levels of governance (national, bilateral, regional, plurilateral or multilateral), taking into account questions of sovereignty and interdependence; what types of governance norms, institutions and mechanisms to utilize, and how to design or reform these in a manner that enables all stakeholders, including weaker players, to have their interests or viewpoints taken into account.

UNCTAD, as the focal point of the United Nations for trade and development and interrelated areas, can make a useful contribution in this regard. Through research and analytical support, technical assistance and capacity-building, and intergovernmental consensus-building on issues of interest to developing countries, UNCTAD works to facilitate the integration of developing countries into the global economy in a manner that maximizes development gains and minimizes possible economic, social and environmental costs. It supports the Doha negotiations toward realizing the development mandate and offers a platform for intergovernmental discussions and consensus-building on critical issues on the negotiating table in a non-negotiating context. UNCTAD also provides capacity-building support on trade negotiations and trade policy to help developing countries engage proactively in the Doha negotiations. It further supports countries in the process of acceding to the WTO in all stages of the accession process.

UNCTAD XII, held in Accra, Ghana, from 20 to 25 April 2008, provided the opportunity to move forward on such questions of coherence, governance and solidarity for development, by particularly focusing upon the theme of "Addressing the opportunities and challenges of globalization for development".[17]

Notes

1. See UNCTAD, *São Paulo Consensus*, UN Doc. TD/410, 25 June 2004, para. 63.
2. See UNCTAD, *Report of the Secretary-General of UNCTAD to UNCTAD XII – Globalization for Development: Opportunities and Challenges*, UN Doc. TD/413, 4 July

2007; UNCTAD, Trade and Development Board, *Globalization and Inclusive Development*, UN Doc. TD/B/54/7, 27 August 2007; and UNCTAD, Trade and Development Board, *Developments and Issues in the Post-Doha Work Programme of Particular Concern to Developing Countries*, UN Doc. TD/B/54/5, 6 August 2007.

3. *Agreement Establishing the World Trade Organization*, adopted at Marrakesh, 15 April 1994.

4. Agreement on Trade-Related Aspects of Intellectual Property Rights, Article 7.

5. Doha WTO Ministerial 2001, *Ministerial Declaration*, adopted on 14 November 2001, UN Doc. WT/MIN(01)/DEC/1, 20 November 2001, para. 44.

6. United Nations General Assembly, *United Nations Millennium Declaration*, UN Doc. A/RES/55/2, 18 September 2000; Doha WTO Ministerial 2001, *Ministerial Declaration*; UNCTAD, *São Paulo Consensus*; United Nations General Assembly, *2005 World Summit Outcome*, UN Doc. A/60/L.1, 15 September 2005.

7. See United Nations General Assembly, *International Trade and Development: Report of the Secretary-General*, UN Doc. A/62/266, 16 August 2007, para. 3.

8. "UN Millennium Development Goals", available at ⟨http://www.un.org/millenniumgoals/goals.html⟩ (accessed 18 February 2008).

9. See UNCTAD, *Report of the Secretary-General of UNCTAD to UNCTAD XII*.

10. The Global Initiative on Commodities aims to re-launch the global commodity agenda by identifying key policies and initiatives to be addressed at national and international levels by commodity-producing developing countries themselves, donor country partners, the enterprise sector, civil society and international organizations in order to address the supply capacity limitations under which commodity producers operate; ensure their effective participation in the value chain; help them diversify their commodity production and export base; and foster an international enabling environment including of solidarity with commodity-dependent developing countries in transforming commodity dependency from a problem into a source of development gains. The initiative is support by the Common Fund for Commodities, the African, Caribbean and Pacific (ACP) Group of States, UNCTAD and the United Nations Development Programme.

11. Doha WTO Ministerial 2001, *Ministerial Declaration*, para. 2.

12. See UNCTAD, Trade and Development Board, *Globalization and Inclusive Development*.

13. See UNCTAD, *Trade and Development Report 2007: Regional Cooperation for Development*, UN Doc. UNCTAD/TDR/2007, New York and Geneva: United Nations, 2007.

14. See UNCTAD, *Trade and Development Report 2006: Global partnership and national policies for development*, UN Doc. UNCTAD/TDR/2006, New York and Geneva: United Nations, 2006.

15. UNCTAD, "Cross-border Mergers and Acquisitions database", available at ⟨http://www.unctad.org/Templates/Page.asp?intItemID=3140&lang=1⟩ (accessed 18 February 2008).

16. See, for example, UNCTAD consultant report by S. J. Evenett, *Can Developing Economies Benefit from WTO Negotiations on Binding Disciplines for Hard Core Cartels?*, UN Doc. UNCTAD/DITC/CLP/2003/3), New York and Geneva: United Nations, 2003.

17. See ⟨http://www.unctadxii.org/en/The-Conference/⟩ (accessed 18 February 2008).

9

Globalization, trade and developing countries

Dani Rodrik

Introduction

In this chapter I present a forward-looking evaluation of globalization. A precondition for a successful conclusion to the struggling Doha "Development" Round, or any other future round of trade negotiations, is for all countries to secure results that it is in their interests to sign on to. Developing countries comprise more than two-thirds of the membership of the consensus-based World Trade Organization (WTO). Without a positive outcome for developing countries, there will be no conclusion to the negotiations. Although improved market access will be one important outcome, I will argue that it is critical that developing nations also secure the necessary *policy space* to implement development strategies tailored to their own needs.

Developing countries that have been successful in the past are not those that have adhered to the Washington Consensus. A turn to markets, macroeconomic stability and outward orientation have produced robust growth only when combined with unorthodox investment strategies that stimulated domestic entrepreneurship.[1] Even the simplest of policy recommendations – "liberalize your trade" – is contingent upon a large number of judgement calls about the economic and political context in which it is being implemented.[2] Meanwhile the tendency in international trade negotiations has been to reduce the scope for government action with respect to industrial policies and productive restructuring.

The WTO and global governance: Future directions, Sampson (ed),
United Nations University Press, 2008, ISBN 978-92-808-1154-4

For these reasons, maintaining the necessary policy space to pursue development strategies that reflect the human and institutional infrastructures in developing countries will be key to the success of any future trade round.

In the following, I accept as my premise that globalization, in some appropriate form, is a major engine of economic growth. But globalization's chief beneficiaries are not necessarily those with the most open economic policies. The developing countries that are the most committed to liberal trade have done poorly, relative to Asian countries with more restrictive policies as well as relative to their own performance in the past. And unease about globalization has increased significantly in some of the most important advanced countries. These developments have led to a new conventional wisdom. The new orthodoxy emphasizes that reaping the benefits of trade and financial globalization requires better domestic institutions – essentially improved safety nets in rich countries and improved governance in the poor countries.

This strategy is predicated on the presumption that insufficiently open markets continue to pose an important constraint on the world economy. Its proponents' concerns therefore centre on the question: what institutional reforms are needed at home and internationally to render further market opening politically acceptable and sustainable?

But is this presumption really valid? I shall argue here that lack of openness is (no longer) the binding constraint on the global economy. I will provide a range of evidence indicating that the obstacles faced by developing countries do not originate from inadequate access to markets abroad or to foreign capital. The gains to be reaped by further liberalization of markets are meagre for poor and rich countries alike.

This leads me to an alternative approach to globalization, one that focuses on enhancing *policy space* rather than market access. Such a strategy would focus on devising the rules of the game to better manage the interface between national regulatory and social regimes. A good argument can be made that it is lack of policy space – and not lack of market access – that is (or is likely to become soon) the real binding constraint on a prosperous global economy. This argument can be buttressed both by current evidence from rich and poor countries and by reference to historical experience with the previous wave of globalization.

But what do we mean by policy space and can we really create it without running into the slippery slope of creeping protectionism? By the end of the chapter, I hope I will have given the reader some reason to believe that an alternative conception of globalization – one that is more likely to maintain an enabling global environment than the path we are on currently – is worth thinking about and potentially workable.

The paradoxes of globalization as we know it

In 2001 the World Bank published a volume entitled *Globalization, Growth, and Poverty: Building an Inclusive World Economy*. In it, the Bank identified four countries as star globalizers – countries that had greatly increased their integration with the world economy and at the same time had grown rapidly and made progress with poverty reduction. The countries were China, India, Viet Nam and Uganda. With the possible exception of Uganda, these still constitute Exhibit A of the case for globalization's benefits. But these countries' policies can hardly be described as being of the free-trade type. In fact, by standard measures such as the height of import tariffs and prevalence of non-tariff barriers India, China and Viet Nam were among the most heavily protected countries in the early 1990s. China and Viet Nam were not even members of the WTO and therefore could engage in policies – such as trade subsidies and quantitative restrictions – that are unavailable to other countries. In each of these cases, whatever trade liberalization took place happened with a significant delay *after* the onset of economic growth.

For example, China significantly reduced its trade barriers in the mid-1990s and beyond, but this came after at least 15 years of rapid growth. It is true of course that these countries greatly increased their volumes of trade and inward foreign investment. But that is precisely the paradox. They did so despite – and in fact because of – their heterodox strategies. Simply put, countries that have benefited the most from globalization are those that did not play by the rules.

By contrast, Latin America, which tried harder than any other part of the world to live by the orthodox rules, has on the whole experienced a dismal performance since the early 1990s. This despite the boost provided by the natural bounce-back from the debt crisis of the 1980s. Here the paradox is not just that Latin America did worse than Asia; it is also that Latin America did worse than its pre-1980s' performance. Let us recall that the pre-1980s were the era of import substitution, protectionism and macroeconomic populism. That the region did better with these discredited policies than it has under open-market policies is a fact that is quite hard to digest within the conventional paradigm.

Another paradox is that globalization remains restricted in precisely those areas where further relaxation of barriers would yield the greatest economic benefits. Barriers to labour mobility in particular are inordinately higher than they are anywhere else. Even minor reductions in labour market barriers would generate gains that are vastly larger than those from the conventional areas under negotiation in the WTO and elsewhere. Many tears have been shed about the difficulties of concluding the Doha Round. Meanwhile, multilateral negotiations on reducing barriers to labour mobility are not even on the agenda. A recent proposal in the United States Senate to institute a temporary guest worker programme was eventually killed, alongside the proposed immigration reform.

The new conventional wisdom

A new conventional wisdom has been emerging during the past few years and its main contours can be described as follows:
- Globalization is indeed contributing to rising inequality, stagnant median wages and the growing sense of insecurity in the advanced economies, even if it is still unclear to what extent globalization is the dominant influence. This is in sharp contrast to the views expressed by most establishment economists during the "trade and wages" debate of two decades ago, in which blame was ascribed to skill-biased technological change rather than to globalization. But the rise of China and of global outsourcing has made those earlier views untenable.
- Trade and financial openness are unlikely to lead to economic growth on their own, and may occasionally even backfire in the absence of a wide range of complementary institutional and governance reforms. This is in sharp contrast to the views expressed in the literature on trade and growth of some 10–15 years ago, in which the assertion was that trade liberalization in particular has an unconditional and strong effect on economic growth on its own – even absent other reforms. Once again, the evidence has rendered the older views untenable.
- Therefore, globalization requires a range of institutional complements in both rich and poor countries in order to deliver its benefits in full and remain sustainable. In the advanced countries of the North, the complementary measures relate in large part to improved social safety nets and enhanced adjustment assistance. In the developing countries, the requisite institutional reforms range all the way from anti-corruption to labour market and financial market reforms. This new conventional wisdom finds expression in a multi-pronged effort to deepen globalization in its current form.

One element is the completion of the Doha "Development" Round, with its focus on agricultural liberalization. At present, the Doha process seems dead in its tracks owing to a combination of rich countries' unwillingness to offer substantial cuts in agricultural supports and market access and developing nations' reticence to offer low enough bindings on their own tariffs. Another element is the promotion of "cautious" capital account opening in developing countries, by a coalition of the International Monetary Fund (IMF) and financial interests in the developing countries themselves. A third flank is the governance agenda of the multilateral institutions, focusing on anti-corruption at the World Bank and financial regulation and supervision at the IMF. A fourth is the ongoing discussion in the United States and other advanced countries on a menu of proposals to take the "pain" out of globalization: increased progressivity in taxation, enhanced adjustment assistance, portability of health insurance, and wage insurance to cover part of the income losses resulting from dislocation. Many of these efforts are useful in their own right, of course. Essentially we can conceive of this strategy as the answer to the following question: what institutional reforms are needed at home and internationally to render further market opening politically acceptable and sustainable?

The maintained hypothesis is that the greatest bang for the global reform buck lies in pushing for *increased* openness and market access, while ensuring that the adverse consequences of openness are taken care of. In the next section I will question the validity of this view and suggest that the binding constraint on maintaining a healthy global economy lies elsewhere.

Economic growth and economic integration

Under certain conditions, economic integration can be a powerful force for economic convergence, and it can promote rapid economic growth in poorer regions. The historical experience of the United States is telling in this regard. The United States experienced economic convergence within its own national economy, but did so only after a truly common and integrated set of product, capital and labour markets was established nationally. The European Union (EU) today presents another interesting case. It is currently engaged in a process of legal, institutional political integration that is somewhat similar to the process that took the United States some two centuries to achieve. It displays the significant growing pains associated with efforts to create seamless integration. Even with all the efforts at convergence within the European Union, integration is far from complete and remains a stop–go process.

What are the implications for developing countries? The vast majority of countries do not face the realistic option of full economic integration with their rich trade partners: legal and political integration à la EU or US model is not on offer, and, even if it were, national sovereignty is perceived to be too valuable for many to give up. They need to recognize therefore that they are living in a second-best world, in which international economic integration remains incomplete. And living in a second-best world requires second-best strategies. If markets cannot solve your problems of labour surplus and capital shortage (because labour is not free to leave and capital comes only in small quantities), you need circuitous policies. You may need to postpone import liberalization in order to protect employment for a while. You may need to subsidize your tradables to achieve more rapid structural change. In fact, you may need a whole range of industrial policies in order to build technological and productive capacity at home.[3]

This line of reasoning helps us understand why some countries that sharply lowered their barriers to trade and capital flows are still waiting for the rewards, while others that have been much more cautious have done so much better. Consider, for example, the contrast between El Salvador and Viet Nam. Both countries returned to peace and political stability after a long period of civil war. Viet Nam started its reforms in the late 1980s; El Salvador's reforms came in the early 1990s. El Salvador quickly eliminated all quantitative barriers to imports, slashed tariffs, established convertibility on the capital account and dollarized its economy. It became an open economy in both the trade and financial senses of the term. It also became the recipient of large amounts of remittances from its expatriates in the United States. Viet Nam, meanwhile, followed a Chinese-style reform, based on gradual external liberalization, pragmatism and a concerted effort to diversify the economy through public encouragement and investment where needed. Viet Nam did not rush into the WTO and has only just become a member.

Looking at these policies through a conventional lens, it would be hard to see how El Salvador's policies could have been improved. Yet private investment and growth remained lacklustre in El Salvador. Meanwhile, Viet Nam achieved phenomenal success in terms of both growth and poverty reduction. These examples can be multiplied many times over. Perhaps the most notable development failure of the past 15 years is Mexico. This is a country that has free and preferential access to the US market for its exports, can send several millions of its citizens across the border as workers, receives huge volumes of direct investment and is totally plugged into US production chains, and for which the US Treasury has acted as a lender of last resort. It is hard to imagine a case where globalization gets any better. Yet, even though trade and investment flows have expanded rapidly, the results have been underwhelming, to say the least, where it matters – in economic growth, employment, poverty reduction and real wage growth.

The North American Free Trade Agreement (NAFTA), it turns out, is another instance of shallow integration. The standard response when cases such as El Salvador and Mexico are raised is to point out, in line with the new conventional wisdom I summarized previously, that these countries did not undertake the complementary reforms needed to make globalization work. What specific reforms are in question depends on who is talking and when, but the usual line is that both countries need more judicial and (in the case of Mexico especially) "structural" reform. But this is hardly a satisfactory response in light of the fact that successful countries that did not open themselves up as fully to international trade and finance had, if anything, even worse institutional preconditions.

It is difficult to argue that Viet Nam or China – two authoritarian socialist economies with extensive state ownership and widespread corruption – had the institutional prerequisites that Mexico and El Salvador lacked. This standard riposte reflects once again the habit of using first-best reasoning when circumstances demand second-best thinking. It is of course trivially true, but largely beside the point, that if Mexico and El Salvador had first-world institutions they would be as rich as the advanced countries. Successful growth strategies are based on making the best of what you have – not on wishing you had what you lack.

Given successive rounds of multilateral trade liberalization and the extensive unilateral liberalization that developing countries have already undertaken, the shallow integration model has already run into strong diminishing returns. This is one reason Doha has stalled. There are simply not enough gains to get people excited. The result is that further global trade liberalization is hardly a force for economic convergence.

The need for policy space

Strong diminishing returns may have set in on the prevailing liberalization agenda, but the losses from a real retreat from today's globalization would be catastrophic. A collapse towards protectionism and bilateralism *à la* 1930s can never be ruled out – it has happened before – and would be bad news for poor and rich nations alike. Therefore, we ought to place a high premium on policies that make such a retreat less likely – *even if* they run contrary (in the short run at least) to a market-opening agenda. In order to maintain globalization in some version of its current form, we need to make a good diagnosis of the problems that confront it. These problems do not arise from liberalization not having gone far enough – unless, that is, we are ready to envisage deep integration as a feasible option.

They originate instead from something that is closer to the opposite, namely the clash between the liberalization agenda and the weakness of the institutional underpinnings that make open markets functional and politically sustainable. Once we put the problem this way, the challenge becomes not "how do we liberalize further" but "how do we create the

policy space for nations to handle the problems that openness creates". The policy space in question would allow:
- rich nations to address issues of social insurance and concerns about the labour, environmental and health consequences of trade; and
- poor nations to position themselves better for globalization through economic restructuring and diversification.

In this section I will make a case for such policy space by showing that globalization's constraints do bite where legitimate economic and social ends are concerned in these two sets of countries – and will bite even more if we continue to pursue a market-opening agenda. I begin with the advanced countries.

Consider the following dilemmas that our present arrangements pose:
- **Labour standards:** Domestic labour laws protect workers from being displaced through "unfair" employment practices at home, such as the hiring of child labour or the employment of workers under hazardous conditions. WTO rules do not make room for similar protections when displacement occurs through trade. But why should trade be allowed to contravene an established domestic norm?[4]
- **Environmental, health and safety standards:** If European citizens want to apply a higher precautionary standard than other countries, should trade rules prevent them from doing so because this has an effect on trade?
- **Regulatory "takings":** Why should foreign firms in the United States receive greater protection from policy changes that affect their profits than domestic firms (as NAFTA and bilateral investment treaties may require)?
- **Redistributive provision of social insurance:** If taxation of capital and skilled professionals has historically helped fund social insurance programmes and generate equity, should their international mobility be allowed to undercut this "social compact"?
- **Currency policies and "unfair trade":** WTO rules recognize the concept of "unfair trade" in cases of explicit subsidization of exports and allow importing countries to respond through countervailing duties. Should countries that undervalue their currencies, and hence subsidize their exports in non-fiscal ways, be allowed to get away with it?
- **Trade versus technological change:** Domestically, research and development and technological progress are highly regulated (see, for example, the stem cell controversies). Why should trade, which is analogous to technological change, be left unregulated as a rule?

These are all difficult questions, without clear-cut answers. They will likely increase in salience with the explosive growth in services offshoring. The appropriate locus for their discussion and resolution is most likely the national polity, given the wide variety of standards and norms that prevail across the globe. And, if it is, countries will need the policy space in which they can act on their deliberations. Sometimes dilemmas of the kinds illustrated above are dismissed by economists as instances of self-interested pleading on the part of lobbies adversely affected by imports. But there is a variety of evidence that points to more than narrow self-interest being at work in rich countries.

For example, when Alan Krueger examined where the support for a Congressional bill aimed against child labour was coming from,[5] he found that the support was strongest not in districts with a concentration of low-skilled labour but in well-to-do districts with preponderantly skilled labour. People were against child labour not because it meant more competition but because they felt it was wrong. Similarly, recent research documents significant willingness-to-pay by US consumers for improved labour standards in developing nations.[6] And, in our analysis of attitudes to trade in a large cross-section of countries, Anna Maria Mayda and I found that individuals with negative attitudes towards trade and globalization were motivated only partly by labour market concerns and monetary issues.[7] Values and norms mattered too. In particular, we found that individuals with high levels of attachment to their neighbourhood and immediate community were more likely to have negative views on trade.

When economists talk about comparative advantage and gains from trade, they typically ignore whether trade opportunities involve exchanges that most people would consider unacceptable if they took place at home. It is immaterial whether the gains from trade are created, say, by a company shutting down its factory at home and setting up a new one abroad using child labour. But the archetypal person on the street reacts differently to trade-induced changes in distribution than to technology-induced changes (i.e. to technological progress). Both increase the size of the economic pie, while often causing large income transfers. But a redistribution that takes place because home firms are undercut by competitors who employ deplorable labour practices, use production methods that are harmful to the environment or enjoy government support is procedurally different from one that takes place because an innovator has come up with a better product through hard work or ingenuity. Trade and technological progress can have very different implications for procedural fairness. This is a point that most people instinctively grasp but economists often miss.

So globalization is a key issue in the advanced countries not just because it affects some people financially; it is controversial because it raises difficult questions about whether its outcomes are "right" or "fair". That is why addressing the globalization backlash purely through compensation and income transfers is likely to fall short. Globalization also needs new rules that are more consistent with prevailing conceptions of procedural fairness.

Turning to developing countries, where do the constraints bite? As I have already argued, successful development strategies often require second-best and therefore unorthodox policies. Current thinking has moved considerably away from a standardized Washington Consensus-style approach to a diagnostic strategy that focuses on each country's own binding constraints.

Differences in the nature of these constraints shape the appropriate economic strategies. For example, investment-constrained economies respond differently to capital inflows than do savings-constrained economies, and need to have a different policy stance vis-à-vis the capital account. Moreover, as the example of East Asian countries shows, desirable policy reforms often take heterodox forms because they try to make the best of pre-existing institutional capabilities and configurations. In China, non-standard policies such as dual-track pricing, township-and-village enterprises (TVEs) and special economic zones (SEZs) provided effective price incentives, some security of property rights and outward orientation, but did so in highly unusual ways. Successful heterodoxy is a reflection of the need to overcome second-best complications. Trying to apply uniform best-practice rules or harmonizing policy differences away does not serve the needs of developing and transitional economies. The need to maintain "space" for developmental policies is now recognized even by ardent supporters of free trade.[8]

The key areas where globalization's constraints bite for developing nations include the trade regime. For example, the WTO agreements on subsidies, trade-related investment measures and intellectual property rights entail a considerable narrowing of space for the conduct of "industrial policies" and preclude the adoption of strategies that worked well for growth superstars such as South Korea, Taiwan and China. Although determined governments can find ways around these restrictions, developed countries are demanding further tightening of restrictions in these and other areas. One reason developing countries such as India and Brazil have lost interest in Doha is that they are being pushed to lower their own tariff bindings significantly. Bilateral and regional trade agreements, especially those negotiated with the United States, often contain clauses on intellectual property rights and investment that go significantly beyond what is in the WTO.

Once again, these are areas where there are difficult trade-offs to consider. The point is not that there is an obvious right or wrong in each of these areas. My argument is that we need to recognize these frictions and focus our efforts on devising rules that can manage them, instead of proceeding with a market-opening agenda as if they were of little consequence.

Enhancing policy space

The question of whether policy space can be enhanced without doing more damage than good lies at the heart of the matter. The conventional view is that there is a slippery slope whereby even the slightest relaxation of international disciplines spawns further demands for protection – to the point that the system of free trade and finance eventually unravels. This view sometimes finds expression in the "bicycle theory" of international trade, which states that maintaining an open economic regime requires constant efforts to liberalize. In this line of reasoning, policy space is a recipe for mischief. National polities cannot be trusted to work out reasonable internal compromises among competing domestic political forces with varying views on globalization. They need to have a straitjacket imposed from the outside.

Yet there is little evidence that favours the slippery slope hypothesis in our contemporary political economy. The political balance in most countries, including developing countries, has tilted sharply in recent decades towards groups that favour links with the global economy. Notable departures from free trade, such as the Multifibre Arrangement and the voluntary export restrictions of the 1980s, did not spawn increasing protection. In fact, they were removed once they had served their primary purpose of increasing the comfort level of rich country citizens. There are also some provisions of the GATT/WTO regime that are highly open to protectionist abuse, but these have had only limited impact on trade. The anti-dumping (AD) provisions of trade law (the Anti-Dumping Agreement) are particularly notable in this respect, because they provide easy access to protection in circumstances where the economic case for protection is weak or non-existent.

Although countries do make use of AD, it is hard to argue that the world economy has greatly suffered as a result. In retrospect, what is striking is not that AD is used but that it is used so infrequently in light of the flexibility of the rules and that it has caused so little damage. Indeed, we could argue that AD has made the trade regime more resilient by providing a safety valve for protectionist pressures. These pressures might have had more damaging consequences otherwise, if they had had to make their way outside international rules rather than within them. That is precisely the principle behind the "policy space" approach: negotiated opt-outs, with internationally agreed procedural constraints, are better than disorganized, unilateral opt-outs. It is better for the rules to recognize that sometimes countries need their own manoeuvring room than to leave such a possibility outside the scope of the rules.

An even better illustration of this principle at work is the WTO's Agreement on Safeguards (Article XIX). The Safeguards Agreement allows countries to re-impose tariffs or quantitative restrictions in certain circumstances and for a limited time period, when they experience a surge in imports of specific products and when such imports are determined to "cause or threaten to cause serious injury" to an industry at home. Aside from being temporary, the restrictions in question must be applied on a most-favoured-nation (MFN) basis, i.e. non-selectively, and affected exporters must receive compensation. Whereas the principle behind Safeguards is clear, the restrictions currently placed on it make less sense. Why limit the application of the clause to instances of injury to producers, for example, or require that it be triggered only by a surge in imports? It could be that the "injury" in question is a conflict with deeply held values at home (say in the case of the import of goods made using child labour or imposing environmental costs). And such injury could well be triggered by new information rather than by an import surge per se: consumers at home may discover unsavoury facts about labour practices abroad or there may be new scientific information about safety or harm to the environment. In these instances, applying safeguard action on an MFN basis will not necessarily make sense (child labour may be a problem in Viet Nam but not in Mauritius).

Requiring compensation may not be appropriate either. In effect, the Agreement vests too many of the residual rights in trade interests and too few in the broader interests at stake. We can envisage broadening the Safeguards Agreement to a wider set of circumstances in which the legitimacy of trade is at issue, subject to institutional and procedural prerequisites that minimize the risk of protectionist capture (in particular by empowering interests that would be harmed by trade restrictions). We can also imagine a similar "development box" provision to facilitate the pursuit of developmental policies that might conflict with existing rules (e.g. subsidies). In effect, rich and poor nations would then be in the game of exchanging policy space instead of market access. Negotiators would be tasked not with maximizing the flow of trade and investment but with designing rules that managed the interface among different regulatory environments.

I discuss an approach I have previously outlined to provide a concrete illustration of how these principles could be put into practice.[9] A broadened safeguard agreement – call it an agreement on social and developmental safeguards – would enable countries to opt out from their international obligations in specified circumstances. The process for obtaining such an exemption would be a domestic one, as in the case currently of the Anti-dumping and Safeguards Agreements, but it would be subject to multilateral review to ensure procedural requirements are met. Any interested party would be allowed to seek an exemption or opt-out. One requirement would be for the plaintiff to make a compelling case that the international economic transactions in question are in conflict with a widely shared social or developmental norm at home. For example, a non-governmental organization might try to make the case that imported goods using child labour violate domestic views about what is an acceptable economic transaction. Or a consumer body might want to ban imports of certain goods from a country because of safety concerns.

A second procedural requirement would be to ensure that producer and other groups that have a stake in the international exchanges in question are able to present their case as well. In particular, the investigative body would be required to seek the views of those groups that would be adversely affected by the exemption. This is to ensure that anti-protection views are given full hearing. One of the most important problems with Anti-dumping and Safeguards proceedings at present is the lack of such a requirement. This prevents the full story from coming out and creates a protectionist bias in the system. When there is a truly widely held norm or principle at stake, it would be difficult for the pro-trade groups to mount an effective defence. It is hard to imagine that a business lobby representing importers would defend free trade when it involves, for example, slave labour or exceptionally harsh and exploitative working conditions. But in other instances there are real trade-offs to consider, and a well-designed set of procedures – whether administrative or judicial – would help bring out the relevant considerations on all sides.

Finally, the ultimate decision would rest with a semi-autonomous government body that would consider the testimony given to it and determine (a) whether there is sufficiently broad support for the exercise of some kind of opt-out; and (b) what the best remedies are in cases where the answer to (a) is affirmative. The decision would be subject to periodic review to ensure that protection does not become permanent. It would also be open to review in a multilateral setting (say the WTO) to ensure that multilaterally agreed procedural requirements have been met.

A main advantage of the proposed scheme is that it forces deliberation and debate at the national level on the nature of the international economy, the economic gains it generates and the circumstances in which domestic practices and needs come into conflict with it. This differs from the traditional, technocratic manner in which international governance is approached. It may seem overly messy and idealistic, but it has the virtue of bringing democracy to bear on these questions, and as such it has the potential to enhance the legitimacy of the global economy.

Concluding remarks

My argument is that deep economic integration – a truly "flat" world economy, to use Thomas Friedman's evocative phrase – is rendered infeasible by the fragmented nature of political sovereignty around the globe. Jurisdictional discontinuities impose transaction costs on international trade and finance that remain in place even when conventional barriers in the form of import duties and financial restrictions are removed.

Of course, deep integration could still be attainable if national sovereigns were to restrict their actions to those that are fully compatible with its requirements, as with the classical gold standard era of the nineteenth century. This is a model that rules out democracy, since it requires that political authorities be unresponsive to national policy imperatives and domestic needs. It is not a coincidence that the gold standard collapsed following the expansion of mass franchise and the spread of democracy in the major industrial powers. Facing the conflicting needs of employment creation and of parity with gold, a democratic Britain made its choice in favour of the former and went off gold in 1931.

We could also theoretically combine democracy with deep integration by eroding national sovereignty and carrying democratic politics to the global level. This corresponds to the US or EU model writ large, on a global scale. Needless to say, this outcome does not seem practical anytime soon.

The only alternative we have left, therefore, is the Bretton Woods compromise, named after the golden era of 1950–1973 in which the world economy achieved unprecedented economic growth under a shallow model of economic integration. I have argued in this chapter that the main challenge at the moment is to recreate this compromise by designing a global architecture that is sensitive to the needs of countries – rich and poor alike – for policy space. This requires us to move away from a market-opening mindset and to recognize that what nations need to do in order to maintain social peace and spur economic development in our second-best global economy often conflicts with the free movement of goods, services and capital. The only way to save globalization is not to push it too hard.

Acknowledgements

This chapter is based on and draws heavily from Dani Rodrik, "How to Save Globalization from Its Cheerleaders", *Journal of International Trade and Development*, Vol. 1, No. 2, 2007.

Notes

1. See, for example, Dani Rodrik, "Growth Strategies", NBER Working Paper No. 10050, National Bureau of Economic Research, Cambridge, MA, 2003, p. 12.
2. The outward-oriented strategies of the newly industrializing East Asian countries have been cited on occasion as examples of economic success through liberalization. For a critique, see Rodrik, "Growth Strategies".
3. See Dani Rodrik, "Industrial Policies for the Twenty-First Century", John F. Kennedy School of Government, Harvard University, Cambridge, MA, September 2004.
4. Rodrik, "Growth Strategies", p. 12.
5. Alan B. Krueger, "Observations on International Labor Standards and Trade", NBER Working Paper No. W5632, National Bureau of Economic Research, Cambridge, MA, June 1996.
6. Michael J. Hiscox and Nicholas F. B. Smyth, "Is There Consumer Demand for Improved Labor Standards? Evidence from Field Experiments in Social Labeling", Department of Government, Harvard University, Cambridge, MA, 2006.
7. Anna Maria Mayda and Dani Rodrik, "Why Are Some Individuals (and Countries) More Protectionist Than Others?", *European Economic Review*, August 2005.
8. Martin Wolf, "The Growth of Nations", *Financial Times*, 21 July 2007.
9. Dani Rodrik, "The Global Governance of Trade – As If Development Really Mattered", UNDP Background Paper, United Nations Development Programme, New York, 2001.

10

Aid for Trade and global governance: An ITC perspective

Patricia R. Francis

Introduction

In January 1995, the World Trade Organization (WTO) became the successor to GATT (the General Agreement on Tariffs and Trade). The new organization was the result of years of negotiations under the auspices of the Uruguay Round; new rules were created for the conduct of international trade and existing ones revised. As a consequence, the WTO emerged as a far more powerful organization than its predecessor.

The outcome of this is that the WTO has undoubtedly secured a place for itself on centre stage as a principal agent of global governance. The rules that govern international trade now reach deep into the regulatory structures of all WTO countries dealing with intellectual property rights, financial services, fishing subsidies, domestic support schemes for agriculture and numerous other equally sensitive subjects.

But in very practical terms, apart from its far-reaching rules, it is well known that the working hypothesis of the WTO is that trade liberalization and improved market access for exports are important contributors to economic growth. This too ensures a major role for the WTO in global governance, determining the distribution of world wealth and the structure of world trade and production through trade liberalization. Thus, although the WTO has the capacity to deliver on this front, the critical question in practical terms is whether or not countries can indeed take advantage of new market openings negotiated in the WTO. What are

The WTO and global governance: Future directions, Sampson (ed),
United Nations University Press, 2008, ISBN 978-92-808-1154-4

their needs in entering new markets and are the resources and skills at hand available for them to succeed?

Nowhere is the answer to this question more relevant than in the case of developing countries. Indeed, the consensus grows that trade can be a very important tool to reduce poverty. The world's 50 poorest countries have only a 0.7 per cent share in world trade. Increasing their share by just 1 per cent could help lift 130 million people out of poverty. Opening up trade is a first and necessary step, and one that many leaders in both developed and developing countries are taking of their own accord. But although this is a necessary condition, it is not a sufficient one. If businesses in these countries do not have the skills and capacity to produce goods and services that are competitive in world markets, trade liberalizing market openings alone will not help.

My personal view is that, of the many challenges facing a successful conclusion of the Doha Development Agenda, the most important area of policy concern for developing countries is securing the promised trade expansion through negotiated liberalization that will promote their economic development. In other words, for the WTO to succeed in its role as an agent of global government, the end result of the Doha Agenda – and any other trade liberalizing initiatives in past rounds and elsewhere – depends on the capacity of developing countries to expand their exports as a result. At the moment, too many developing countries simply do not have this capacity. In simple terms, developing countries need to be able to produce goods and services competitively and to maintain and further develop the international competitiveness of companies, including related issues of quality, SPS requirements, supply assurance and access to retail supply chains. As a consequence, the trade agenda is concerned no longer only with border issues such as tariff reduction but also with behind-the-border issues.

I could not agree more with WTO Director-General Pascal Lamy when, in his report to the high-level session of the Global Aid for Trade Review on 20 November 2007, he remarked: "We agree that making trade possible is only half of the challenge – making trade happen is the other half, which requires infrastructure, technology, know-how, financing and competitive exporters. And we agree that the future of an open world economy – and the multilateral trade system that underpins it – depends on all countries sharing in the benefits more equitably."[1]

The role of the International Trade Centre

The totality of the work of the International Trade Centre (ITC) serves as Aid for Trade. It has been this way since the creation of ITC by the

General Agreement on Trade and Tariff (GATT) in 1964. Indeed, GATT created ITC as "a technical cooperation organization whose mission is to support developing and transition economies, and particularly their business sectors, in their efforts to realize their full potential for developing exports and improving import operations with the ultimate goal of achieving sustainable development. ITC deals specifically with the operational aspects of trade promotion and export development." The ITC is a joint venture between the United Nations, through the United Nations Conference on Trade and Development (UNCTAD) and the WTO.

The term "Aid for Trade" means different things to different people and needs to be properly defined to facilitate the dialogue among so many players. Let me say up front that, in my view, there are four broad areas that constitute Aid for Trade. The first relates to policy. The policies needed to support trade development must have national, inter-country and global dimensions. National strategies for trade, including export strategies, as part of national development plans are required. along with cross-border facilitation, global facilitation and rule-making. The second area is infrastructure: physical infrastructures must be created and improved to support trade, including assistance to industrial facilities. Third, there must be compensation for tariff reduction, preference erosion, the cost of conforming to standards and the like. Finally, trade-related technical assistance is critical as a pragmatic means to help with supply-side constraints and to build a human and institutional capacity to trade.

If the focus of assistance up to now has been on trade policy negotiations, then the Aid for Trade initiative is changing the balance. The link between exploiting market access through creating the right conditions for business is no less a key influence on the process of global governance than the negotiation of market access itself. If the governance role of multilateral trade liberalization is to be effective and equitable, it is essential to look at the adjustment costs for industries that will lose jobs, to build infrastructure that will help businesses and to give businesses the skills to compete.

Aid for Trade must address issues that are close to business, because the ultimate actor in trade is business. The business sector is also a driver for development. A dynamic private sector is the key to mobilizing savings and investment, creating meaningful jobs, meeting consumer demand, generating exports and contributing to government tax revenues.

More and more, developing countries understand that, to help their firms grow, they must move beyond connecting producers with buyers, beyond supplying coffee beans to the agro industry or handicrafts to tourists. They need to add value to their exports, look for new market opportunities and define the marketing and branding strategies that will help them create new, profitable businesses that produce sustainable jobs.

Getting the framework right

Trade can promote economic development only if we get the framework right. Expanded trade is not the automatic result of negotiations that improve opportunities to access potential markets. The right framework is one that is broad enough to address legitimate concerns about globalization and to help developing countries build the skills they need to be competitive in world markets. Accessing markets requires these skills and other resources for private enterprises to take advantage of the market opportunities. This calls for an ability to listen to business leaders, trade institutions and policy-makers and to design a range of innovative approaches that are targeted to the needs at hand.

Despite many years of progressive liberalization in GATT and WTO rounds, some developing countries are worse off than they were 30 years ago. The framework has not been right. Part of the problem derives from existing trade and international financing conditions, which, for the weakest partners, require urgent amelioration. The gap to be filled in all of this is the need to develop more effective marketing (and sourcing) strategies on the basis of an assessment of trade opportunities at the regional and global levels. The global economic reality has changed substantially and rapidly during recent years, fuelled by a globalization of the production process – a process that has been driven by trade liberalization and technological progress. This process has divided up the value chains and has led to an integration of trade and to a geographical fragmentation of production. Global production and distribution networks are key drivers of this process. Some of the most notable characteristics of the new globalized production patterns are production fragmentation and production-sharing. The effects on local production have also revealed that a country cannot be competitive in manufacturing if it is not competitive in producer services such as transport, telecommunications and other network infrastructure services. The increased importance of services in the globalized economy has led to improved prospects for the export of personal as well as producer/industrial services (such as tourism and health services and business processes outsourcing). It has also meant that a local presence of competitive producer services is a precondition for the internationally competitive production of goods and services.

Aid for Trade in practice

Of the four key areas of Aid for Trade that I mentioned above, the ITC's contribution is mainly in the key area of *trade-related technical assistance*, but it also includes *policy* considerations. Within its mandate, ITC applies a holistic and integrated approach to its technical assistance through building trade capacity at three levels:

- at the level of the policy- or strategy-makers, the objective is to enable them to integrate business priorities in national trade policies and negotiations and to achieve effective collaboration between public and private sectors;
- at the trade support institution level, the objective is that export service delivery channels are enabled; and,
- at the small and medium-sized enterprise (SME) level, ITC's aim is that potentially competitive new enterprises are created and that the competitiveness of existing enterprises is strengthened.

ITC's fundamental role is to support developing and transition countries to understand destination markets and create opportunities for export success. In order to achieve this, ITC needs to build the capacities of its clients to understand what their existing and potential consumers want and to demonstrate compliance with consumer requirements.

From our past experiences in this work we have learned a great deal. For example, technical assistance works best when it is requested by recipients themselves and influenced in its design them. Further, all kinds of needs assessment and development of strategies in the trade field can be done in a meaningful and sustainable way only through inclusive and consultative processes, in which the private sector must play a vital part. Additionally, the business community – the true exporters – needs pragmatic technical assistance. It has little time for theories about optimal conditions for trade.

A further lesson relates to technical assistance aimed at building export skills. Developing countries are demanding more and more help in enhancing competitiveness designing and implementing export strategies and acquiring basic knowledge about WTO rules, all of which are ITC specialties. Better business and government dialogue is essential in achieving results with trade-related technical assistance, and a greater awareness of the potential of business advocacy helps the business sector of the developing world to maintain its faith in the multilateral trading system.

But what is critical in delivering aid for trade is getting the priorities right. This is not easy, as I will explain, as both process and substance are involved.

Before I develop this further, let me first note that talking about the "delivery" of Aid for Trade is the wrong terminology! The existing system of implementation of Aid for Trade needs to be improved by ensuring stronger ownership and deeper commitment by the beneficiary countries ... not its delivery. A major effort is required in local capacity-building for enhancing the national arrangements and constituencies in charge of trade development and, consequently, the capacity of the developing countries to absorb trade-related technical assistance more effectively.

As with all development needs assessments, trade demands practical and participatory processes involving representatives of commercial business (large and small), government agencies and civil society. These processes need to be designed in such a way as to attract and engage all the participants, with appropriate external co-facilitation where desired. These processes need to help people illustrate (literally) the linkages in a country between trade, services, communities and prosperity to gain new insights into opportunities and to deconstruct prejudices.[2]

It is imperative also to draw on previously available needs assessments, prepared under such initiatives as the Diagnostic Trade Integration Studies of the Integrated Framework for Trade-Related Technical Assistance to Least Developed Countries. Similarly, the World Bank, the International Monetary Fund, the WTO, UNCTAD, ITC and other UN and non-UN bodies have undertaken surveys of needs in developing countries, and these should be used as reference and built upon. In the optimal scenario, the expertise of different agencies should be combined. However, the involvement of external partners in needs assessment at the national level should be light and essentially facilitatory. These processes cannot be driven from the outside.

In terms of substance, there are many critical and interrelated facets. Building human and institutional capacity to ensure good local governance is essential, as is the development of the right sort of infrastructure and logistical requirements. This means responding to new demands in relation to the labour market and related requirements for an adequate and constantly evolving skills base. Only this will ensure an appropriate environment for enterprise development. Product development is vital, along with the assurance of export markets and products of a quality that will enable them to penetrate those markets. Product standards, rapid innovation, adaptability and speedy responses are some of the key factors companies all over the world have to consider in order to improve, or at least maintain, their competitiveness and survive in the increased global competition.

Countries are different with different needs

Bearing all this in mind, a further complication is ensuring that the right assistance gets to the right groups. Developing countries, although they face many common challenges, are not a homogeneous group. Even within regions there are varying levels of development and the requirements are different.

A region with which I am very familiar, the Caribbean, which is often perceived as prosperous, with economies based on tourism, services and selected agricultural products, is in fact much more diverse. Gross domestic product (GDP) per capita ranges widely from US$16,728 in the Bahamas to US$420 in Haiti. Correspondingly, the nature of the economies and their needs varies greatly. Cuba, the Dominican Republic and Jamaica have relatively diversified economies; other countries have narrow productive structures with high transaction costs. Tourism is a significant source of income for most countries. Most also face structural challenges following trade liberalization. For example, industries such as sugar, bananas and textiles have suffered preference erosion. What is important is for each government to identify the infrastructure and regulatory requirements for facilitating the transformation of its national economy to emphasize new sectors, with inputs from the private sector.

However, the experience has been that the design of coherent trade development strategies has taken a back seat to negotiating trade pacts. Reaping the benefits of free trade agreements must involve coordinated policies to identify ways to diversify exports and target markets. For small countries, regional cooperation, such as through the Caribbean Community, is key to exploiting synergies in the design of successful strategies. In this process, small economies cannot afford to develop on their own the range of trade support institutions needed for economic transformation. Regional agencies are required to achieve economies of scale in areas such as trade finance, standards and quality assurance, logistics and marketing. National agencies should still be created or strengthened, however, to provide crucial services requiring local knowledge.

Once the broad lines of trade development are in place, efforts should shift to designing sector-specific trade strategies in knowledge-based and education services and creative industries – sectors with a competitive advantage. In this context, many countries are re-profiling workers and exploring opportunities in service sectors. But transformation is slow. Firms are mostly small and unable to meet demand, even when they offer goods or services that are internationally competitive. The lack of local opportunities and a global demand for skilled workers has resulted in a brain drain. Some firms have succeeded in foreign markets by focusing on unique or specialized products or services. We need to research these cases and help others, especially small and medium-sized enterprises, draw lessons from these examples. International cooperation can also provide targeted assistance in strategic business planning and improving business practices.

Monitoring and evaluating Aid for Trade

Although monitoring systems for trade-related technical assistance (TRTA) have recently been put in place, particularly via the Doha Development Agenda database, it is still difficult to obtain a clear picture of the world of TRTA. This difficulty is largely owing to the manner in which descriptors have been identified and the way in which different agencies report to the database. Monitoring mechanisms clearly need to be strengthened and this can be done, first and foremost, by building monitoring capacities within relevant institutions at country level. ITC has already made a proposal for funding under the enhanced Integrated Framework for building capacities at country level to manage, coordinate and monitor TRTA effectively.

On the subject of evaluation, it can be said that all TRTA providers grapple with the issue of evaluating the results and impact of TRTA on trade development in particular and on development in general. Although it is evident that trade can potentially have a strong impact on development, it has not always been possible to demonstrate the linkages in a clear and convincing manner.

So how can this be done? In terms of implementing results-based management, the most important challenge is the upgrading of the partnership with organizations that design and distribute ITC's technical assistance to enterprises to include monitoring and evaluation functions. My personal conviction is that trade-related technical assistance will have a positive impact if, and only if, the monitoring and evaluation functions are fully owned by the beneficiaries. This is why ITC's activities must also aim at mobilizing local resources.

Needs and responses: The role of the private sector

The "business sector" ranges from the smallest micro-enterprise to the largest multinational. When providing assistance to business, countries need to decide on target groups, so they can tailor programmes to their needs. Trade-related technical assistance has focused on export-ready small and medium-sized firms, as the group most likely to achieve results. More recently there have also been successful programmes targeting very poor communities. These communities are becoming part of international trade through, for example, community-based tourism or organic herb and spice production.

Most of the benefits of development derive directly from the activities of the private sector, including the largest and the very smallest enterprises and local non-profit agencies. Governments are involved to a steadily diminishing degree. They often remain responsible for major public infrastructure programmes, but even here their roles are being reduced.

It is therefore logical that the private sector should have an equal, if not even a pre-eminent, role in determining the development needs of a country, in order to emphasize the importance – in the broadest sense – of the "business environment" and to help to define the facilitatory and regulatory roles of the public sector, which would include opportunities for public–private partnerships. For reasons of sustainability too, private interests must be invoked since it is they that principally drive the development process, with or without donor support.

ITC's primary aim has always been to assist enterprises. It does this in three ways. First, it helps to make the policy environment more friendly for export business by strengthening policy-makers' ability to integrate business into the global economy. Second, it strengthens the institutions that provide services to exporters. Third, it helps small export enterprises to become more competitive.

ITC can support policy-makers with tools to analyse and define negotiating positions. Various databases and methodologies help negotiators assess scenarios and better incorporate the views of the private sector, and allow policy-makers to focus on the actions needed to improve the trade framework. ITC can offer its expertise in the development of national export strategies, based on consultation between the private and public sectors. This process can identify obstacles to successful export promotion and propose efficient mechanisms to address them. ITC also offers specific technical assistance to address macro-level challenge facing enterprises. It designs activities and coordinates with leading trade support institutions (TSIs), in particular with export promotion organizations, to deliver services to small and medium-sized firms. This approach focuses on strengthening the capacity of TSIs to deliver to the largest possible audience.[3] Further efforts will help coordinate the work of individual TSIs, so their assistance can be more targeted to their clients and their inputs to national strategies can be better considered.

It is critical to improve the competitiveness of SMEs and to support efforts to add value to products and services for export. Useful activities in this area include promoting the development of national and regional enterprise networks and improving capacities in business planning and management. Programmes can also be devised to encourage the clustering of SMEs to enhance their participation in global supply chains and to link large national firms with local SMEs to increase the transfer of know-how and value addition. As part of the emphasis on marketing it is necessary to strengthen the capacity of enterprises to understand and anticipate demand and to promote the development of new products and target new export markets. This should be done in collaboration with higher-level educational institutions to develop programmes to increase export skills and increase awareness of export opportunities among service providers as well as to develop training and mentoring for women producers and exporters. This involves researching and disseminating lessons from successful exporters and linking producers in poor communities to export markets and helping them to organize themselves. The ITC is active in all these areas.

Conclusion

To achieve the goals elaborated above, it is important to reinforce the principles of aid effectiveness and coherence as agreed in the Paris Declaration on Aid Effectiveness in March 2005[4] and as embodied in individual IMF/World Bank Poverty Reduction Strategies. Aid for Trade should reinforce the principles of the Paris Declaration and Poverty Reduction Strategies (PRS) by strengthening national development strategies. It should facilitate the integration of trade considerations into national development planning, including PRS, and it should do so through appropriate participatory processes.

Further, it is essential that Aid for Trade be fully consistent with the development needs of partner countries. ITC and other specialized trade agencies can help to articulate needs in the trade sector. At the same time, Aid for Trade programmes should be fully accountable, not just upwards to donor agencies but more especially downwards to the true beneficiaries. As in other areas, Aid for Trade programmes supported by donors should be fully coordinated and coherent. ITC strongly advocates the practice already begun of having one donor play a leading and coordinating role in helping to harmonize assistance with individual UN agencies. Where Aid for Trade is multilateral in intent, it should fully respect the principles of multilateralism rather than being "steered" by individual donors to favour their own bilateral proclivities.

Aid for Trade should respect the best principles of capacity development, including the facilitation of change, rather than the grafting on of external solutions, and compatibility with local standards, norms and capacities. Aid for Trade should be targeted at all relevant sectors, including in non-governmental and private sector interests. The fuller participation in aid programmes of many different interests is the best insurance against corruption and misuse of resources.

So what can we conclude from all this. First it is important to identify the outstanding gaps that need to be filled for an Aid for Trade initiative to be successful. This involves improving outreach to SME associations and the business community outside capital cities while transferring quality standards requirements and implementing responses in enterprises. There is a need to directly support groups of businesses to develop market offers, and support the integration of indigenous SMEs in exporters' value chains as a lever for their growth. There must be the development of trade financing and investment support for SMEs and practical upgrading of trade facilitation processes and an involvement of other interests – particularly non-governmental organizations – in trade programmes, such as in the context of fair trade.

The ITC's mission is to enable small business export success in developing countries by providing, with partners, trade development solutions to the private sector, trade support institutions and policy-makers. Its three main strategic objectives correspond exactly to three of the five items on the Aid for Trade agenda: trade policy and regulations; trade development; and building productive capacity. ITC can also provide a forum for public–private dialogue on trade policy. It will continue efforts to translate the content of trade agreements into business language to help the private sector understand the opportunities they afford.

As a final word, I firmly believe that, in fulfilling the ambitions of the Aid for Trade agenda, sight must not be lost of the need for greater coherence in global policy-making. This item figured prominently in discussions in the Consultative Group of 18 in the GATT in the 1980s, and led to a result in the Uruguay Round. In Marrakesh in April 1994, ministers stressed that growing interactions between national economic policies meant that cooperation in each aspect of policy-making was necessary for progress in other areas. In particular, if the origins of difficulties are outside the trade field, they cannot be redressed through trade measures alone. What was called for were consistent and mutually supportive policies at the global level.[5] Only by adopting this course of action can the WTO satisfactorily fulfil its role as a true agent of global governance.

Notes

1. See ⟨http://www.wto.org/english/news_e/sppl_e/sppl81_e.htm⟩ (accessed 30 January 2008).
2. As it happens, ITC has considerable experience in this area and has developed a range of methodologies that are fully adaptable to local circumstances.
3. The services that SMEs need include: access to relevant trade information, statistics, trends and analysis; assistance to improve quality standards, packaging and product design; addressing lack of knowledge about information and communications technology solutions for business; development of sector strategies and integration in global supply chains; building export-oriented managerial and marketing skills; fostering the creation of coalitions of export service providers; identifying and meeting the needs of women exporters developing export programmes for poor communities.
4. *Paris Declaration on Aid Effectiveness: Ownership, Harmonisation, Alignment, Results and Mutual Accountability*, High-Level Forum, Paris, 2 March 2005, available at ⟨http://www1.worldbank.org/harmonization/Paris/FINALPARISDECLARATION.pdf⟩ (accessed 19 February 2008).
5. For the origins and outcome of the discussion on coherence in the Uruguay Round, see Gary P. Sampson, "Greater Coherence in Global Economic Policy Making: A WTO Perspective", in A. Krueger, ed., *The World Trade Organization: Its Effectiveness as an Institution*, Chicago: University of Chicago Press.

11

The future of the WTO and free trade

Ted Turner

I like free trade. I've been a free trader ever since I debated the topic back in my high school days. I pushed for free trade when I travelled around the world, from country to country, urging them all to open up their media markets to CNN.

If we don't have free trade that gives every country a chance, we're never going to build a better, more prosperous world. That's why I think the World Trade Organization (WTO) is one of the best ideas humanity's ever had. We human beings have been trading with each other ever since we started coveting our neighbours' goods. But we didn't create the General Agreement on Tariffs and Trade (GATT), and then the WTO, until we'd been around about a million years. It was about time!

Today we're in a crisis – for the WTO, for trade and for the future of the world. In 2001, the Doha Round of trade negotiations began with a commitment to increase the benefits of free trade for developing countries. It was a great plan: developed countries would reduce their agricultural subsidies and tariffs, and developing countries would lower their tariffs to allow imports, improve their industries and attract investment. The Doha Round is struggling to survive and a lot of commentators share the view expressed in the *Financial Times* that, if Doha fails, it could be "the last effort of its kind".[1]

"The last effort of its kind"? If we give up and quit on this round, we may not ever try anything like it again? No more global trade agreements? The role of the WTO in global affairs would change for ever. No longer would it be fulfilling its role in global governance by liberalizing

The WTO and global governance: Future directions, Sampson (ed),
United Nations University Press, 2008, ISBN 978-92-808-1154-4

trade and bringing common sense to the structure of world trade and production. That would be a disaster! Poor countries are going to remain poor countries until they can find a way to sell goods to rich countries. But to do that, poor countries have to improve their industries, open their markets, draw new investment and get trade rules that are fair. That's what this Doha trade round is all about – to give developing countries a better chance to trade on a more equal footing with rich countries.

If we give up on global trade agreements, we know what will happen. The big countries will go off and do separate bilateral and regional deals with their favoured trading partners – and guess who will be left out? The very people the WTO was created to include: the developing countries. They will be left to bargain alone against the giants of international trade. We've already seen where that leads – it leads right back to where we are today: to a world where billions of people live in poverty.

It's one of the biggest moral failures in the history of humanity that we allow half the world's people to live in intolerable conditions, on less than US$2 a day. A billion live on less than a *single* dollar a day. A billion have no safe drinking water.

Poverty is cruelty. And poverty persists in part because the trade that has created so much prosperity for the world's wealthy countries is by-passing poor countries: 54 countries are poorer than they were 15 years ago. And poverty doesn't just mean doing without food and shelter. For many of these countries, poverty means conflict. When there isn't enough to go around, people start to fight: of the 20 poorest nations on Earth, 16 have suffered civil war over the past two decades.

If we can't reverse it, poverty is going to crack the world apart. If the world ends up hopelessly split between rich and poor, we will never get the global cooperation we need to deal with the problems the whole world has to solve together.

We're running through the assets of this planet that took billions of years to create. The fossil fuels that we're burning are turning up the world's temperature. We're overpopulating the earth. We're using up our oil, coal, gas, forests, rivers and arable land, with no sign of slowing down and little idea what to do when these resources are gone.

We're spending more than US$1 trillion a year on military budgets – *more than 50 times what we spend on the United Nations*, our best tool for peace. Nearly 20 years after the end of the Cold War, the United States and Russia still have thousands of nuclear missiles on hair-trigger alert, ready to launch within minutes. We have hundreds of tons of poorly secured highly enriched uranium – and groups of terrorists desperate to get the materials, build them into bombs and use them.

We can't solve any of these problems unless all countries work together. We created the United Nations to give ourselves this option. We created the WTO for the same reason. But we're not making the most of what we have.

The world's leaders in both business and government aren't looking at the future; they're looking just a few days ahead – at the next day's news stories, the next quarter's earnings, the next poll, the next election. We need to learn the difference between long-term value and short-term gain.

I got rich making long-term decisions. My competitors were all thinking about the TV ratings from last night, and I was thinking about where I was going to be 10 years later. The first TV station I ever thought of buying was losing US$70,000 a month. My board told me that if I bought it I would bring the whole company down. I bought it. Then I bought another one – worse than the first – and my accountant quit in protest. Eight years later, I sold that station and started CNN. If I had had to show a profit every quarter, I never would have built anything.

I think young people ought to be raising hell with older people about this. Most of the people making big decisions in the world today are over 50. Many are over 60. They're taking out loans, and they're not even going to be around when the debt comes due. They have to lift up their eyes and see the future: either we change our ways or we're going to destroy ourselves. We have to go for the long-term gains we'll get from building a world in which every country participates. The more countries participate in the global economy, the more they will have an incentive to build a better world – and the more they will have the *capacity* to build a better world.

That's why developing countries *have* to have a bigger stake in global commerce. Expanding trade is the best way to get it. And the Doha Round is the only instrument the world has to make that happen. We have to revive these talks and get an agreement.

Global trade agreements have made a huge economic impact since the GATT. They've cut tariffs; they've increased trade, they boosted economic growth. For the United States, the European Union and Japan it has meant hundreds of billions of dollars a year.

But the benefits of global trade are uneven. And now WTO governments need to rewrite the rules so they help poor countries the way they've helped rich countries. That's the purpose of the Doha Round.

If we give up on Doha, we're giving up on fighting poverty.

If we *don't* give up – if we revive Doha and get a strong agreement – we can immediately increase incomes in the poorest countries of the world. There is nothing the international community could do that would strike a quicker, wider blow against global poverty. No handout, no programme, nothing. If you're against poverty, you're for a strong Doha agreement. If you're against a strong Doha agreement, you're probably not too worried about global poverty.

Now, we're not going to get this deal until the trade negotiators get an agreement that every country can live with.

Sure, global agreements are a pain. The more people who have to agree, the longer it takes to get an agreement. But there's an African proverb that says: "If you want to go fast, go *alone*; if you want to go far, go *together*." I believe that human beings are not going to go much further *unless* we go together.

Right now, we're not going *anywhere*. The Doha Round is stalled because rich countries and poor countries are split on the question of agricultural subsidies. In the United States, government farm supports are 16 per cent of total farmer income; in Europe, they're 32 per cent; in Japan, they're 56 per cent. In West Africa, cotton farmers on some of the richest land in the world make only US$400 a year, because developed countries drive prices down with their cotton subsidies. In fact, developed countries spend about US$2 billion every week on trade-distorting tariffs and subsidies.

Why do we even *have* subsidies? That's simple. We have subsidies because we have overproduction. Supply is greater than demand, and prices fall below what farmers need to make a living. Farmers in rich countries are supported with subsidies. Farmers in poor countries just suffer.

The fight over subsidies is not, for developed countries, just an economic matter. At the time the GATT was adopted, agriculture represented half the trade in the world. In 2007, it was 8 per cent. When the entire system of global trade agreements is put in jeopardy by a disagreement over 8 per cent of all trade, you can suspect the reason is more politics than economics.

If developed countries negotiated away agricultural subsidies, politicians in rich countries would have to tell farmers in rich countries to find something else to do. At which point, the farmers would tell the politicians that *they* have to find something else to do. That's why these talks are stalled – politicians in the developed countries do not want their farmers to fire them in the next elections.

If agriculture were always going to be the same, then the question of subsidies would be a problem without a solution. But agriculture is changing. Farmers have always grown crops for food and fibre. Today, farmers can grow crops for food, *fuel* and fibre. This changes the future. There is now a huge and growing unmet demand for farm products such as corn, sugar beets and sugar cane that can be converted into ethanol. There's a huge market for palm, soy and rapeseed oil that can be made into biodiesel. Agriculture is changing from an industry that faces limited demand to an industry that faces *un*limited demand; from an industry facing low prices, to one facing high prices.

And that's what's so ironic about this trade impasse. The Doha negotiations have come to the point of collapse over agriculture. But the negotiators are deadlocked over agriculture the way it was in 1999 or 2000, not the way it is today, and certainly not the way it might be in the coming years.

There is a huge and growing opportunity in agriculture for farmers who can grow fuel. Since 2000, global ethanol production has more than doubled. Biodiesel production is up nearly fourfold. And demand is so great that, even though Brazil produces almost a quarter of the world's sugar, it still struggles to meet its own domestic demand for ethanol. A sugar grower in Brazil recently told the *Washington Post*: "We would never be able to supply the United States with any substantial quantity of ethanol."[2] If the world's largest biofuels producer doesn't have enough to supply the world's largest energy consumer, this is what I would call a business opportunity.

It is also an opportunity to do something for the earth and humanity. Biofuels are far better for the planet than fossil fuels. They can dramatically cut greenhouse gas emissions. And biofuels are renewable. You don't have to spend billions of dollars finding new oil fields in the ocean. You don't have to put new wells in national parks. And you don't have to negotiate with countries oceans away. You have to plough and plant seeds. We've been doing that for a long time.

This is a natural stage in human evolution. Humans have gone from hunter-gatherers to farmers to produce their *food*. Now we're going from hunter-gatherers to farmers to produce our *fuel*. It's much better than coal and oil. When you want more fuel, you don't have to wait for the next geological age. You just have to wait for the next growing season.

The emergence of biofuels creates something like a merger between two industries: agriculture and energy. When agriculture (an industry with slow-growing demand) is merging with energy (an industry with fast-growing demand), it's a very bullish change for agriculture. This gives developed countries a chance to end the stalemate over agricultural subsidies by giving farmers incentives to grow biofuels and by giving consumers incentives to use them. If, over the next 10 years, WTO nations adopt policies that support an entirely new market in bio-based energy – and if production expands to provide 15–20 per cent of global fuel needs, the market in global agriculture could double or triple in value.

In this market of unmet demand, the effect of government incentives for biofuel production will be totally different from that of normal crop subsidies. The unmet demand for transportation fuel is almost endless. This means that support for domestic production will not displace foreign competitors or reduce the prices paid abroad. Farmers will be getting their income from the market, not from the government. Even farmers who *don't* switch to energy crops will do better financially because other farmers will have switched their land to biofuel production. This will reduce supply and raise prices for conventional crops.

If farmers see that agriculture is changing, and see how that change can benefit them, the politics of subsidies changes. This change is crucial to reviving the Doha Round and getting an agreement. But first the trade negotiators have to *explain* this change to their constituents, who are the only ones who can give negotiators permission to go back to the table and make a deal.

A growing market in biofuels could reduce or even end the need for agricultural subsidies in the developed world. But this isn't just an opportunity for rich countries. Developing countries can benefit even more. Poor countries that are dependent on oil imports have been hit especially hard by rising energy costs. Ten years ago, when the world agreed on debt relief for the poorest countries in sub-Saharan Africa, the price of oil was US$22 a barrel. Between 2003 and 2007, the price has more than tripled. Higher oil prices now cost Ethiopia five times as much as it is gaining from debt relief. Other developing countries that import oil face the same burdens. Gambia spends six times as much money on fuel as it does on health. Sierra Leone spends twice the money on fuel as it does on all efforts at poverty reduction combined. Now the price of oil is more than US$120 a barrel.

And the energy problems of developing nations go beyond higher budget expenditures. Most of sub-Saharan Africa has no electricity at all. In many countries, women gather and carry loads of firewood for miles each day. By investing in biofuels, developing countries can start solving these problems. They can produce their own domestic transportation fuels, cut their energy costs, improve public health, create new jobs in the rural economy and, ultimately, build export markets. By converting part of their output from food and fibre to fuel, they will be entering a market with higher prices and rising demand and are more likely to attract the kind of foreign investment that can modernize their agricultural practices – and increase their food production as well.

This is a critical point, because there should be no food vs. fuel debate. We can absolutely produce both – all that's required is investment. Economic growth, especially in rural areas, will help developing countries meet their food needs more easily. The answer to hunger is not more food; it is less poverty.

Some enterprising companies and towns are already showing the way on biofuels:

- 40 per cent of the energy for the Bolivian town of Riberalta comes from a plant powered by Brazil nut shells;
- an Indonesian company switched from firewood to a biomass gasifier to dry its cocoa beans. The gasifier is fuelled by palm nut shells – a waste product from the business's other operations;
- women's groups in the African nation of Mali are using biofuels (processed from locally grown crops) to run diesel generators to power grinding mills;
- biofuels are also catching on in the Caribbean, where Jamaica is investing millions of dollars in ethanol;
- the Dominican Republic is looking at jatropha – a bush that grows well in hostile conditions and has great potential as an energy crop;
- Malaysia, India and Thailand are preparing to make big commercial investments in palm oil.

On a grand scale, of course, nobody beats the example of Brazil. Its biofuels have saved the country some US$50 billion in oil imports and created 1 million new jobs.

The opportunities will get better as the technology improves – and that's happening right now. In the future, we should be able to produce new fuels such as cellulosic ethanol, a biofuel that could be extracted from virtually anything grown anywhere. We will be able to genetically alter biofuel crops to make their conversion more efficient. And we will be able to create better bio-refineries, increasing the returns on biofuel investment.

The global demand for biofuels is huge and rising. That's why I'm confident that, in the near future, farmers' incomes will be assured, not by subsidies and tariffs, but by market forces. And that's why it makes so little sense to throw away the Doha Round over agricultural subsidies and tariffs. We shouldn't give up a great future to cling to the past.

Developed countries have the greatest responsibility for putting this Round back together. Over the past 60 years, free trade has added trillions to their economies. Now they have a chance to grow even richer while giving developing countries new opportunities through trade to help boost their economies and reduce poverty. In the process they will also be creating new markets for themselves.

Developed countries should agree to phase out tariffs and reduce their subsidies for food and fibre crops and replace them with support for biofuels. The right approach would allow a transition period, say 5–10 years, to phase in the changes. As soon as the deal is struck, farmers – instead of pressuring politicians to preserve subsidies – will be pressuring politicians to quickly make the changes necessary to convert farms profitably to biofuel production.

Developing countries also need to do their part for the Doha Round by reducing tariffs and opening their markets – especially to each other. If they keep their markets closed to protect domestic industries, it might help for a time. But if they don't open their borders and allow imports, their products will never compete, they're never going to draw much investment, and they won't capture the much bigger market beyond their borders.

Officials in all countries should not only explore options for production of biofuels, but also adopt policies that promote consumer demand and build an infrastructure that can guarantee supply. These steps will help meet energy needs, reduce greenhouse gas emissions, revive the agriculture industry and help eliminate the conflict over subsidies that is stalling crucial advances in world trade.

The WTO negotiators need to remember the point of what they're doing: they're just trying to reach out and bring in more people – into trade, into prosperity, into opportunity, into community. Those first TV stations of mine that I mentioned earlier. I bought them cheap, because they had an inferior signal – a UHF signal – that couldn't reach very many homes at all. How was I going to make any money if I couldn't even get my TV signal to all my neighbours? Well, we had an idea. Instead of broadcasting from a tower 1,000 feet high that sends a signal out 50 miles, we started broadcasting from an antenna 24,000 miles out in space that covered a quarter of the surface of the earth with one signal. The satellite. I guess that's when I really started to think globally; when I realized I had to bring more people in, or I really wasn't going to make it. The world is facing the same situation today. We've got to bring everyone in, and stop leaving so many people out.

*   *   *

The economist Eric Beinhocker says that the "critical advantage" that humans had over Neanderthals was trade. We had trade; Neanderthals didn't. We're still here; they're extinct. What's the lesson? Trade is good. Trade helped save us.

We need trade to save us again.

The key is right here in the hands of the trade negotiators. Right now they don't have permission to negotiate cuts in agricultural subsidies. But their constituents will never support a deal if they know *only* what they'd be losing and don't understand what they'd be gaining. If the WTO wants to change public policy, it has to change public opinion. It has to explain to people that adding energy crops will create economic opportunities. It will create stronger markets for food crops. It will help boost incomes in the poorest countries in the world. And it is crucial for the environment.

We're polluting our planet, and we've got to do something about it. We're not going to stop using energy, so we've got to start using a different *kind* of energy. This is our chance to make a big push – and do something that will save the earth for our grandchildren.

Convincing people is a big job, but it has to be done. If we give up on trade, we're giving up on ending poverty. We can't give up because the role of the WTO in bringing sense to the structure of world production and trade would change forever. To keep this vital role for the WTO in global governance we've got to keep fighting.

At the gym where I used to box when I was a teenager, there was a sign on the wall that said: "Fight one more round." You could look at that sign at the start of the fight; you could look at it at the end. But the message was always the same: fight one more round. No matter how bloody and exhausted you are, fight one more round – because if you're always willing to fight one more round, you're never beaten.

Acknowledgements

A version of this chapter was presented at the World Trade Public Forum, WTO on 25 September 2006. Please see ⟨www.unfoundation. org/bioenergy/PDF?Ted_Turner_Speech_WTO_Public_Forum.pdf⟩ (accessed 6 August 2008) for more details.

Notes

1. Alan Beattie, "Last Round? Intransigence on trade calls into question the multilateral approach", Financial Times, 16 November 2005, available at ⟨http://www.ft.com/cms/s/ 0/bd1a9db8-5645-11da-b04f-00000e25118c.html?nclick_check=1⟩ (accessed 11 August 2008).
2. Monte Reel, "Brazil's Road to Energy Independence", Washington Post, 20 August 2006, available at ⟨http://www.washingtonpost.com/wp-dyn/content/article/2006/08/19/ AR2006081900842_pf.html⟩ (accessed 11 August 2008).

Part IV

Dispute settlement and governance

12

Some thoughts on the WTO dispute settlement procedure

Mitsuo Matsushita

This chapter is not intended to be an elaborate scholarly analysis of the WTO dispute settlement procedure. It is basically an essay in which I wish to state some thoughts on the workings of the WTO dispute settlement system. I served as a member of the WTO Appellate Body in the period 1995–2000 and more recently acted as a panellist in a case in which environmental issues were involved. The following views are partly based on my experience as a member of the Appellate Body and a panellist and partly based on my research as an academic. However, they in no way reflect the views of the Appellate Body or panels and are purely personal in nature.

Accomplishment of the WTO dispute settlement procedure

It is fair to say that the WTO has successfully established a rule-oriented international trading order in which "rules" rather than economic and political powers play the central role. The General Agreement on Tariffs and Trade (GATT) 1947 consisted of some legal instruments, and the rule of law played a role in maintaining international trade order to a certain extent. However, rules under the GATT 1947 were less elaborate and detailed compared with those under the World Trade Organization (WTO), and the dispute settlement procedure under the GATT 1947 was less powerful in enforcing the rules as compared with the dispute settlement procedure under the WTO. In contrast, the WTO dispute settlement

The WTO and global governance: Future directions, Sampson (ed),
United Nations University Press, 2008, ISBN 978-92-808-1154-4

system is designed to operate more efficiently and forcefully. It is equipped with a two-stage procedure: panels and the Appellate Body. Panels are engaged in fact-finding and also determining the consistency of the measures in question with the rules of WTO agreements. Parties dissatisfied with the findings of panels can appeal to the Appellate Body for a review of panels' findings. The Appellate Body reviews the legal findings of panels and upholds, modifies or reverses them. Reports of panels and the Appellate Body are adopted by the Dispute Settlement Body (DSB) by negative consensus, whereby reports are adopted unless opposed by unanimity. This guarantees an automatic adoption of panels and appellate reports.

Since the establishment of the WTO and DSB in 1995, about 400 dispute cases were petitioned to the WTO dispute settlement procedure and approximately 80 decisions were made by panels and the Appellate Body. This figure is impressive when one compares it with the figure under the old GATT dispute settlement system, in which about 300 cases were filed during 1947–1994, a period of nearly 50 years. There are cases in which the WTO faced difficulty in implementing the recommendations of the DSB based on panel and appellate reports. However, among the total number of dispute cases before the WTO, in only a handful of cases was there such difficulty. It shows that the WTO dispute settlement system has gained the confidence of members.

In the WTO dispute settlement procedure, what counts is the legitimacy of the legal claims of the parties rather than their economic and political powers. Even a small country or a developing country that is at a disadvantage in trade negotiations compared with developed countries with more resources can prevail over its more powerful opponents as long as its legal claims and arguments are right. This contributes to the establishment of a rule-oriented international trading order.

There are several examples of small country members prevailing over large and powerful members in dispute settlement. One such example is the US *Underwear* case[1] in which the United States imposed quantitative restrictions on imports of underwear from Costa Rica. Costa Rica brought a claim against the United States in the newly established WTO dispute settlement procedure and argued that the US measures were contrary to the provisions of the Agreement on Textiles and Clothing (now defunct). The panel and the Appellate Body accepted Costa Rica's claims and arguments and recommended that the United States lift the import restrictions.

A more recent example is the *US–Gambling* case[2] in which Antigua-Barbuda, a country with a population of about 70,000, took the United States to WTO dispute settlement because the United States had violated its commitment to liberalize trade in recreational services by prohibiting the cross-border supply of gambling (Internet gambling). One of the important subjects of dispute was the extent to which the United States had made concessions with regard to recreational services. The United States stated in its concession that it would liberalize recreational services "except for sporting". Although there was a difference of views between the panel and the Appellate Body, both decided that the United States had made a full concession to liberalize recreational services and its prohibition of Internet gambling was contrary to this concession and, therefore, violated the General Agreement on Trade in Services (GATS). There were some other issues, including whether US measures would be justified by the exception incorporated in the GATS regarding public order and morals. In the end, the Appellate Body decided that, although the US measures fell within the exception, they were still a violation of the GATS since the United States allowed interstate provision of gambling services while prohibiting their international provision, and this amounted to discrimination contrary to the national treatment principle. Thereupon, the United States was requested to make its measures conform to the WTO norms.

The above two cases are good examples that even a small country can prevail over a large country as long as it can present persuasive and legitimate legal claims. In the above cases, if there had not been the WTO dispute settlement system, Costa Rica and Antigua-Barbuda would have had to negotiate with the United States individually in order to resolve the trade disputes. Owing to the differences in political and economic power between the United States and those countries, negotiations would have been difficult and it is doubtful whether Costa Rica and Antigua-Barbuda would have accomplished as much as they did by using the WTO dispute settlement system.

One of the serious trade problems before the coming into being of the WTO was that of voluntary export restraints (VER). A VER is a trade deal between an exporting country and an importing country whereby the former "voluntarily" refrains from exporting to the latter. Often de facto pressures were used to coerce an exporting country to make this concession. VERs were often used in the 1980s and 1990s between Japan on the one hand and the United States and the European Communities (EC) on the other, as shown in such examples as the Steel VER, the Auto VER, the Textile VER and the Semiconductor VER. VERs were carried out without any specific rules under the GATT 1947 and was probably contrary to its norms. However, it was exercised anyway.

A VER distorts the natural flow of trade and causes a misallocation of economic resources. Also, one VER precipitates another VER. For example, when Japan and the United States agreed on a VER whereby Japan imposed export restraints on the total quantity of steel exports to the United States, Japanese exporters concentrated on exporting specialty steel, which was high-valued and its price per unit was higher than that of regular steel products so that exporters would gain more profit by exporting within the limit set by the VER on the total quantity of exports. This, however, led to a surge of exports of specialty steel into the United States, injuring specialty steel producers in the United States. Therefore, US producers of specialty steel put pressure on the United States government to negotiate a VER with Japan on the export of specialty steel from Japan to the United States. This led to another VER agreement between the United States and Japan.

The WTO successfully dealt with issues of VERs. Article 11:1(b) of the Safeguard Agreement explicitly prohibits VERs. Not only does it prohibit VERs exercised by governments but also it prohibits governments from encouraging private enterprises to engage in practices having a similar effect to VERs. Since the establishment of the WTO, VERs have disappeared from international trade.

The WTO dispute settlement procedure has successfully dealt with issues surrounding unilateral measures imposed by the United States on its trade partners in the 1980s and 1990s. During this period, the United States often invoked Section 301 of the Trade Act and imposed unilateral sanctions on its trade partners for engaging in "unfair practices". A good example is the US–Japanese semiconductor dispute in which the United States imposed trade sanctions on Japanese products. In this case, the American Semiconductor Institute claimed that the Japanese government exerted control over the semiconductor industry in Japan, consolidating the major companies into an oligopoly to which subsidies were provided. According to this claim, the international competitiveness of the Japanese semiconductor industry was artificially increased, Japanese products were dumped into the US market and the Japanese semiconductor market was closed to foreign products.

In response to the claim by the American Semiconductor Institute, the United States government invoked the Anti-dumping Act and required Japanese chip producers to enter into suspension agreements with the US Department of Commerce whereby the Japanese producers maintained a certain price-level in the US market. In addition, the US government invoked Section 301 of the Trade Act and required the Japanese government to invoke laws to maintain a certain level of export prices of Japanese chips to be exported to third-country markets so that they would not flow into the US market via third-country markets. The US government also requested the Japanese government take measures so that the market share of foreign chips in Japan would rise to 20 per cent or above. Both governments decided to resolve the dispute through negotiations and the US–Japan Semiconductor Agreement was signed in 1986, whereby Japanese chip producers entered into suspension agreements with the US Department of Commerce and the Japanese government exercised control over the prices of chips to be exported to third-country markets and promised to do its best to improve the market share of foreign chips in Japan.

However, the US government decided to impose trade sanctions by way of high tariffs on certain products exported from Japan to the United States because Japanese chips were being exported to third-country markets at lower prices than those that had been stipulated and the market share of foreign chips in Japan had not reached the desired level. A second Semiconductor Agreement resolved the issue and, thereafter, a third Semiconductor Agreement, which lasted until the establishment of the WTO in 1995.

This is just one example of unilateral trade sanctions imposed by the US government on the basis of Section 301. Unilateral trade sanctions were a problem in international trade because, in invoking such sanctions, the US government was acting as a challenger or prosecutor and, at the same time, as judge or arbiter, and objectivity was somewhat lacking.

In the Uruguay Round of trade negotiations, the European Communities, Japan, Korea and others that had been affected by Section 301 of the US Trade Act worked together and succeeded in incorporating Article 23 of the Dispute Settlement Understanding (DSU), which states that WTO members must resort to the WTO dispute settlement procedure to resolve all trade disputes arising from WTO agreements. Under this provision, all WTO members must have recourse to the WTO dispute settlement procedure to resolve any dispute arising from the interpretation and application of WTO agreements, and any imposition of unilateral sanctions without the authorization of the DSB is prohibited.

After the establishment of the WTO, the United States changed its policy and has never since resorted to unilateral trade sanctions. Whenever disputes arise with other trade partners in relation to matters covered by WTO agreements, the United States petitions the DSB to get them resolved. As a consequence, the United States has become the biggest user of the WTO dispute settlement system. At the same time, this signifies that the WTO dispute settlement system has successfully resolved the issue of the unilateral imposition of trade sanctions under Section 301 of the US Trade Act.[3]

Governance of international trade and WTO dispute settlement

Cooperative relationships between WTO agreements and other agreements relating to international trade

The WTO regime does not exist in a vacuum, it needs cooperative relationships with other international agreements governing economic relationships among trading nations.[4] For example, the WTO regime needs a stable international currency relationship to be governed by the International Monetary Fund (IMF). Issues of how to promote economic development in developing country members are becoming increasingly important for the WTO regime. In this respect, the WTO and the World Bank have a common objective. In fact, the WTO dispute settlement procedure deals with issues of international balance of payments when dealing with developing country issues, as exemplified by the *India – Quantitative Restrictions* case.[5] Article 18 of the GATT allows a developing country member to invoke an import restriction when that country is confronted with a basic imbalance of payments. In the above case, India invoked an import restriction in accordance with this provision. One of the issues dealt with by the Appellate Body was whether or not India suffered a basic imbalance of international payments. This is an international currency issue and the IMF has expertise in this matter. Therefore, Article 18 states that, when the WTO dispute settlement procedure deals with this issue, it should defer to the judgment of the IMF. This is an example of a cooperative relationship between the WTO and the IMF. In fact, the WTO and the IMF entered into an agreement whereby officials of the WTO participate in IMF meetings as observers, and vice versa. There is a similar agreement between the WTO and the World Bank.

In the intellectual property area, the WTO Agreement on Trade-Related Aspects of Intellectual Property (TRIPS) incorporates by reference the Paris Convention, which deals with industrial property rights, and the Bern Convention, which deals with copyrights. Therefore, WTO members are bound by the rules of the Paris Convention and the Bern Convention even if they are not members of those conventions. This dramatically widens the scope of TRIPS, as well as providing "teeth" to those conventions since violations are dealt with by the dispute settlement procedure of the WTO as they are seen as violations of TRIPS.

Other examples of cooperative relationships between the WTO regime and other international agreements are found in the areas of technical barriers to trade (TBT) and sanitary and phytosanitary measures (SPS). Article 2.4 of the TBT Agreement states that WTO members must base their compulsory domestic standards on international standards. Such international standards include rules established by the Codex Alimentarius and the International Standard Organization (the ISO). If a member's compulsory standard is based on an international standard recognized by the WTO, this standard is presumed to be compatible with the GATT and the TBT Agreement or the SPS Agreement, as the case may be.

On the other hand, in some other situations, the relationship between the WTO and other international agreements may not be so harmonious.

For example, the Cartagena Protocol on Biosafety, which is a supplementary agreement to the United Nations Convention on Biological Diversity, provides for the precautionary principle, according to which members of the Protocol can invoke a measure prohibiting the production and sale of products containing genetically modified organisms (GMOs) even if a risk associated with GMOs is not scientifically proven. In contrast, the SPS Agreement provides that, when members prohibit the sale and import of a GMO product, members should conduct a risk assessment and adduce sufficient scientific evidence to prove that there is a risk associated with it. Although Article 5.7 of the SPS Agreement also provides for the precautionary principle, its scope is much more limited than that of the Cartagena Protocol.

In the *EC–Approval and Marketing of Biotech Products* case, in which the United States, Canada and Argentina challenged a moratorium of the European Communities on the approval of the sale of biotech products and safeguards applied by six EC members that temporarily prohibited the sale of biotech products, the European Communities argued that the UN Biodiversity Convention and the Cartagena Protocol should be applied to the dispute in this case.[6] The panel rejected this claim on the basis that one of the parties to this dispute, the United States, was not a party to the Cartagena Protocol, which therefore was not applicable to this case. The relationship between the SPS Agreement and the Cartagena Protocol was thus not an issue in this case. However, in a situation in which the parties to a dispute in a WTO proceeding are also parties to the Cartagena Protocol, there would be a serious conflict between the SPS Agreement and the Protocol because one requires that a measure to prohibit a GMO product needs to be based on scientific evidence whereas the other permits the application of the precautionary principle. It seems that, in the event of such a conflict, panels and the Appellate Body have no choice but to apply the SPS Agreement over the Cartagena Protocol. However, this would not resolve the conflict, which ultimately has to be resolved through negotiations among trading nations as to the proper scope of each agreement.

A similar conflict may arise between WTO agreements and multilateral environmental agreements (MEAs) such as the Kyoto Protocol. Although the Kyoto Protocol does not require that members restrict international trade and, therefore, WTO disciplines and the Kyoto Protocol do not necessarily come into conflict, there could be tension. For example, a member of the WTO might put into effect a measure to encourage electric cars over cars run on gasoline or diesel in order to reduce carbon dioxide emissions through taxing cars run on gasoline more heavily than electric cars. If cars run on gasoline or diesel oil are imported from abroad, this preferential tax could be challenged by other members as a violation of the "national treatment" principle if those two kinds of cars are like products. On the other hand, if a WTO member imposes an environmental tax on a product and producers of the product in this country want to export the product to member countries that do not impose the same or a similar tax on this product, then these producers are disadvantaged to the extent that they have to pay the environmental tax on the product. The exporting country member may then refund the environmental tax on the product or exempt the producer on the condition that the product is exported. This may raise the question of whether or not such a refund or exemption contingent on export of the product might constitute an export subsidy, which is generally prohibited by the SCM Agreement.

In such cases, the issue of conflict between WTO disciplines and environmental agreements may be resolved by applying the exemptions incorporated in Article XX, especially Article XX (b) or Article XX (g). However, the scope of exemption under those articles as applied to environmental issues is not entirely clear and is left to future panels and the Appellate Body to decide this relationship. Ultimately, this issue will need to be addressed in future negotiations.

The interface between the WTO regime and national sovereignty

Another important aspect of the relationship between the WTO dispute settlement procedure and global governance is the relationship between WTO agreements and national sovereignty. When WTO members join the WTO, they give up their sovereignty to some extent. The question is, how much sovereignty has each member given up? The WTO is composed of a set of international agreements in which negotiators agreed on certain matters where members submit their sovereign rights of control over their domestic matters to the WTO. The problem thus arises of how to demarcate the border between the realm of the WTO and that of each member's domestic control of sovereignty.

Panels and the Appellate Body, especially the latter, have been criticized as focusing too much on the text and being too literal in interpreting WTO agreements. Panels and the Appellate Body always cite the *Oxford English Dictionary* and the *Webster Dictionary* when determining the meaning of terms in an agreement and they try to follow the precise meaning of these terms. Criticisms that the Appellate Body has adhered too much to the literal meaning of the text of an agreement may be valid up to a point. However, the purpose of adhering to the literal meaning is to abide by the intentions of the negotiators as expressed in the text and not to infringe the sovereignty of WTO members by interpreting the text too broadly.

This tension between WTO agreements and national sovereignty is especially acute in such agreements as the SPS Agreement and the TBT Agreement. Both the SPS and the TBT agreements require that domestic standards on food safety and product safety be based on international standards, whether such domestic standards are applied to imported products or to domestically produced products. In this sense, these agreements cut deeply into the domain that had traditionally been allocated to national sovereignty. For this reason, the determination of the boundary between the domestic and the international control of such matters involves a delicate question of interpretation.

This issue is shown in the *EC–Sardines* case,[7] in which Peru challenged the European Communities' Regulation that the term "sardines" should be used only for canned foods made of fish caught in the North Sea, the Black Sea and the Mediterranean Sea, whereas the Codex Alimentarius, an international standard, permits the use of "sardines" on canned foods made of fish caught in different sea areas as long as a prefix such as "Peruvian" or "Pacific" is affixed before "sardines". In this respect, there is a contradiction between the EC regulation and the Codex standard. The EC Regulation in question was issued in 1980 and the TBT Agreement came into being in 1995. Article 2.4 of the TBT Agreement states that members should base their compulsory domestic standards on international standards if they exist or if their completion is imminent. The Appellate Body decided that Article 2.4 of the TBT Agreement would apply even when the compulsory domestic standard in question had been formulated and issued before the coming into being of the international standard.

It seems, however, that the text of Article 2.4 reflects a compromise between the requirement, on the one hand, that international standards be the basis of domestic standards and, on the other hand, that the domain for domestic control be respected. This compromise is reflected in the wording stating that domestic standards should be based on international standards when international standards exist or if their completion is imminent. This wording does not seem to cover situations where a domestic standard is already in existence when an international standard is enacted. This implies that, if domestic standards were in place when the international standard was agreed upon and promulgated, they need not be based on the international standard. This is an attempt to strike a balance between international disciplines and domestic regulations.

The above view is just one way to interpret the relationship between domestic and international standards and I do not claim that it is necessarily a correct interpretation.[8] However, I present this example to show that subtle relationships between WTO agreements and national sovereignty are often expressed in the text of an agreement, which is why a textual or literal approach in interpreting WTO agreements is followed.

Improvement of the WTO dispute settlement procedure in the face of difficulties encountered by developing country members

One of the important goals of the Doha Development Round is to promote the capacity-building of developing country members. This encompasses building up the capacity of developing countries in trade negotiations in the WTO and their legal capability in handling WTO dispute cases. The latter aspect will be discussed below.

The WTO dispute settlement procedure is premised on the assumption that all members are equal in their legal capacity to present their position in dispute settlement. In this regard, the WTO dispute settlement procedure is likened to the process in civil and commercial litigation in which parties are equal and it is their responsibility to adduce sufficient evidence and to present persuasive legal arguments. If a party is unsuccessful in producing good evidence and persuasive legal arguments, that party fails. The question, however, is whether WTO members are truly equal in their legal capacity in dispute settlements. In fact, there is a great deal of difference between developing country members and developed country members with respect to their legal capacity and this may hamper developing country members in effectively utilizing the WTO dispute settlement procedure.

Some WTO agreements are extremely complex and require a lot of legal knowledge, skill and experience if effective arguments are to be based on them. Much of this expertise is concentrated in the governments of developed country members such as the United States and the European Union and also in some large trade law firms in the United States and Europe. Developing country members often receive advice and assistance from such law firms when they are engaged in dispute settlements in the WTO. However, because of costly legal fees, some developing country members experience difficulty using those law firms. In some situations, developing country members are unable to win cases because of the lack of legal capacity that they could have exploited successfully if enough legal expertise were provided. In the *US–Gambling* case touched upon earlier, Antigua-Barbuda presented a jumble of pieces of US laws and claimed that the "totality" of these pieces of legislation constituted a violation of the provisions of the GATS. The panel sorted out some laws from among this jumble and constructed a meaningful claim for Antigua-Barbuda. If a developed country member presented this kind of claim, panels would refuse to accept them.

In order to address this gap between developing country members and developed country members, the Advisory Centre on WTO Law (ACWL) was established to assist developing country members in their use of the WTO dispute settlement procedure. The ACWL is staffed by some 10 lawyers who provide advice to developing country members on WTO litigation and sometimes represent them before panels and the Appellate Body. In fact, in the *EC–Sardines* case mentioned above, lawyers from the ACWL represented Peru and successfully pursued the litigation. However, the human resources of the ACWL are rather modest making it is hard to meet the needs of developing country members in dispute settlements at the WTO. In the rest of this section I wish to address some institutional aspects of the dispute settlement procedure in order to explore whether changes or modifications would help to address this imbalance.

In principle, panels deal with the facts, legal claims and arguments presented by the parties. I would suggest that panels utilize their power under Article 13 of the DSU and engage aggressively in fact-finding. Although the facts presented by the parties need to be accorded due respect, panels are authorized to seek information from anyone, including the governments of the parties and private entities. The vigorous exercise of this power seems to be useful when one of the parties to a dispute is a developing country member whose fact-gathering ability is somewhat handicapped compared with the other party which is a developed country member and is fully equipped with the legal and economic resources to present sufficient facts. Through this exercise, any imbalance in the fact-gathering abilities of the parties may be somewhat eased.

In the *US–Gasoline* case,[9] the first case to be referred to the WTO dispute settlement system, the Appellate Body requested after the oral hearing that all parties submit a post-hearing memorandum in which they set out their final statements of facts and legal arguments. In my experience, this post-hearing memorandum was the most detailed and clear statement of the parties' arguments. One advantage of a post-hearing memorandum is that the parties can take into consideration what they said and heard in the oral hearing and incorporate additional material. By these means, developing country members are given an opportunity to present another version of their views to the Appellate Body after the whole process has finished. This request for a post-hearing memorandum was made only once and was not renewed. I submit that the Appellate Body should reconsider the matter with a view to institutionalizing it.

In the judicial process of the European Union, the Advocates General of the European Court of Justice participate in legal proceedings with the disputing parties and present independent legal opinions regarding the matter in question. Advocates General do not represent any of the disputing parties; they only set out legal opinions that are neutral and based on a public interest standpoint. Often the views expressed by Advocates General play an important role when judges decide the case. I wonder if a similar system might be introduced into the WTO dispute settlement procedure. In this system, a special legal officer from a pool of legal experts in the WTO would be appointed to present a neutral legal opinion in each dispute case. Such officers would not represent the position of the claimant or that of the respondent. They would only state an objective interpretation of the WTO agreements in question. They would not be involved in the fact-finding aspects of the case. Although the views of these officers would not necessarily provide an advantage to developing country members when they are disadvantaged vis-à-vis a large developed country member in the WTO dispute settlement procedure, they might have the effect of restoring the balance between the claims and arguments of a claimant and a respondent when, owing to a lack of resources, a developing country member is handicapped in asserting its claims and arguments.

At present, the views expressed by third parties in a dispute settlement procedure sometimes have a comparable effect of keeping a balance between the different views expressed by the disputing parties. At the same time, however, it is often true that third parties have their own national interests and side with either the claimant or the respondent. In this situation, their views are not neutral in the real sense of the term but are close to advocating one of the positions in a dispute.

The role of scientific evidence in WTO dispute settlements

Some of the WTO agreements deal with highly scientific matters, as exemplified by the Agreement on Sanitary and Phytosanitary measures (SPS Agreement) and the Agreement on Technical Barriers to Trade (TBT Agreement). The SPS Agreement is concerned with such items as food safety and agricultural quarantine and the TBT Agreement provides for product safety, product testing and product representation. In the *EC–Hormones* case,[10] in which the SPS Agreement was at issue, a question relating to the role of scientific evidence was presented, which raises an interesting problem of whether a minority view expressed by a scientist should be respected.

In the *EC–Hormones* case, the European Communities imposed a ban on the use, sale and import of hormone-treated beef on the ground that this might cause cancer. The United States and Canada filed claims against the European Communities with the WTO for the reason that this ban was not based on a proper risk assessment and was contrary to articles of the SPS Agreement that require that, when a member imposes a ban on a substance, it must run a risk assessment and provide sufficient scientific evidence proving that a health risk is involved. The SPS Agreement also states that a domestic standard for food safety should be based on an international standard if there is one, and, when a domestic standard is based on an international standard, this is presumed to be compatible with the GATT 1995.

With regard to the safety of beef, there is an international standard (the Codex Alimentarius), according to which there is no health risk as long as the residue of hormones contained in hormone-treated beef remains within the range stipulated in the Codex Alimentarius. The total ban imposed by the European Communities goes beyond this international standard and the European Communities needed to prove with scientific evidence that this higher standard for safety was necessary in spite of the fact that the Codex Alimentarius provides that there is no risk as long the hormone residue stays within the stipulated range.

The panel dealing with this case requested several scientists to present their views on the safety of hormone-treated beef. The majority of scientists expressed the view that there would be no danger to the life and health of humans as long as the hormone residue contained in the beef remained within the range stipulated by the Codex Alimentarius. However, one scientist expressed the view that, even if the hormone residue remained within the stipulated range, there was still a one in a million risk of humans getting cancer from eating such beef. This is a small risk but it is a risk nevertheless. The panel accepted the majority view and determined that the European Communities had not proved with scientific evidence that a domestic standard more stringent than the international standard was necessary.

The European Communities appealed to the Appellate Body and argued that the panel's disregard of the minority scientific view violated Article 11 of the DSU, which requires that panels engage in an objective assessment of the law and the facts, and that the panel had ignored and distorted the evidence. The Appellate Body stated that the panel's treatment of the evidence was in accord with Article 11 and dismissed the claim of the European Communities. However, the Appellate Body added a sentence stating that a minority view needs to be respected in some circumstances.

This decision of the Appellate Body seems to raise an important question of evidential issues relating to SPS cases, i.e. whether a minority scientific view should sometimes be accepted. Simply put, the question is as follows: If the issue is related to human life and health, should a minority view be set aside so easily? Should the panel not respect the minority view and base its decision on it? This raises another question about whether or not a majority view on food safety matters should be set aside. It is common-sensical that, in most cases, the majority opinion on a scientific matter should be adopted. However, if the matter that a panel is dealing with is related to human life and health, common sense may not always prevail.

Often scientists differ in their views on food safety issues, where there is rarely an absolute scientific truth. Therefore, it is often a matter of a policy decision rather than a scientific decision to choose which scientific evidence to accept. In this respect, Article 5:3 of the SPS Agreement is suggestive. It states:

> In assessing the risk to animal or plant life or health and determining the measure to be applied for achieving the appropriate level of sanitary or phytosanitary protection from such risk, Members shall take into account as relevant economic factors: the potential damage in terms of loss of production or sales in the event of the entry, establishment or spread of a pest or disease; the costs of control or eradication in the territory of the importing Member; and the relative cost-effectiveness of alternative approaches to limiting risks.

The word "human" is lacking from this provision. One interpretation that can be drawn from this provision is that there is a difference between matters involving human life and health and those involving only animal and plant life and health. In the former, one may argue that a precautionary principle needs to be considered more seriously than in the latter and a strict regulation is allowed.

The role of economics in interpreting WTO agreements

Article 3:2 of the DSU states that panels and the Appellate Body should interpret WTO agreements in accordance with the principles of treaty interpretation as established in public international law. Such principles are incorporated in the Vienna Convention on the Law of Treaties. Panels and the Appellate Body interpret provisions in WTO agreements in compliance with Articles 31 and 32 of the Vienna Convention. Article 31 of the Vienna Convention requires that a treaty interpreter interpret the provisions of a treaty in accordance with the wording of the treaty in the ordinary sense of the terms, context and the purpose and objectives thereof. Article 32 states that, if an absurd or unreasonable result comes by relying on Article 31, then the interpreter can rely on the preparatory works of the treaty in question. These principles of interpretation are not so different from the principles of interpretation of statutes as developed in civil law countries.

I wonder if there is any role for economics in interpreting WTO agreements. WTO agreements are based on a certain kind of economic policy and they deal with economic questions. If the rulings of panels and the Appellate Body do not make any economic sense, what is the use of

WTO agreements? Of course, panels and the Appellate Body are entrusted by the membership of the WTO to interpret WTO agreements
as intended by the negotiators and framers and not to introduce their
own likes and dislikes into them. The principles of interpretation expressed in the Vienna Convention are designed to guarantee objectivity
in the interpretation of treaties.

Nevertheless, I think there is a role for economics in interpreting WTO
agreements. There may be situations in which panels and the Appellate
Body interpret a provision in a WTO agreement by relying on the wording, context, objectives or preparatory works of the treaty in question
and yet are not able to arrive at a definitive answer. After all, WTO
agreements are the result of political compromise and some element of
ambiguity is inevitable.

In the *EC–Bed Linen* case,[11] an anti-dumping case in which the Appellate Body established the rule that "zeroing" is unlawful under the Anti-
dumping Agreement, India, the claimant, argued that the European
Communities violated provisions in the Anti-dumping Agreement by cal-
culating the constructed value of the exporter by relying on data about
the general expenses of only one other exporter. Article 2.2.2 of the
Anti-dumping Agreement states that, if the general expenses of an exporter pertaining to the product in question cannot be determined, they
should be calculated on the basis of actual data pertinent to production
and sales in the ordinary course of trade of a like product of the exporter.
It further states that, if the general expenses of the exporter cannot be
determined by the above method, then the amount may be determined
by the weighted average of the actual amount incurred and realized by
other exporters and producers subject to investigation in respect of the
production and sales of the like product in the domestic market of the
country of origin.

In the *EC–Bed Linen* case, the European Communities relied on the
data of one other exporter in India, which was subject to investigation
because data on the Indian exporter in question were not available. India
objected, arguing that Article 2.2.2 of the Anti-dumping Agreement requires that, in the absence of data pertinent to the exporter in question,
the amount should be determined by the "weighted average" of the
actual amount incurred and realized by other "exporters", and that this
provision envisions that there are several other exporters and the
weighted average of those exporters' data should be used, whereas, in
this case, the European Communities relied on the data of only one other
exporter. In fact, there was only one other exporter in India exporting
bed linen to the European Communities.

The panel stated that the European Communities measure could be
upheld because "plural" includes "singular" and the above-cited provision of the Anti-dumping Agreement encompasses the situation where

there is only one other exporter. The Appellate Body reversed this ruling and held that the provision envisages the situation where there is more than one other exporter and the weighted average of the data on those exporters should be used as the basis for constructing the value of general expenses.

On the surface, this may look like a grammatical question of how the words "singular" and "plural" should be distinguished and applied. However, there is an underlying economic question. When data on the general expenses of an exporter are not available, Article 2.2.2 of the Anti-dumping Agreement allows the use of data pertaining to other exporters. One interpretation of the reason the wording "weighted average of other exporters" is used may be that, if there is only one other exporter in the market of the exporting country, this is not sufficient to constitute a market of the product in question. To calculate a value in the above way is to construct an artificial value. It is necessary to approximate this artificial value as closely as possible to the economic reality. In order to do so, it is necessary to use data on exporters that operate in a real market. If there is only one other exporter, it can hardly constitute a market and, if one uses the data on this exporter, these may reflect idiosyncratic features that are not representative of the market in question. If one looks at the situation in this way, one may argue that there is an economic reason for using the term "weighted average of other exporters" in Article 2.2.2 of the Anti-dumping Agreement. I would suggest that panels and the Appellate Body give economic meanings to the words used in WTO agreements in addition to the grammatical meanings that can be attached to them. It is not always possible to do this. However, if panels and the Appellate Body explain the economic rationale of the rulings they make, this will contribute toward enhancing the persuasiveness of their reports.

Another interesting example in this regard is the *Chilean Price Band* case.[12] The Chilean government had formulated a complex scheme for imposing a special levy on agricultural products. It had established a price band for agricultural products based on the average of international prices of agricultural products and, whenever the import price of a particular agricultural product went below the band, a special levy was imposed on it in addition to the regular tariffs. However, it was provided that the totality of imposition (special levy and regular tariff) could never go above the concession rate of the agricultural product in question.

This imposition of a special levy based on a price band system was challenged by Argentina, and the Appellate Body held that this imposition was contrary to Article II of the GATT 1994 because it was not a part of the regular tariffs and was similar to a variable levy, which was prohibited under the GATT. The Appellate Body reached this conclusion by analysing the wording of Article II of the GATT and its linguistic implications.

The conclusion of the Appellate Body was probably correct. However, it may be questioned on the basis that, under the Chilean scheme, the imposition of the levy plus regular tariffs on an agricultural product never went above the concession rate and the totality of the imposition was likely to be lower than the maximum of the concession rate, which the Chilean government conceded. Since the Chilean government was justified in raising tariffs to the maximum set out in the concession, why did this imposition of a levy distort international trade more than the imposition of maximum tariffs would have? Chile could have abandoned this imposition system and just imposed the maximum tariffs on agricultural products under the concession. Would this not have had a more restrictive effect on the import of agricultural products than the imposition of levy?

On the other hand, one could argue that the imposition of a levy by the Chilean government based on the average import prices of an agricultural product would make the prospect of trade unpredictable. It is this inherent unpredictability that causes distortion in international trade.

One way or another, it is an economic question. It seems that, when the Appellate Body made this ruling, it could have explained why the ruling was sensible from an economic standpoint. This would have made the ruling more persuasive. My sense is that this Appellate Body ruling can be explained economically by using unpredictability theory, i.e. that it is more harmful to trade if the conditions for trade are uncertain and unpredictable than if they are restrictive. If they are restrictive, traders can take the restrictiveness into account and make plans to circumvent it, overcome it or reduce its severity. If conditions are unpredictable, it is harder for traders to deal with them.

Is there any need for a reform of the Appellate Body?

Many people have commented that the Appellate Body has worked well and has been instrumental in establishing important jurisprudence for the WTO. I agree wholeheartedly with this view. The Appellate Body has also faced criticisms, i.e. that its interpretation of WTO agreements is too literal and textual, on the one hand, and that it has "made law" rather than interpreted law as commissioned by the membership of the WTO, on the other. Although there may be some truth in both of these criticisms, the principles of interpretation established by the Appellate Body are really noteworthy. Therefore, the basic policy of the WTO dispute settlement system, including the Appellate Body, is to "do no harm".[13]

However, there is weakness in any human institution and the Appellate Body is no exception. I would like to mention one particular issue. Under the current system, reports of panels and the Appellate Body are adopted by negative consensus and, therefore, automatically. This makes a decision by the Appellate Body de facto the final decision-making in the WTO dispute settlement process. In this respect, the position of the Appellate Body can be likened to that of a supreme court in domestic jurisdictions.

In domestic jurisdictions, legislatures can make new law and correct decisions of supreme courts if their decisions are wrong, unreasonable or politically unpalatable. In the WTO, such a role should be played by the General Council and the Ministerial Conference, where the policies of the WTO are made. If the rulings of the Appellate Body are wrong, unreasonable or politically unacceptable, resolutions can be made to overturn them and make new rules. However, the political situation in the Ministerial Conference is such that it is very difficult to make decisions to change rules and consequently the Ministerial Conference is not operating as a corrective mechanism to deal with wrong decisions that the Appellate Body might make.

This means that no effective checks and balances operate in the WTO decision-making process. It is an unfortunate situation for the Appellate Body in the sense that any mistake it might make will not be corrected by any other decision-making body. Unless the Appellate Body assumes infallibility in its decisions, this puts a heavy burden on the Appellate Body, and who can claim infallibility?

Two tendencies might result from the lack of checks and balance in decision-making. First, the Appellate Body might restrain itself from making broad interpretations of WTO agreements so that its interpretation does not go beyond what has been entrusted to it by the membership. This course would mean the adoption of a literal, textual and narrow approach in interpretation, emphasizing the wording and context of a provision in an agreement as prescribed in Article 31 of the Vienna Convention. This is a safe approach. Although, there is not much room for creative and imaginative interpretation.

On the other hand, the Appellate Body might emphasize a teleological approach and engage in broad and creative interpretations that could contribute toward the establishment of WTO jurisprudence. However, this might lead to "making law" rather than interpreting law and to judicial activism, which some members of the WTO would oppose.

In fact, the Appellate Body has been criticized by some members of the WTO and by commentators for engaging in either one or the other of these approaches. In my mind, the Appellate Body has not committed a grave sin either way. On the whole, the Appellate Body has tried to stay in the middle of the road and avoid extreme approaches. However, it is useful to think about some ways in which the Appellate Body system could be improved.

Some critics argue that the WTO dispute settlement process has become too judicialized and it is time to reintroduce a more political decision-making process.[14] However, this seems to be a regression rather than progress. Given the achievements of the Appellate Body since the establishment of the WTO, the judicial-type dispute settlement system should be maintained.

What may be needed is to introduce a mechanism of checks and balance in the decision-making process of the dispute settlement procedure. Article XI:2 of the Marrakesh Agreement states that the Ministerial Conference and the General Council can adopt exclusive interpretations of WTO agreements by three-quarter majority votes. Therefore, constitutionally, any mistakes that the Appellate Body may make can be corrected by using this authority. However, it is difficult to get a three-quarter majority to adopt an exclusive interpretation and this provision has not yet been invoked. One could propose that such an exclusive interpretation should be adopted by a two-thirds majority or a simple majority. It should be remembered, however, that the Ministerial Conference and the General Council are political bodies and it is not desirable to construct a system in which political bodies can easily overturn judicial decisions. From this perspective, a two-thirds majority might be a better idea.

Another softer approach can be proposed. In this approach, there would be a small group of experts on WTO law and economics and this group would periodically review the rulings of the Appellate Body. This group would be established within the WTO as a sort of advisory group and would have no power to overturn the rulings of the Appellate Body. Its function would be limited to reviewing the decisions of the Appellate Body, assessing them in terms of jurisprudential and economic soundness and publishing its views. This group would be composed of academics, lawyers, judges and economists of established renown and authority. Reviews of decisions of the Appellate Body made by this group should be based on neutral, jurisprudential and economic theories and should not be based on the political desirability or otherwise of the rulings of the Appellate Body.

Critical analysis of Appellate Body reports is made by academics and other commentators. However, a group established within the WTO to review Appellate Body reports would play a different role from academic comments and criticisms, and the Appellate Body might pay special attention to its views.

Notes

1. *United States – Restrictions on Imports of Cotton and Man-Made Fibre Underwear*, WT/DS241/R/DSR, adopted 25 February 1997 (Panel); WT/DS241/AB/R/DSR 1997, adopted 25 February 25, 1997.
2. *United States – Measures Affecting the Cross-Border Supply of Gambling and Betting Services*, WT/DS281/R, adopted 20 April 2005 (Panel); WT/DS285/AB/R, adopted 20 April 2005 (Appellate Body)
3. The European Communities brought a case against the United States at the WTO on the ground that the existence of Section 301 of the Trade Act in the United States was per se contrary to the Dispute Settlement Understanding (DSU), which is part of the WTO agreements. The panel held that Section 301 of the Trade Act was not a violation of the DSU in itself. However, depending on the way it is put into effect, it can be held to be inconsistent with the provisions of the DSU. See *United States – Sections 301–310 of the Trade Act of 1974*, WT/DS152/R, adopted 27 January 2000 (Panel).
4. For details, see Mitsuo Matsushita, "Governance of International Trade under World Trade Organization Agreements", *Journal of World Trade*, Vol. 38, No. 2, April 2004, pp. 185–210.
5. *India – Quantitative Restrictions on Imports of Agricultural, Textile and industrial Products*, WT/DS90/R, adopted 22 September 1999 (Panel), as upheld by the Appellate Body Report, WT/DS90/AB/R.
6. *European Communities – Measures Affecting the Approval and Marketing of Biotech Products*, Complaints by the United States (WT/DS291), Canada (WT/DS292) and Argentina (WT/DS293).
7. *European Communities – Trade Description of Sardines*, WT/DS231/AB/R, 23 October 2002 (Appellate Body).
8. For details of my view of this case, see Mitsuo Matsushita, "'Sovereignty' Issues in Interpreting WTO Agreements: The Sardines Case and Article 2.4 of the TBT Agreement", in Dencho Georgiev and Kim van der Borght (eds), *Reform and Development of the WTO Dispute Settlement System*, London: Cameron May, 2006, pp. 191–199.
9. *United States – Standards for Reformulated and Conventional Gasoline*, WT/DS2/R, adopted 29 April 1996 (Panel); WT/DS2/AB/R, adopted 29 April 1996 (Appellate Body).
10. *European Communities – Measures Concerning Meat and Meat Products*, WT/DS26/R/US, WT/DS48/R/CAN, adopted 13 February 1998 (Panel); WT/DS26, 48/AB/R adopted 13 February 1998 (Appellate Body).
11. *European Communities – Anti-dumping Duties on Imports of Cotton-Type Bed Linen from India*, WT/DS141/R/DSR 2001: VI, 2007, adopted 12 March 2001 (Panel); WT/DS141/AB/R/DSR 2001: V, 2049, adopted 12 March 2001 (Appellate Body).
12. *Chile – Price Band System and Safeguard Measures Relating to Certain Agricultural Products*, WT/DS207/R/DSR 2002: VIII, 3012, adopted 23 October (Panel); WT/DS207/AB/R/DSR 2002: VIII, 305, adopted 23 October 2002 (Appellate Body).
13. *The Future of the WTO: Addressing Institutional Challenges in the New Millennium, Report by the Consultative Board to the Director-General Supachai Panitchpakdi*, Geneva: World Trade Organization, 2004, p. 49.
14. The most prominent such criticism is Claude Barfield, *Free Trade, Sovereignty, Democracy: The Future of the World Trade Organization*, Washington, DC: AEI Press, 2001.

Index